YOUNG FRIENDS
Schools and Friendship

Also available from Cassell:

J. Brierley: *Growth in Children*
B. Byrne: *Coping with Bullying in Schools*
C. Cullingford: *The Inner World of the School*
P. Lang, R. Best and A. Lichtenberg: *Caring for Children*
D. Nyberg and N. Nyberg: *Improving Children's Personal Relationships*
V. Varma (ed.): *Coping with Unhappy Children*

Young Friends

Schools and Friendship

Sue Roffey, Tony Tarrant and Karen Majors

CASSELL

Cassell
Villiers House
41/47 Strand
London WC2N 5JE

387 Park Avenue South
New York
NY 10016-8810

First published 1994

British Library Cataloguing-in-Publication Data

A catalogue record for this book is available from the British Library.

ISBN 0-304-32940-1 (hardback)
     0-304-32989-4 (paperback)

Typeset by Action Typesetting Ltd, Northgate Street, Gloucester
Printed and bound in Great Britain by Redwood Books, Trowbridge, Wiltshire.

Contents

Acknowledgements

We would like to thank the following people:

Our respective partners, David, John and Lorna, for their support and encouragement.

John Nolan and David Roffey for their computer expertise and the many hours that they gave helping to unravel the mysteries of the word processor.

Ralph Pesapane and the staff of Milton Avenue School, Chatham, New Jersey and Elizabeth Gillies for information about the United States and 'Magic Circles'.

The pupils of the following schools in the London Borough of Haringey for their artwork:
Lordship Lane Junior School
Risley Avenue Junior School
Devonshire Hill Primary School
Earlham Junior School.

Our colleagues in Barking and Dagenham, Haringey, Southwark and the Institute of Education.

Our friends and families for their tolerance − we now hope to spend more time with them in some friendly interactions of our own.

To
Children Everywhere

Introduction

'... there is an expanding body of knowledge documenting that social skills during childhood has significant short and long term consequences. Socially skilled children feel good about themselves, perform well at school and are more likely to be socially adjusted as adults. On the other hand, socially deficient children receive little positive reinforcement, are subject to academic and behavioural difficulties and may be more likely to experience a variety of poor adult outcomes ...'

(Michelson and Mannarino, 1986, p. 374)

THE NEED FOR FRIENDSHIP

People need to learn to get along with each other for many reasons: for collaboration, for companionship, and for mutual support. The quality of our interpersonal relationships affects the quality of our lives, both in a personal sphere and in a working context. The support and company of friends can make difficult times more bearable and good times more enjoyable. Positive close relationships which work well make us feel good about ourselves and promote psychological health.

THE NEED FOR FRIENDLINESS

Friendly behaviour not only opens doors to close friendships: it also fosters a warm and welcoming environment, gives positive value to differences and provides alternative ways of dealing with disagreement and conflict. Schools often work hard to develop strategies to deal with unacceptable behaviour but may not actively promote friendship skills between children or teach them appropriate assertion strategies.

Large companies sometimes invest in training for their staff to give them greater 'people' and 'team-building' skills — they realize the difference it makes when there is good communication, positive feedback and co-operation. Their ultimate aim might be to make a profit but they are also looking at how their organization can be most effective and how to maintain a high level of motivation. Schools similarly benefit from paying attention to developing a friendly ethos. Their aim is to maximize the effectiveness of the learning environment and encourage children's enthusiasm to participate.

LEARNING FRIENDLY BEHAVIOUR

Good social and friendship skills don't just happen. They need to be learnt in the same way as many other skills. Those individuals who are successful in their relationships are likely to have had positive experiences from an early age which have given them a high level of self-esteem and confidence. They will probably have had good models of social behaviour, opportunities to meet with others and develop friendships, and have been in a supportive environment when there were difficulties.

Those individuals who have not been so fortunate will not have learnt so well how to manage relationships or how to cope successfully in a variety of social situations. At one end of the spectrum these are the people who have not learnt to take account of others and who sometimes cause great distress as a consequence. By helping children to have a higher level of esteem and confidence, to develop the ability to relate well to others, to be aware of both their own and others' feelings and perceptions, to communicate and assert themselves effectively, we are likely to affect more than just those individual children.

THE ROLE OF THE SCHOOL

Although parents and families are the primary influence in social development, children spend a lot of time in school in their formative years. Teachers, friends and the ethos of a school generally can all greatly influence pupils with regard to their self-esteem, confidence, ability to interact with others, and understanding of their social world.

There is a great emphasis in education in the present day on curricular targets and attainments. Teachers feel that their time is taken up ensuring that pupils reach appropriate levels within the curriculum. There is, however, also concern about behaviour in school, exclusions, truancy and bullying. Pupils who are in a school environment which deals positively and pro-actively with social issues are more likely to achieve success on academic measures, because there will be better co-operation, higher motivation, less disruption and less truancy.

SOCIAL SKILLS ARE AN INTEGRAL PART OF THE CURRICULUM

There are, therefore, solid reasons for exploring ways that schools can promote friendship and friendly behaviour. This book is not just about social skills, although there are activities here which can be found in social skills programmes. It is about looking at the whole area of the social curriculum in schools, at both a formal and an informal level. It is about not leaving things to chance but making sure that positive things happen. Although we have included a number of activities and games to promote skills and understanding, they need to be introduced to children within a context which is promoting a positive ethos generally and looking in some depth at how pupils are relating to each other.

ALL CHILDREN HAVE A RIGHT TO FRIENDSHIP

We begin by looking at what friendship means to children and why it is important. There is good evidence to suggest that there are serious and negative consequences for children who are friendless in school and we consider therefore that access to friendship should be a right for all children. We talk about children having a right of 'access to the curriculum' within the context of special needs, cultural diversity and gender. We also need to talk about 'access to friendship', what that means and how we can go about providing it.

FRIENDSHIP BUILDING IS NOT JUST ABOUT BEHAVIOUR AND SKILLS

Relationship building is developmental, and children need different things from their friends at different ages. Encouraging and promoting positive, appropriate behaviour can usefully be done from an early age, but children need to have reached a certain conceptual level before they can begin to develop more complex social skills which take into account the perceptions of others.

Throughout this book we talk not only about those behaviours which are more likely to bring about positive responses but also about how to develop awareness of self and others so that behaviour can be flexible and thoughtful, not automatic and rigid. Many activities are designed to encourage children to think through their perceptions and understanding of others.

We have not restricted our discussions to any one age group because of the need to have a developmental perspective. Many of the activities we have outlined, however, are most appropriate with children in middle childhood, between the ages of about 8 and 13, when they have reached the developmental level which enables them to view interactions from perceptions other than their own. Some of these activities are also appropriate for use with young people in their teens.

FROM THEORY TO PRACTICE

We have tried to combine our experience as teachers and psychologists with knowledge that is rooted firmly in research. This provides a theoretical underpinning for each chapter. We have good reasons for believing that our views and ideas are useful and linked with the development of an effective school.

In writing a book with as wide a brief as this one, the most difficult decision is what to leave out. What we have chosen to do, therefore, is to make it as 'user-friendly' and as immediately relevant to practising teachers as possible. We have done this by combining theory and knowledge with practical applications. The 'taking action' section of each chapter often includes looking at policies and ways to develop these. The activities we give are examples and we hope that they will stimulate teachers to create others, perhaps specifically designed for their own classes, groups or for individual children. We have included a resource section in each chapter for those who wish to follow up further ideas.

A BRIEF OUTLINE

Although teachers may wish to dip into chapters that are most relevant to their immediate needs, there is a sequence to the book.

We begin by looking at social interactions in a developmental framework which indicates which approaches are likely to be most useful with children at different ages. This chapter also includes what the 'provisions' of friendship are and why we need our friends.

The development of a positive self-concept and good self-esteem is crucial in developing positive relationships with others. Many individuals have difficulty because they need to protect their own vulnerability. Chapter 2 explores ways in which teachers can promote self-awareness, confidence and self-esteem for children in their classes.

The third chapter is about the opportunities and skills that are needed to establish a 'threshold' for friendship. These include the more straightforward social skills of giving friendly verbal and non-verbal messages.

From individual strategies we then look at groups and what is involved in being part of a group – the positive aspects of this and also the more difficult.

Communication is a vital ingredient in developing social interactions and good relationships. 'Poor communication' is often cited as a reason for the breakdown of relationships. Chapter 5 deals with what is involved in communication for the development of friendships.

Friendship is a right which should be available to all. How do we ensure that every child, regardless of ability, race, gender or background, is provided with opportunities to make friends and access to social relationships? This is discussed in Chapter 6.

The following two chapters are concerned with difficulties in social relationships. Chapter 7 looks at individual conflicts, loss of friends and the importance of friends in times of crisis. Chapter 8 focuses on bullying and ways in which schools can become safer places.

What happens in the playground between pupils affects what happens in the classroom – and vice versa. A substantial proportion of the school day is 'breaktime'. This chapter looks at what does and does not happen in the playground and at lunchtime and makes suggestions about what could happen.

Finally – and most importantly – we explore the environment within the classroom which promotes friendliness and co-operation between pupils. It is in the classroom that many of the activities we suggest will happen. They will be more effective if there is a positive social climate. What this means and how to promote it is covered in Chapter 10.

BEING EFFECTIVE

This book is not about ensuring that everyone makes close friends, nor is it about getting everyone to conform to a rigid standard of socially acceptable behaviour. It is about having access to a wider range of alternative behaviours and being able to choose. It is about providing opportunities, devising policies and strategies that will enable children, groups and individuals to have better relationships with each other. Teachers struggle to do this all the time, and we hope that the suggestions we have made and the perceptions we have given will help them to do this more effectively. We hope that a friendlier ethos will lead to greater effectiveness in schools and greater happiness and better psychological health for children.

REFERENCE

Michelson, L. and Mannarino, A. (1986) Social skills training with children: research and clinical application. In P.S. Strain, M.J. Guralnick and H.M. Walker (eds) (1986) *Children's Social Behavior. Development, Assessment and Modification.* Orlando: Academic Press Inc.

Chapter 1

What Friendship Means to Children

Angela, aged 3	'Why is Julio your friend?'
	'Because I like him.'
	'Why do you like him?'
	'Because he's my friend.'
	'Why else do you like him?'
	'Because he lives next door.'
Simi, aged 6	'Why is Martina your friend?'
	'Because she sits next to me and lends me her pencil.'
	'Why else is she your friend?'
	'Because she comes to my party and I go to hers.'
Daniel, aged 9	'Why is Peter your friend?'
	'Because we have a laugh together.'
	'Are there other reasons?'
	'He helps me when I can't spell something.'
Sabina, aged 13	'Why is Amber your friend?'
	'Because I can trust her with my secrets.'
	'Why else is she your friend?'
	'Because we think the same way about things.'

THE DEVELOPMENTAL STAGES OF FRIENDSHIP

As with all aspects of development there are significant changes in the social world of children as they grow older. This applies to the ways in which children interact with each other, the purpose and meaning of those interactions and the concepts that children have about what it means to have a friend and what might be thought of as friendly behaviour. There are complex interactions between cognitive development (levels of understanding), moral development (ideas about right and wrong in relation to others) and learning experiences which affect social development. The following gives an outline of how children's friendships develop over time. As there is considerable overlap between the stages and some children will be much more socially advanced than others, the ages given here are approximate, especially with older children.

Playmates: the earliest friendships

As all parents and carers will be able to testify, small children from a very early age show an interest in each other. They look at each other curiously and sometimes make overtures by gestures such as handing over a toy, often accompanied by noises or by smiling. 'Play' situations, however, are usually structured by parents or other adults. Children's 'friends' are usually those children who happen to be there, such as the sons and daughters of their parents, friends and neighbours.

From the ages of 2 to 4 years there is an increase in independent interactions where children can go and play together without the close supervision or intervention of an adult. With the development of the ability to predict what someone might do, choose actions and understand what might be expected in a given situation – albeit simply – children rapidly develop a range of social skills. As they do so there is an increase in the amount of time spent in playing *with* others rather than alongside them. 'Playing with' is both associative activity – such as two children playing with cars and the same toy garage – and co-operative activity – where one child pushes the car to the garage and the other pretends to fill it up with petrol. Co-operation, of course, requires an even greater range of skills, and many nursery and infant school teachers find that they need to encourage young children to move from a purely egocentric stance to one that includes taking account of others. It is generally considered that children at this age are unable to see things from an entirely different perspective from their own but they do begin to understand that some games and activities cannot happen unless there is an element of sharing and turn-taking. It has been suggested that the term 'playmate' is a more accurate term than 'friend' at this stage, although there is often an element of choice in who is a preferred playmate. Some studies have challenged the view that very young children don't really have friends and have shown evidence that some individuals do actively seek each other out and that between these children the quality of play and interaction is richer (Vandell and Mueller, 1980). True reciprocity as a feature of friendship, however, is not understood until much later, and using moral arguments with pre-schoolers about how they ought to behave is not usually effective. Helping children to understand what the consequences of co-operation and non-cooperation will be for themselves is likely to meet with more success.

There is some evidence to suggest that infants who have opportunities to mix with other children or with older brothers and sisters from an early age benefit from the experience in terms of their social development (Rubin, 1980). There is also evidence to indicate that children who have secure parental attachments have an advantage in the confidence that this gives them to explore both their physical and their social worlds (Bretherton and Waters, 1985).

These earliest friendships are important for a number of reasons:

- They provide a better framework and reference point for social reality than adults. Baby Jane may have been over-indulged and given the impression that everything she does is perfectly wonderful. Other children are unlikely to be so adoring and will provide a new perspective on the world which is closer to what will be found when she eventually goes to school. For children who have had less supportive or more restrictive parenting the opposite can happen and friends can provide a boost to self-esteem and an encouragement to explore and extend experiences.

- Children learn for the first time ways of dealing with conflict and differences between equals. Parents who are having difficulty coping with their pre-schooler's behaviour might learn some useful management strategies from 4-year-olds: they tend to ignore children who behave in ways they don't like! Learning to relate in a way that is acceptable to peers provides a strong basis for the future development of relationships.

- It is clear right from the beginning that some children find it easier to relate positively than others. The skills that appear to be important are those that include taking positive initiatives, for example 'Come on, let's go and get on the slide', and being more accepting, accommodating and positive to others, for example 'Let Frankie on, he can get on here'. Children who intervene in others' activities in a more disruptive way and are negative in their responses for much of the time tend to be avoided by their peers.

Teaching pre-school children social skills, such as guiding them into ways of joining in activities or encouraging them to include others, may be useful but parents, carers or teachers can be even more effective in helping a young child make friends if they concentrate on the following:

- Modelling ways of behaving which are positive and welcoming. Children learn by watching and copying and in the first instance they tend to copy much of the behaviour that they have experienced from the adults around them. A young child who is regularly reprimanded with a smack will learn that when other children don't do as she says then the thing to do is to hit out. An adult who is able to include several children in an activity and says positive things to them will be teaching those children how to go about being friendly.

- Showing that there are a variety of strategies for dealing with conflict. Similarly, parents and teachers can help children learn to share, to take turns and to begin to realize that there are two sides to an argument although it might be some time before they will be able to do these things independently. At this stage children need to see that the resolution of conflict is in their interests.

- Developing confidence and self-esteem. Children who have had their successes pointed out to them and have been praised for their efforts will be more confident generally. They will also be more confident in their approaches to others than those who have come to understand that little of what they do is viewed positively. Low self-esteem may lead to a reluctance to engage with others or to a simultaneously aggressive yet defensive stance which inhibits the development of friendships.

- Being empathetic and commenting on or explaining social behaviour in a simple but clear way, for example 'If you push Andy over every time you get in the sand pit together he won't want to play with you', or 'That was a nice thing to do, letting Tanya play with your animals. Perhaps you could be the vet and she could bring the sick ones to see you?'

All of the above will do much to enable pre-schoolers to behave in open and friendly ways with their peers without the need for further instruction.

Going to school: likes me, likes me not, likes me, likes me not

When children first go to school, friends are, by and large, still seen as people who do things for you or give you things. A friend is someone who is fulfilling your immediate needs, whether it be for company or for ice-cream! It is not uncommon to hear a 5-year-old shout out defiantly to another, 'You're not my friend any more!' when he doesn't get his own way. It would not be unusual for these same children to be seen playing together again shortly afterwards, as the immediacy of the world is what matters, not what happened yesterday or even an hour ago. There continues to be a 'proximity' element to choice of friend and this would include who sits on the same 'table' in the class as well as friends who may be known in other contexts, such as those who were in the same playgroup. The way teachers set out their classrooms therefore can have quite an impact on the social lives of their pupils in promoting or preventing the development of certain relationships.

From the age of about 6 most children have begun to understand for themselves that there is an element of reciprocity required for maintaining satisfactory interactions, although at first this is confined to material and physical aspects such as lending and borrowing pencils and taking turns with the skipping-rope. A young child's social world tends to be made up of specific social incidents rather than be focused on the notion of friendship itself. This does not mean that a child is unaware of the needs of others or unable to respond to them. In fact, even very young toddlers will often try to comfort a crying baby, and children from their first year of school will regularly bring someone who is hurt to be cared for by a teacher or supervisor.

Children begin to make more independent and overt choices in friendships although they do not set much store by permanence and loyalty at this stage. Making and breaking friends, quarrels, compromise and rough-and-tumble games are all part of practising relationships. Learning to deal with conflict in different ways and being taught that it is possible to have a situation in which there are no clear winners or losers are useful foundation stones for managing disputes in the future. The instinct of most adults is to prevent conflict in children. It would probably be better to provide guidance, appropriate to the child's age and understanding, as to how that conflict could best be managed.

Friendship groups in infant classrooms can shift and change a good deal within a school year, but further up the school friendship choices become more stable. This is because the definition of friendship changes from the immediate function, for example 'someone to play with who lives next door and lets me have a go on her skates' to qualities of personality, for example 'someone who I can rely on to stick up for me and who shows me how to do the hard sums'.

For much of this period and extending into pre-adolescence there is an element of competition in peer-group relations by which children make judgements about themselves by comparing their performance, status, and so on with that of their associates. How they measure up and how they fit in has a considerable effect on their own self-concept and self-esteem. Useful intervention in the social curriculum in schools and classrooms may include looking at ways in which children's perceptions of each other can be positively influenced and how 'peripheral' children can be given a value and place within the group.

Chums in the middle school years: pre-adolescence

Although there is a tendency for children to play with same-sex friends right from nursery days, by the age of about 9 there is an almost exclusive gender split, with girls and boys having separate groups of friends who operate quite differently. Boys' groups tend to be larger and more activity based and the girls' smaller and more 'conversational'. It is tempting to stereotype this split, however, and fail to take account of the number of girls who are keen to play football or the boys who seek out an intimate 'best friend' with whom to talk over their problems. Schools often make provision for the majority but also need to think of ways of accommodating those who may prefer different opportunities. The school yard is frequently dominated by boys playing football or other sports. Given the chance many girls often enjoy active games but are prevented by the status quo of the 'space invaders'. It is possible to influence the extent and effect of this gender split by sensitive teaching, and having mixed groupings and pairs for collaborative work (see Chapters 6 and 9). A preference for same-sex friendship choice is, however, the norm and continues until adolescence, when interest in the other sex takes on a significance not confined to straightforward friendship.

There is also evidence of a tendency to choose friends who are perceived to have similarities in other ways – such as race or ability (Tuma and Halliman, 1979). Encouraging children within a classroom to focus on what they have in common as well as valuing individual backgrounds is likely to foster a friendly environment, as against one which is allowed to become increasingly divided by the differences between people. 'Open' classrooms, where pupils are organized in groups and a greater degree of interaction is encouraged, have been shown to have a more even spread among friendship choices with more flexible and less exclusive social groupings (Halliman, 1976). The physical organization of the learning environment therefore needs to take account of social as well as academic outcomes.

The complexity of play and other co-operative ventures increases with age. Giving children early opportunities to solve problems together, create together and explore together under the guidance of skilled teachers can have benefits both for the individual children involved at the time and also as a future grounding for the workplace, where teamwork is increasingly valued.

The middle school years, from about 9 to 13, are characterized not only by greater selectivity in choosing friends but also by a deepening of relationships and a shift from the simple sharing of activities to shared views and shared intimacies as well. 'Helping' becomes a highly valued activity of friendship, more important even than 'playing', and this help includes not only the practical variety but also psychological and emotional support (Lewis and Roffey, in press). Children become increasingly aware of other people, not only in terms of what they do but also what they might be thinking and feeling. This awareness leads to a greater sensitivity to others where words and actions might be modified to take into account possible responses from others. Whereas younger children may refrain from doing something because of consequences they would prefer to avoid, an 11-year-old might be careful about what he says because it would be hurtful to someone. The spontaneity and immediacy of earlier friendships is replaced by a greater consciousness of behaviour both in terms of how that might be viewed by others and how it might affect others. Having the ability to understand an action or situation from someone else's point of view is a significant developmental step. Valuing the qualities that someone brings to a relationship means that a friendship may take on a more lasting quality as there is increased motivation as well as skills to maintain it.

It is at this age, in middle childhood, that young people begin to understand the themes that underlie adult friendship. Skills learnt now, together with a learning environment that values and encourages positive social interactions, will benefit them in their relationships for the rest of their lives.

Adolescence: cliques, gangs and going out

Trust and loyalty are essential features of a pre-adolescent friendship and to some extent this increases and intensifies in early adolescence. Friends between the ages of about 11 and 14 can be inseparable. They may spend much of their time together sharing and supporting each other in all the trials and troubles of growing up and out of childhood. Sharing intimacies, which may include a high level of self-disclosure, inevitably means that commitments are strong. When these break they cause a lot of heartache and grief, which may be hidden from adults. Because young people have an increased awareness of the gradual deepening of a relationship over time and how it can take a long time to establish a mutually supportive and intimate friendship, losing a close friend at this age may result in anxiety about being alone. A real friend cannot be quickly or easily replaced.

Friends are now valued, not only for what they bring to the relationship in terms of mutual support, but also for their own qualities of personality. It becomes more important that the people with whom they are associating are worthy of their admiration and respect, although the qualities that are esteemed are not necessarily those that would win adult approval. There is also more tolerance of the occasional failings and moods of friends. Teenagers often become very interested in 'what makes people tick', why they are as they are. This applies especially to their own peer group.

Peer group relationships in adolescence take on a significance which often causes alarm to many parents, not to mention teachers. Young people need to establish themselves as separate and independent from their families and they look for support to do that from their friends. As adolescence proceeds there is a move away from going around together simply in pairs and small groups into being part of a larger group or gang. Membership of the 'gang' and one's status within it become a central feature of a teenager's life. Teenagers' points of reference change, so that what is acceptable to and valued by their friends, and more specifically the group to which they belong, becomes of greater importance than the views that their parents hold. This sometimes leads to conflict as parents see to their horror their son or daughter going to 'ruin' under these 'bad influences'. Nevertheless, the quality of some of these teenage relationships is very high, and many young people get a strong sense of belonging and a good deal of harmless enjoyment from their 'gang' membership. Parents need to avoid making hasty judgements which may be based on biased media coverage of teenage behaviour.

This too, however, is only a 'phase', and by late adolescence most young people will have outgrown the need to be with the 'in-crowd'. They will be spending more and more time in couple relationships which are also sexual in nature. In tandem with this there is a growing realization that a friendship does not have to be exclusive, that people have different needs and that these can be met by the qualities of a range of friends.

WHY HAVING FRIENDS IS IMPORTANT FOR DEVELOPMENT

Children have two social worlds in which they operate. One is the world of adults, where the relationship between the child and the adult is based on caring, protection, instruction and basic inequality. The child is in a position of dependence and comparative powerlessness. Adults are bigger, controlling, dominant, and to a great extent define the relationship. Peers, on the other hand, provide companionship, a face of reality and a measure of equality. Children learn primarily from their friends and companions the 'rules' of relationship; which social skills are rewarding and which behaviours are unacceptable.

We have already mentioned that for the youngest children peers provide a different set of expectations from those of their parents. It is these playmates who are often the means by which egocentricity begins to decrease and the world opens up. Children who acquire some of the basic interactive skills of turn-taking, including, initiating and responding at this young age have a good grounding both for early experiences in school and also for developing more complex friendships later on.

During the school years friends influence each other in many ways and fulfil many functions for the developing child. These are summarized below.

Personal identity formation: developing a sense of self

Children identify not only with their family but also with the social group to which they belong, and especially with their friends. They receive feedback about many aspects of themselves from these significant people in their lives. The way children see themselves – their self-image – is altered and shaped by these messages and by comparisons with others with whom they identify. From these associations children learn what might be valued or considered important and what might be less significant or viewed negatively. If a child's self-image fits in with values held by the group this will have a positive effect on his level of self-esteem. If the group, for instance, values kindly behaviour and the child sees himself as caring, he will have a positive self-image. If, however, being kind is held to be 'soft' and does not fit in with a macho value system the same child may not feel so good about himself (see Chapter 2).

With older children, as with adults, friends do much to validate and support each other's personality. They do that by sharing the same way of seeing things, having similar thoughts, and finding the same things funny. The closer the friends, the more they will have in common about the things that really matter to them. They will have similar views about what is right and wrong, what is valuable and what is enjoyable even though they might have different preferences for ice-cream flavours and even support different teams.

Socialization: developing the skills to live in harmony with other people

Although it is the family which is the first and most important agent for the socialization of children, behaviour is also modified by the influence of the peer group and more specifically by friends. If children continue to behave impulsively, as they may do when very young, they may find themselves in continual conflict with their peers. In order not to lose a friend or to lose the support of the group it is necessary to control these impulses, especially aggressive actions, and seek other more acceptable ways of expressing disagreement or distress. Children will be surprisingly tolerant of the occasional outburst, especially if the child having a 'wobbly' is usually self-controlled, but they will have little to do with those who habitually behave in ways that disturb or disrupt the group. The strength of peer influence and its potential for such things as controlling bullying could be used to good effect in schools.

Unfortunately, there is a cycle of distress here as it is often the angry and friendless child who is more likely to behave in an uncontrolled, 'unsocialized' way. This makes it all the more important that children have supported social learning opportunities as early as possible and more intensive help during middle childhood if necessary (see Chapter 7).

Social cognition: developing understanding

Central to a child's educational progress is the ability to think clearly, to grasp concepts and to be able to reason. Egocentric, subjective views are incompatible with critical or logical thinking. This requires a level of objectivity and ability to see things from different perspectives. As early as 1932 Piaget commented on the role of peers in accelerating this process of 'decentration' which, according to him, is crucial in the development of understanding in all areas. In order to maintain and develop social interactions children cannot continue to operate in an egocentric way; they need to take the views of others increasingly into account. They also need to have direct experience of issues such as fairness and co-operation. This is crucial to the development of understanding about human relationships, the development of concepts of morality and understanding of society in general. These are interlinked, as all involve the developing ability to have insights into the reasoning, perceptions and motivation of other people.

Discussions and interactions with peers include exchange of information and the communication of ideas. This becomes increasingly complex with age and is valuable in promoting cognitive development generally. It is possible that these peer interactions have become even more significant over the past few decades as the one-way communication channel of the television inhibits conversation in family life.

Unless children come from large families they have few opportunities to develop relationships with children of other ages. Schools tend to band students in year groups and do not foster cross-age links. This needs to be reconsidered in the interest of promoting skills, knowledge and understanding. Children do not learn only from others their own age; interaction with 'more competent' peers has been shown to be highly effective in inducing cognitive development (Tudge, 1990).

Company and communication: developing language

Going places, doing things and exploring the world with all its possibilities are enriched by sharing them with a friend. This applies both to the small child and to the adult. For children who no longer need to be accompanied by their parents, a friend may become the means by which these activities actually occur; without someone to go with you may choose not to go.

The need to communicate is part of being human. Those for whom language is a struggle nevertheless seek to find ways of communicating. Commentary, sharing ideas, sharing perspectives on events and people, telling jokes, and simply having an audience for stories about personal events are an integral part of having a social life. As children grow older friends provide an increasing focus for this communication and the nature of the communication changes. By the time children are approaching adolescence friends become the people with whom they share their most private experiences and emotions, almost always in preference to anyone in their family.

Good communication skills include awareness of non-verbal messages, active listening and the give and take of conversation. Knowing how to show an interest in someone else, what to say and how to say it are quite sophisticated achievements. Some children pick these skills up along the way by having good models and opportunities to practise but many other individuals never learn these skills at other than a very basic level, and their ability to make and maintain good relationships with others may be impaired as a result. Teaching children how to communicate effectively may not lead to deep friendships but it certainly goes a long way towards creating opportunities and providing a basis for friendship to develop at some later stage (see Chapters 3 and 5).

Maintenance of emotional stability: developing a sense of inner security

Emotional stability is promoted by the simple fact of having someone who values you enough to want to be your friend. It is a reassurance of your worth and a reinforcer for self-esteem.

On another level emotional stability is supported by having someone with whom to communicate and share. Children, and it appears more especially girls, increasingly seek out friends with whom they can discuss their emotional life, their problems and difficulties. To do this safely requires a level of trust and reciprocity. Events that threaten from outside can pull people together, and where a crisis could result in emotional disintegration for an individual, the level of support, 'togetherness' and ability to share difficulties can strengthen both relationships and the individuals within them.

It is emotionally healthy to experience and try to overcome difficulties but not to prolong unduly the time that they are the central focus of thoughts and feelings. Friends, especially in childhood, provide a perspective which is centred on everyday normality, which helps to 'put things in proportion'.

Stability is also provided by having people with whom perspectives on the world can be compared. When friends share a similar view of events and reinforce each other's value systems they are bolstering each other's personal identity. When someone is often in the minority and his opinions are rejected it can lead to self-doubt. A friendship network can provide stable comparisons for our responses to events and provide feedback about where we stand. This helps to integrate the personality and strengthens a positive self-image.

Help and support: developing empathy and responsibility

For children as young as 10, the definition of a friend is more likely to be someone who 'helps' you than someone who plays with you. This can take the form of practical help such as 'showing me how to spell words I don't know' and also psychological support such as 'listening to me when I've got problems'. What is crucial here in maintaining a relationship as a friendship is that there is acknowledgement and opportunity for reciprocity. If the 'helping' is one-way only then the relationship cannot develop because the person on the receiving end has no way of feeling valued for what she can offer.

This has implications for peer support in the classroom. Children who benefit from help with work need to be given ways in which they can balance the exchange so that they can be reassured of their own worth. The prevailing value system may make some children feel that what they have to offer doesn't count. Where this happens these children often find other ways of making themselves feel better. This is not always helpful to the teacher or to others in the class, except perhaps as a welcome distraction.

Teachers could make a difference here simply by raising awareness of the various qualities that individuals have to offer: 'It was good of you, Lynnette, to take care of Joanne [after she has hurt herself in a game]; it must be nice to have a friend like you.' Cross-age 'helping' has also proved a positive innovation in some schools where children who are struggling in their own age group are given the opportunity to support younger children.

A sense of belonging: developing loyalties

To feel that you are part of something, that you belong, that there is a place for you where you are accepted, is necessary for psychological health. The family is usually the central focus for this sense of belonging and where children first learn about acceptance, trust and relying on people for help and protection. Where there is a lack of these experiences children have greater difficulty establishing other meaningful reciprocal relationships because the foundation stones have not been laid. The experiences that children have in school are crucial as they can go some way to compensating for these gaps. Teachers who are themselves warm and supportive of children, support emerging friendships, help individuals to deal with issues of conflict and foster a sense of class identity and belonging are probably doing more than they realize.

The importance of friends for all children in providing this sense of alliance and inclusion increases with age. 'Best friends' at the pre-adolescent stage can often be highly possessive of each other as if the 'belonging' has overtones of ownership. It takes another step to maturity to recognize that friendship does not have to be exclusive. The need to identify with a group is at its strongest during the teenage years as young people move away from their families.

Loyalty means 'sticking up' for someone or supporting a group, but this does not have to be exclusive. Although a feeling of 'belonging' is healthy and comfortable it is important that children learn to find a balance which allows for pride and security in the groups to which they belong — be it family, friendships, school, gang, team or country — but does not encourage superiority, chauvinism or hatred of outsiders (see Chapters 4 and 6).

POPULARITY IS NOT FRIENDSHIP

Children who are popular and liked by many others usually have skills to make others feel good about themselves. They are therefore able to make good and close friendships to meet the social need for companionship and the psychological need for support and intimacy. There is, however, a danger of confusing popularity with friendship and social success with successful relationships. It is understandable that parents want their children to be popular and well-liked but the promotion of potentially superficial popularity can detract from meaningful, strong friendships and lead to competitive rather than collaborative behaviour.

Famous and successful people who always seem to be surrounded by admirers sometimes give a different impression of their lives in magazine interviews. For some, their apparent popularity hides a personal life of broken relationships and loneliness.

Popularity is concerned with quantity, not quality

Anna is a popular girl; she has many people who say they are her friends or would like to be. She is always invited to parties and everyone wants her on their team.

Graeme isn't so popular. He is a quiet boy whom no one notices much. He isn't much good at sport so he doesn't join in with the ball games at lunchtime. Within the class context Anna has many superficial friends and Graeme has none.

Both of these children, however, have close friendships which are highly rewarding. Anna's friend goes to another school but lives nearby and the girls see each other every evening and weekend. Graeme has a long-term and close friendship with a boy in a different class, whom he has known since his earliest school days. These relationships, both for Anna and Graeme, are significant in that they provide opportunities to share many interests and activities, talk over worries, celebrate others' successes and reinforce a shared view of the world and its meanings. The fact that Anna has many other children to play with during the school day and that Graeme relates only to his friend at playtime and lunchtime is a superficial difference unless it affects his self-esteem and ability to collaborate with others when he needs to.

It is the more intimate and rewarding relationships which provide emotional security and fulfil the 'provisions of friendship' which have been outlined in this chapter. In addition, it is the making and maintaining of close friendships which facilitates the development of higher-level social skills and interactions. The ability to deal successfully with future relationships will be enhanced by having had significant reciprocal friendships at a younger age.

We have already mentioned the gender difference in which sociable girls tend to form close, intimate friendships and sociable boys have larger but looser circles of friends. Graeme's close friendship with another boy is less common than Anna's relationship with her friend. It isn't surprising to find that as adults men and women often both prefer to confide in and be intimate friends with women. An area which might benefit from further research is the ways in which boys can learn skills of intimate friendship, how to support each other more effectively and consequently be more supportive of others when they are older.

Children who do not have friends

As it is important to separate the concept of popularity from the concept of friendship it is also necessary to clarify what constitutes aloneness. For some people solitude is a choice; they enjoy their own company and would prefer to be alone for much of the time. A few children do not actively seek companionship and appear to be content within their own world. This is often true of particularly able children who have no one with whom to share the depth and complexity of their thinking. Such children often have a rich imaginative world which they find satisfying although they also need to have opportunities for developing relationships and learning the skills that go with making and maintaining friendships.

Other people find themselves alone when they crave companionship. Such loneliness can be devastating and lead to increasing withdrawal and passivity. If someone has no one with whom to share thoughts, reflect upon experiences and show interest and caring then that person might consider that it is not worth bothering with anything. The physical existence of other people does not necessarily alleviate these feelings of loneliness if the provisions of friendship are not being met. Loneliness in a crowd may, in fact, be the worst kind.

The extent to which adults − and children − need friends, however, differs from one individual to another. Teachers sometimes find that they worry about pupils who spend more of their time on their own. It only becomes a problem, however, if the children concerned are unable to collaborate with others when required to do so or become unhappy with their state. For other children, even the existence of several friends cannot assuage feelings of loneliness, especially if no one can provide the levels of intimacy that are desired. Such individuals may have a long history of unmet emotional needs.

Children who have no friends because they are actively rejected by their peers constitute one of the most vulnerable groups in schools. They achieve poorly, often truant and may become involved with delinquent behaviour. It has been found that the one factor in childhood that consistently correlates with poor mental health in adulthood is rejection by classmates (Cowen *et al.*, 1973). Norah Frederickson, in writing about the rejected child (Frederickson, 1991), emphasizes the need to address the perceptions and behaviours of others as well as helping the individual concerned to learn new skills and develop more useful perspectives (see also Chapter 7).

Friendship and school attendance

Much of the research that has been carried out in the field of school attendance has focused on family concerns, curriculum issues or school ethos. All of these factors are relevant but friendship also exerts a strong influence on attendance. Having someone to come to school with, looking forward to social activities with friends, and having a sense of belonging are all powerful reasons for wanting to come to school, regardless of the academic curriculum. Likewise, being bullied, feeling isolated and having no way to maintain your self-esteem are understandable reasons for staying away.

Friendship in school is important

Friendship is not something which is either incidental or insignificant. Making and maintaining friendships, feeling you belong somewhere, learning to collaborate with and support others are crucial not only to people's happiness but also to their attainments, their successes and their ability to cope with life. Friendship needs to be given greater attention in schools and be a much higher curricular priority than is presently the case. Those schools that do see that the social curriculum is an integral part of the academic curriculum will recognize that attendance and attainments improve where children are encouraged to value each other. Making provision for pupils to learn the skills involved in making and maintaining relationships will foster an environment where friendship flourishes.

FINDING OUT

Most of the activities outlined in this book are concerned with bringing about change. This section offers ways of identifying where interventions should take place and evaluating changes that occur.

It is easy to make assumptions about how children are relating to each other, especially in the hurly-burly of the school day when teachers have a hundred and one things to do. Nevertheless, if any intervention is being considered within the social curriculum, whether it is with an individual child, a group of children or with the whole class, it is well worth doing some groundwork first. This will give some guidance as to which strategies are likely to prove the most effective and provide a base-line against which any change or development can be measured.

Here we describe a number of investigation techniques which teachers can use, either independently or with others, to enable them to find out more about the social dynamics in their classes or year groups and to identify the problems that some children may be having in making or maintaining friends.

Informal observation

All the time teachers are making informal observations in one way or another. Here we mean observing more closely with a particular focus in mind, perhaps to check out hunches or to get a better idea of what is going on. Asking someone else to make some observations is often useful. It can both validate concerns and provide insights that may be hidden to the teacher who is herself part of the class interactions. It is valuable to carry out such informal observations in a variety of contexts, such as the classroom and the playground, and to note similarities and differences between situations.

Semi-structured observation

The need for more specific observations may follow an informal observation. For example, an informal observation may confirm that a particular child is being left out of groups, both in the class and at break-times. A more structured observation will focus on that child to find out more about what is happening. Are overtures being made and being rejected, is there an influential leader who is determining the behaviour of others, is there anyone who seems to be friendlier than others, and are supervising adults intervening or even reinforcing this situation?

Looking at the issues around conflict may also be enlightening, especially with regard to any emerging patterns of behaviour. Behavioural difficulties can often and valuably be perceived in the light of inadequate or inappropriate friendship skills. Including strategies which address social learning needs may therefore be useful when planning intervention.

Structured observation

The 'soft data' gathered in informal and semi-structured observations provide information on which to base more quantitative investigations. These provide the 'hard data' by which to measure change. They also give clear indications about where and how to focus interventions.

Structured observations are not difficult to carry out once you know what you are looking for. Some of those to be made in the classroom, however, will require the assistance of another person as it is not possible to teach at the same time.

The more structured an observation is the more reliable it will be. These are some ways of structuring observations:

1. *Making a tally.* This is the easiest way of establishing a base-line. The observer simply makes a note of every time a certain behaviour occurs within a given time-period. It may be useful to do this throughout a day or a week to see whether there is a pattern over time.
2. *Timed interval.* The observer has a list of behaviours that appear to be significant. At timed intervals – possibly of a minute – the observer ticks the category of the behaviour that is happening. This technique could be used, for instance, to look at the balance between on- and off-task behaviour within different social groupings.
3. *Field notes.* These observations go into even more detail by recording exactly what is happening in a given context. Categories may be used either at the time or for later coding. This would be useful for seeing what actually happens in a paired 'collaborative' activity.
4. *Checklist.* This could record whether something happens or how often, or simply the physical features of a situation. An investigation into playground behaviour, for instance, might look at questions such as how many seating areas there are, what children are playing with, and so on.

Interviews

If you want to know what is going on it is a good idea to ask the people concerned. Interviews to some extent follow the same pattern as observations in that they move from the informal and unstructured, which can give a general idea of the situation, to something more detailed and specific. Structured schedules of questions serve the same sort of purpose as checklists in observations.

Parental interviews

If a teacher is particularly concerned about an individual child in her class for any reason it is essential that she should talk with that child's parents or carers. This should be done with sensitivity so that anxieties are not unduly heightened and parents do not feel that they are being blamed in any way. Asking whether they also have concerns and finding out what the child is like at home will be very helpful in deciding what to do.

Often parents will be the ones to initiate a discussion. This may be focused around the behaviour of others, such as bullying. Teachers might feel that parents are being over-protective or that their child is equally to blame for situations. Parents will feel, however, that they are being taken seriously if teachers agree to investigate the situation carefully and keep everyone informed of their findings. Discussing the usefulness of possible interventions with parents is also likely to be helpful in gaining their support and maximizing the effectiveness of strategies.

Questionnaires and surveys

When you need to find out the views of a large number of students a questionnaire is helpful. Surveys can sometimes be carried out by pupils themselves. There is some information about carrying out a survey into bullying in Chapter 8.

Sociometric surveys

Sociometric surveys are ways of looking at the sociometric composition of a class and identifying the children who are popular or rejected. They are also helpful in evaluating changes. Some researchers are reluctant to use these methods, especially when children are asked to nominate unpopular peers, for fear of reinforcing a negative situation. It is possible to adapt some of the methods described below to minimize this possibility.

1. Children are asked to name the child they would most like to play with and then their second choice. Sometimes they are also asked for their third choice. In some surveys children are also asked which child they would not like to play with. Children may be asked slightly different questions, such as who they would most like to 'work' with as well as or instead of 'play' with. This survey will enable the teacher to 'score' children in terms of their popularity and will quickly identify children who may be vulnerable.

2. The names of all the children in the class are listed and there are four columns next to each name, containing a smiley face, a frowning face, an 'indifferent' face and a blank face respectively. Children fill in the columns according to whether they would like to play with this person or not, whether they don't mind, or whether they don't know this person well enough to know. This method shows which children are accepted and rejected as well as which are popular, and also gives guidance as to which children would be most responsive in strategies to intervene.

Picture representation

If children are asked simply to draw a picture of themselves with their friends and to write something about it, most children find it an enjoyable and unthreatening activity. It provides some information about the reciprocity of friendships, what activities are seen as central to the friendships, and, to some extent, the importance of these relationships to the individuals concerned.

REFERENCES

Berndt, T. J. (1983) The features and effects of friendship in early adolescence. *Child Development* **53**, 1447–60.

Bigelow, B. J. and La Gaipa, J. J. (1980) The development of friendship values and choice. In H. C. Foot, A. J. Chapman and J. R. Smith (eds) *Friendship and Social Relations in Children*. Chichester: Wiley.

Bretherton, I. and Waters, E. (eds) (1985) Growing points of attachment theory and research. *Monographs of the Society for Research in Child Development* **50** (1–2).

Cowen, E. L., Pederson, A., Babigian, H., Izzo, L. D. and Trost, M. A. (1973) Long-term follow-up of early detected vulnerable children. *Journal of Consulting and Clinical Psychology* **41**, 438–46.

Duck, S. (1977) *The Study of Acquaintance*. Farnborough: Saxon House.

Duck, S. (1991) *Friends, for Life: The Psychology of Personal Relationships*. Hemel Hempstead: Harvester Wheatsheaf.

Fontana, D. (1981) Concept formation and development, and Values and moral development. In *Psychology for Teachers*. Basingstoke: Macmillan and British Psychological Society.

Frederickson, N. (1991) Children can be so cruel: helping the rejected child. In G. Lindsay and A. Miller (eds) *Psychological Services for Primary Schools*. Harlow: Longman.

Halliman, M. T. (1976) Friendship patterns in open and traditional classrooms. *Sociology of Education* **49**, 254–65.

Hartup, W. W. (1978) Children and their friends. In H. McGurk (ed.) *Issues in Childhood Social Development*. London: Methuen.

Kohlberg, L. (1981) *Essays on Moral Development*, Vol. 1. New York: Harper & Row.

Kohlberg, L. (1984) *Essays on Moral Development*, Vol. 2. New York: Harper & Row.

La Guipa, J. J. (1981) Children's friendships. In S. W. Duck and R. Gilmour (eds) *Personal Relationships 2: Developing Personal Relationships*. London: Academic Press.

Lewis, C. L. and Roffey, S. (In press) Developing the friendly school. Paper presented at the Division of Education and Child Psychology Conference. British Psychological Society, 1993.

Maxwell, W. (1990) Friendship in the primary school. In P. Kutnick and C. Rogers (eds) *The Social Psychology of the Primary School*. London: Routledge.

Parten, M. B. (1932) Social participation among pre-school children. *Journal of Abnormal and Social Psychology* **27**, 243–69.

Piaget, J. (1929) *The Child's Conception of the World*. New York: Harcourt Brace Jovanovich.

Piaget, J. (1932) *The Moral Judgement of the Child*. London: Routledge & Kegan Paul.

Rubin, Z. (1980) *Children's Friendships*. London: Open Books.

Selman, R. L. and Jacquette, D. (1977) Stability and oscillation in interpersonal awareness: a clinical-developmental analysis. In C. B. Keasey (ed.) *The Nebraska Symposium on Motivation*, Vol. 25. Lincoln: University of Nebraska Press.

Smith, P. K. and Cowie, H. (1992) *Understanding Children's Development*. Oxford: Blackwell.

Sullivan, H. S. (1953) *The Interpersonal Theory of Psychiatry*. New York: Norton.

Tudge, J. (1990) Vygotsky, the zone of proximal development and peer collaboration: implications for classroom practice. In L. C. Mull, *Vygotsky and Education*. Cambridge: Cambridge University Press.

Tuma, N. and Halliman, M. (1979) The effects of sex, race and achievement in school on children's friendships. *Social Forces* **57**, 1265–85.

Vandell, D. L. and Mueller, E. C. (1980) Peer play and friendships during the first two years. In H. C. Foot, A. J. Chapman and J. R. Smith (eds) *Friends and Social Relations in Children*. Chichester: Wiley.

Westwood, P. I. (1987) *Commonsense Methods for Children with Special Needs*. London: Croom Helm.

About my picture: Me and my friend's playing football I am quit good At football I am in The school football team I play mid filed The name's of my friend's are osman, chris, mario, Amar, Hasan, Elisha, Moshan Andrew, Demetris, Jermaine, Ben, Garry, Ianan, Marcus, peter, Mark.

Chapter 2

Self-Concept, Self-Esteem and Confidence

'There's just no stopping her; she's able to do anything.'

'Once she stopped thinking we were all out to put her down, it was much easier to be friends.'

'I can't go to the party, they don't really want me there.'

'Maria comes up to me time after time to check that she's doing something correctly.'

'He won't even try — he just thinks of himself as a failure.'

'I really tried to help Ian get on better with the others in the class. I even took a small group at lunchtimes to try and teach him how to have conversations but he didn't seem to have any motivation or interest, so I just gave up.'

SELF-ESTEEM: THE ROUTE TO FRIENDSHIP

Even the most able and sensitive teacher will have difficulty in helping a student to learn appropriate social skills if that pupil has a low level of self-esteem and confidence which prevents her from focusing outwards.

Self-concept and self-esteem are key factors in influencing how successful a child will be at initiating and sustaining friendships. When someone has a positive view of herself and her self-esteem is high, she is likely to have sufficient confidence to make and respond to overtures of friendship. Someone who anticipates failure or ridicule will be less likely to take the risk. One definition of shyness is the focusing on the self in a situation rather than on others because of anxiety about performance. It takes quite a lot of self-confidence not to think or be anxious about how you are doing but to be genuinely interested in other people.

Children with high levels of self-esteem and confidence are more able to make and keep friends, communicate effectively and be independent. When there are problems with relationships these children are more likely to be prepared to tackle the difficulty and 'bounce back'. Children with a low level of self-esteem and who are lacking in self-confidence are more vulnerable. They are more likely to react badly when things don't go smoothly, sometimes by withdrawing altogether or by making inappropriate and sometimes even aggressive responses. Moreover, failure to overcome these problems serves to reinforce their feelings of worthlessness and inadequacy.

All teachers will be familiar with the child who at first appears to be anything but lacking in self-confidence. He sits at the back of the class, making more noise than the others, always wanting to be first in line and over-reacting to any assumed insult. It soon becomes clear that his confidence is, in reality, very thin and masks a low level of self-esteem. Not surprisingly this can affect educational progress and social adjustment. A significant proportion of school refusers show low levels of self-esteem as well as records of poor academic attainments (Reid, 1982).

Successful friendships are reciprocal, involving 'give and take'. This can mean exchanging jokes, listening to and telling secrets and helping someone out when they are in trouble. Having a realistic view of yourself and generally liking yourself are prerequisites for having good friends. A child who has a very low opinion of herself is unlikely to believe that other children will like her and will therefore tend to avoid opportunities for friendship.

DEFINITIONS

In this chapter, we discuss how children can be helped to develop a sense of self and self-confidence. Before we go any further in discussing ways of developing the confidence and self-esteem of pupils, it may be as well to clarify what is meant by these terms.

A sense of self

When describing the self we are entering potentially vague territory as there are several terms which are often used interchangeably:

- self-image or self-concept
- ideal self
- self-esteem
- self- or social confidence

Although these different terms are very much related they do have distinct meanings and it is useful to be clear about what we are talking when we use each of them.

Self-image or self-concept

The self-concept is about how people see themselves. It is the core of a person's individual identity. For instance, someone may view himself as assertive, able to listen to others, good at mathematics and a weak swimmer, along with many other things that make up the person he considers himself to be. The way we see ourselves is dependent on factors which include gender, race, age, abilities, physical and personal character-istics and even our name, together with influences such as social class, culture and religion.

An important part of developing a sense of self is identifying with the groups to which we feel we belong. Children at a very early age are aware of gender, for example, choosing, for example, same-sex playmates, and children at the ages of 3 and 4 can often identify members of their own racial group, distinguishing them from other racial groups (Milner, 1984). Children are also developing an awareness of attitudes towards different groups and how different groups in society are treated. This may be a positive experience, serving to reinforce their sense of identity and self-esteem, or it may have negative and potentially damaging consequences. These are important equal opportunity issues which significantly affect self-identity and opportunities for friendship, and are explored further in Chapter 6.

The self-image is powerfully shaped by how others see us (and indeed how we think others see us). This also begins right from the earliest stages of development. A child who overhears comments on his musical ability such as 'he's really taken to playing the guitar', and is told by others, 'you've got a talent there', is more likely to think of himself as musical, even if he is not particularly talented in that direction. The chances are, of course, that he will become interested and able musically. The girl who constantly hears comments such as 'You've broken it — you're so clumsy' and is discouraged from attempting to do things independently will eventually think of herself as helpless.

We are unique individuals with our own thoughts and feelings. Our perceptions, however, about ourselves and the world are shaped by the experiences we have and how we interpret them. Our self-image is acquired, not inherited. It helps to under-stand others if we can get an insight into how *they* perceive themselves in the world, and what sort of persons they think they are.

Ideal self

As the term implies, the ideal self is the picture someone has in his mind's eye of how he would really like to be. Perhaps he would like to be popular, good at basketball, or even-tempered in trying situations. It is worth reminding ourselves that not everyone has the same ideal self, and what is important for one person, such as being really successful at school, may not figure very much on someone else's agenda. A child's ideal self (or at least part of it) may be modelled on another person, such as a parent or esteemed adult or a popular figure such as a sports personality or entertainer.

Self-esteem

Giving ourselves credit for what we are and what we have done is helpful to our health and well-being. Self-esteem is concerned with how we feel about ourselves and our perceived characteristics. If there is a big difference between the self-image and the ideal self, there is likely to be a markedly low level of self-esteem.

Correspondingly, the closer the match between self-image and the ideal self, the more likely that there will be a high level of self-esteem. Children with low levels of self-esteem often focus on the things they cannot do, rather than on those they can. Adults, therefore, need to provide opportunities for children to become more aware of their strengths and to learn to value the good things about themselves. They also need to be helped to acknowledge and express feelings and to accept themselves as they are. Raising self-image in these ways is a powerful step towards improving self-esteem.

Social confidence

Confidence as a feeling is important to everyone. Realistic and reliable confidence gives us peace of mind.

Angela is respected by other children for her ability and liked because she is modest and will help others if they ask her. Yet in science and maths she becomes very anxious and can hardly start her work at all.

Her parents see Angela as confident and competent, especially when she is with younger children. They do not know that she would rather not go into shops where she has to ask for what she wants and that she always goes to supermarkets if asked to do any shopping. Inside, Angela does not feel good about herself and prefers to avoid social contact and many situations. She is therefore at risk of social stresses and possibly of completing formal education without fulfilling her potential.

Like most people, including children, Angela feels confident with some things and in many situations. Her problem is that she does not feel confident in herself generally, and this affects her social opportunities. She is well liked but does not confide her feelings to anyone. She does make comments to other children which sound negative, but they interpret them as modesty. No one sees that Angela has any problems, so they are not being addressed. They are as likely to grow as to fade as she gets older.

Angela has kept up the appearance of being confident, successful and socially skilled, but her feelings overall and attainments do not reflect this. Helping her develop her social confidence further would also involve raising her level of self-esteem.

THE LINK BETWEEN SELF-ESTEEM AND LEARNING

Several studies have revealed an association between self-esteem and academic achievement. Children with greater levels of self-control and autonomy showed correspondingly high levels of self-esteem and academic achievement (Lawrence, 1987). It would seem that there may be a downward spiral for some children linking their self-esteem and reading ability. The child with lowered self-esteem is likely to approach the learning situation with increased levels of anxiety and can afford to take fewer risks to learn. Indeed, such children often display a noticeable passivity in class, which may be in stark contrast to their behaviour in other settings (Holt, 1964). In these situations, adult reaction to the failure can significantly influence a child's self-esteem. Parents are rightly concerned about their children's progress. There are occasions, however, when parental anxiety regarding their child's failure to read, for example, can be counter-productive. The child can come to feel that she is failing not only herself, but also her family, as the attention of everyone is focused on the negative aspects of the situation. Teachers have a powerful role to play in providing learning and social opportunities where positive feedback can be given to foster self-confidence. It is important that we acknowledge that children cannot develop self-esteem on their own. Adults important to the child have a major part to play, as do other children with whom the child comes into contact.

MAINTAINING A LOW LEVEL OF SELF-ESTEEM

Children with low self-esteem will risk less and use avoidance and compensatory strategies in order not to fail. Many teachers will be aware of the child who becomes the class clown or entertainer to avoid attempting work that is seen as too difficult. For the child, failing because you haven't tried is infinitely less stressful than failing when you have tried.

Jerry is often in trouble; he will hide children's belongings and sometimes scribble on other children's work. He continually makes up stories about where he has been and what he has been doing, which sound interesting until you find out that they are not true. Jerry never owns up to a problem, even when there are adults who have been at the scene.

Jerry has very low self-esteem. Like other children with poor self-esteem, he does not accept responsibility for his actions. Children like Jerry frequently tell lies to protect themselves and blame others; they may show quite boastful behaviour, and may bully others. Although these strategies may seem effective for the child in protecting a vulnerable level of self-esteem, they make it difficult for others to intervene in helping to raise it. A child's self-concept and self-esteem are often quite resistant to change. Damaged confidence needs a great deal of careful mending, which takes time and effort.

LEARNING TO COPE

Children who have experiences of positive and responsive parenting from babyhood learn early on that they can effect change. This helps them to feel more secure and more willing to interact with others. It is these expectancies which shape ability and social skills together with specific experiences. In the following years, children begin to explore their worlds and attempt to do things independently, for example feed themselves, ride a bicycle and make contact with significant adults. These adults need to give support, encouragement and praise for the child's efforts. Perceived disapproval or rejection may lead to a poorer self-concept and a lower level of self-esteem. The world becomes an uncertain place, where it is harder to take risks and the expectation of failure is often fulfilled. Children in these situations have often learnt to believe that they can have very little control over the world around them. Their behaviour is perceived to be governed by adults or by events happening to them. We say that they have developed an 'external locus of control'. All teachers will have met children who find it hard to accept responsibility for their own actions. For some children with low self-esteem, this not only includes their poor behaviour but also their achievements.

Happily, many children learn that they *can* make things happen and when this occurs we say that they are developing an internal locus of control. These are two very contrasting approaches to life. Whether a child is developing an inner or external locus of control will determine self-concept and self-esteem, the development of successful relationships and academic achievements (see Chapter 7).

ADULTS AS ROLE MODELS

Not only are adults important in providing support and encouragement, they also model behaviour. If an adult relates well to others, is considerate, firm and friendly, this provides a good model for the child. If an adult behaves in an aggressive way, however, over-reacting and not communicating well, this is not a good model, and it will be hard for a child to develop appropriate and satisfactory social skills. One interesting study was carried out where the researcher observed adults communicating with other adults and adults communicating with children (Yule, 1985). It was found that when adults were together they spent more time exchanging conversation and smiling. When adults were communicating with children, they were less likely to smile and spent more time scolding. Adults may not be fully aware of the models they are providing.

The importance of adults being supportive and positive cannot be underestimated. Jay Carter (1989) refers to people whom he calls 'invalidators'. People who invalidate others may (or may not) appear to be caring and helpful, yet on other occasions will say things which might seem quite trivial but which will undermine another person's self-esteem, such as:

> 'That's a lovely painting ... what's it supposed to be?'
> 'I asked you to make sure you shut the gate properly. Now the dog's got out. Honestly, I can't leave you for five minutes.'
> 'Steven's just not musically minded. Mind you, he insists on practising every night.'

Making judgements and generalizations about a child's personality that go much further than the specifics of the situation are the hallmarks of an invalidating message. Invalidating may be conscious or unconscious. As adults, we need to be aware of our relative position of power, because children will be very much more susceptible to the messages behind the comments that we make.

POWER AND CONFIDENCE

The balance of power is a significant factor affecting social confidence. For example, most adults would find cooking a meal for friends more relaxing, and so perhaps more likely to be enjoyable, than cooking a meal for the boss and partner! There is unequal power between adults and children. In our society, children are less powerful, not only because of their physical immaturity and lack of experience, but also because of restrictions on their rights and choices. For example, children do not have a right to vote or to own property, or to choose which school they will go to (Lansdowne, 1993). This powerlessness can make children more vulnerable and increases the need for adults to be supportive and to act in the best interests of the child. Children also need to be helped to express their own views on matters affecting them in accordance with their age and understanding.

Those pupils who need to boost their self-esteem often benefit from opportunities to play with or look after younger children. In these situations they are able to feel more powerful and can be helped to regain confidence in their skills and abilities to relate positively to others.

FEELINGS AND PERCEPTIONS

Many children with low self-esteem are unable to express feelings, fearing disapproval or rejection. When feelings are denied over a period of time, a child's sense of who he is can become lost. He can begin to feel powerless. A child who feels rejected and excluded by other children might deny these feelings and also the events surrounding this. He may find it less painful to reinterpret the situation.

'I don't like Harry, Sean or David ... I'll never be friends with them.'

The child is unlikely to make attempts to join a group with these children, even if friendly gestures are made towards him. If the child does show social behaviour which offends other children, for example always wanting to be first and wanting to control the game, or hitting others without provocation, then the real difficulty is hidden and therefore less accessible to change.

A child can be helped, however, to acknowledge his feelings;

'I feel miserable/lonely/hurt when they won't let me play.'

He can also be encouraged to try to see why this is happening:

'I did hit David, I wanted to go first.'

Discussion about why this doesn't help can lead to looking at alternatives:

'I'll let someone else go first and say we should take turns.'

In this way, helping a child to express and share his feelings about a situation leads to the next step of helping him to acknowledge and 'read' a situation more accurately. This is of crucial importance. The more able a child is to perceive a situation accurately, the more able he is to use the social skills he has appropriately and effectively. Most teachers will know of children who have difficulties relating to others because, while often desperate for friendship, they misread the situation and so show inappropriate behaviour (see Chapter 7).

Teachers can help these skills to develop. When a child is able to recognize and express her own feelings, she can then be encouraged to empathize with the feelings of others. This can be done by talking through situations as they arise, by providing opportunities to discuss and role-play stories, and through other curriculum-related activities. The ability to appreciate the situation from another point of view is an important cognitive skill. Children can be shown how to empathize and express concern for others: 'Chantelle is feeling sad because her pet dog has died. Let's think of things we can say or do to help her feel a bit better, to show that we care.'

Teachers who have high levels of self-esteem themselves are often more able to take risks in trying new things with children. They can take the view that a little success is better than doing nothing. It makes a considerable difference if the school has a good ethos and staff have a high level of expectation for themselves as well as the children. Pupils are then more likely to have good levels of self-esteem. If this is not the case, teachers need to look at whole-school approaches to developing a more productive and welcoming environment for everyone. This may include making sure that a challenging and interesting curriculum is provided, where co-operative learning is important and valued. (See Chapter 10, where ideas for encouraging co-operative learning are discussed.)

PERCEPTIONS ARE NOT ALWAYS ACCURATE

As we have seen, perceptions of self and others are not always accurate. We have discussed how self-concept, self-image and self-esteem are shaped not only by our own perceptions but also by our perceptions of how we think others see us. Perceptions are our constructs and interpretations of the world and the people about us, how we make sense of it all. The nearer our constructs are to the real situation, the more effective and appropriate will be our response to other people and events. For example, people with anorexia nervosa often have a distorted body image; although they may in reality be thin and underweight, when they look in the mirror they perceive themselves as being overweight – a perception which is accompanied by feelings of self-loathing.

A child may be focused upon what she considers to be the negative aspects of herself. She needs to be supported in redressing this biased perception to a more balanced image, so that a more accurate and less negative self-concept is formed, with a consequent rise in self-esteem.

DEVELOPMENT AND CHANGES

Our perceptions need to be flexible – adapting and developing as situations around us change. When there are major changes in our lives, attention needs to be paid to our general level of self-esteem and confidence. In general, positive changes in perceptions indicate that a person is in control of her life, even though there may be temporary set-backs. The transfers between schools from first to middle school, primary to secondary school, or middle to senior school are important transitions in life. Some children may experience lower self-esteem for some time as their self-concept is redefined in terms of new challenges and the making of new friends. Others may look forward to a new situation with confidence in the hope that it will offer a 'new start'.

Issues of self-confidence for young people are often linked with the development of their bodies. Being well co-ordinated and good at sports contributes to being popular. For some, physical characteristics undermine rather than promote confidence and social success. Without general confidence, social development is restricted and quality of life affected. If young people feel good about their bodies, then issues of hygiene and dress may help to reinforce their self-esteem. If they feel unattractive then the way they dress and their personal hygiene may make them feel worse and also impede their friendship building. The onset of puberty is also a significant developmental stage leading to physical and emotional changes. For a while, lower self-esteem may occur while a new body image is being formed. It is when children are not able to adapt their perceptions flexibly to changes that more persistent difficulties may emerge.

As was discussed earlier, some children may fail to learn to read despite the help and support they are given and it may be that their fixed image of themselves as non-readers may be a barrier to progress:

'I'm not clever, so I can't read.'

This self-image may be unconscious or conscious. Pupils' fixed perceptions of themselves as non-readers, together with low self-esteem, do not allow for the possibilities of change. To try to learn to read risks further failure; it is more comfortable to stay with the self-image as a non-reader. The same thing may happen with respect to making friends. To change into someone who helps others may put at risk a fixed self-image which is about being tough. Adults need to be aware of a child's perceptions of himself in order to help the child to increase his own awareness and to enable these perceptions to be challenged. This is an important step in helping a child to take more control and develop more effective strategies both in learning and in social relationships. Children with reading difficulties who receive counselling to improve self-esteem tend to make more progress than those receiving reading tuition alone (Lawrence, 1985).

LABELLING CAN HAVE SERIOUS CONSEQUENCES

Adults need to make sure that their perceptions are flexible and not fixed so that they can take into account all aspects of a person's behaviour and the situations in which they occur. Perceptions can be distorted through the use of labels and stereotypes. Labels do not reflect the complexity of a person. The child who has been labelled a 'bully' could possibly be a victim of bullying in other situations, for example by older brothers or sisters. It is important to label the behaviour and not the child (Robinson and Maines, 1988); for example:

'Ashraf, I'm surprised at you ... swearing at those younger children this morning. You normally behave well at break-times.'

Identifying specific behaviour is more likely to leave self-esteem intact. The teacher here gives positive reinforcement of other behaviour as well as maintaining the expectation of appropriate behaviour.

The influence of adult expectations is considerable. Improved behaviour is likely to be a consequence of positive expectations and encouragement. If a teacher thinks that a child will be unable to do something this expectation is likely to lead to a self-fulfilling prophecy. Teacher expectancy is a powerful tool which can be used to raise a child's level of self-esteem, but can also be quite damaging if used in a negative fashion.

BUILDING SELF-ESTEEM AND SELF-CONFIDENCE IN THE CLASSROOM

To develop a child's self-esteem, we need to look closely at the child's self-concept, and to be aware of the defences that may be in operation to protect self-esteem. For example, day-dreaming, not attempting work, being boastful and blaming others may all be strategies to avoid possible feelings of failure or inadequacy.

Indicators of high self-esteem	*Indicators of low self-esteem*
self-confidence	low self-confidence
willing to try	gives up
independent	dependent on adults
makes friends	has difficulty relating to others
uses constructive feedback	finds it hard to accept criticism
has a realistic view of skills	has a negative view of capabilities
is able to trust others	lack of faith in others
motivated	avoids tasks
confident in own ideas	copies others

Teachers can help to develop a child's self-esteem by becoming a significant person to a particular child and by creating a positive, safe and caring environment in the classroom. In order for a teacher to become a significant other, she will need to spend time getting to know the child in order that a relationship built on trust and acceptance is developed. The first step in developing a child's self-esteem is to help the child to recognize that she is accepted for who she is and can learn to accept herself. Some of the activities which follow are aimed at self-acceptance.

The teacher will also need to be able to recognize and value the good characteristics of the child and gain an understanding of the child's self-concept. She will need to be able to make a consistent effort to help the child feel better about herself.

There are teacher qualities which make any such strategy more effective. These are genuineness, warmth and empathy, which is the ability to understand how another person views her situation and to communicate that understanding (Rogers, 1967). It needs to be conveyed to the child by her teacher that she is respected and valued as an individual. This is not necessarily a straightforward task, especially when a child's behaviour poses difficulties for others, or where a child's level of self-esteem is so low that she is hardly able to accept praise. High school teachers in particular might be slightly wary in their more public responses to pupils, as it can embarrass them. Praise and offers of help need to be discreet.

Clive had recently been appointed as a geography teacher at a large high school. He took pride in having high expectations and ensured that school and homework were completed to a high standard. Clive felt that he had a good relationship with his pupils and had reached the stage where he could relax more in class and tell a joke or two without discipline breaking down. Initially Clive was pleased with the work of his pupils but towards the end of the first term he noted that some pupils seemed restless and less motivated. This was particularly so for a few pupils with poor writing skills. Clive was perplexed and disappointed as he had spent a lot of time helping these particular pupils. He had hoped that they would become more confident and take pride in their work. Had Clive been more in tune with the feelings of these students, he would have found some valuable clues as to the change in behaviour.

Sarah, one of the pupils with literacy difficulties, comments:

'Mr Clarke takes time to explain things to us if we don't understand ... but he makes me feel stupid. He calls me out to his desk in front of everyone and goes through my work pointing out the spelling mistakes. Sometimes he says, "Good work, Sarah, now why can't you do it all the time?" He makes me feel useless.'

Teachers need to make sure that intended compliments are positive.

Be precise in your praise!

Precise positive feedback and growth in self-esteem go together. The effect of compliments may be lost if they are too general. Comments such as 'that's much better' written on an essay do not give precise feedback that can be acted on. Specific, positive comments written about an essay are not only helpful to develop learning skills, they give the message that a pupil's efforts (and, by extension, the pupil herself) are valued. For example:

'You have presented your ideas clearly and convincingly. Well done!'

'I can see that you've spent time on checking for spelling errors — there aren't any! This is a very good piece of work!'

We know of a sociology teacher who significantly raised the self-esteem and achievement of his pupils through specific positive comments written on the essay. He often finished with comments to really boost morale, for example:

'Well done, Linda. Far from starting to flag, you're storming home!'

Continual low-key reinforcement which is genuine is likely to have a positive outcome. Sporadic praise which is not always justified is not believed or valued by the child (or adult) and so has little impact.

Acknowledging success

It is more usual to compliment, praise and reward children in the primary school. Colourful displays of children's work are public affirmations of achievement. Such public exhibitions are less evident in high schools, where pupils move from class to class, from teacher to teacher, and more frequently work from textbooks. While the handing out of certificates and prizes on 'prize day' is rather a thing of the past, this system of reward has not been replaced. Regular occasions to mark and celebrate the effort and successes of individuals and groups in senior schools would be useful. Such occasions raise the self-esteem of individuals and contribute to a positive school ethos in which people feel valued and their efforts recognized. Many secondary schools are now taking time to develop impressively presented Records of Achievement to record pupil progress. Public displays of achievements which cover effort, progress, responsibilities and so on as well as academic, sporting or musical success can be very uplifting and improve self-esteem. Some tutor groups in senior schools have a display board to be used by the pupils, where letters of thanks for fund-raising, certificates, and message of support and good luck are displayed.

Learning to be assertive

As children become more able to express their feelings and to read social situations more accurately they are more able to act assertively. Teaching children how to be assertive empowers them and helps them to approach problems in all areas of their lives with more confidence. It is a reinforcing cycle. When children are assertive they are learning that they can influence events and people around them. As a consequence their self-esteem and social confidence are increased. We are all exposed to situations where we need to be assertive. For children these could be:

- approaching someone to be friendly when others are present
- dating issues
- asking to join a well-established group
- refusing to join an undesirable activity
- approaching an unfriendly or uninterested adult
- refusing dangerous or threatening activities
- dealing with threats of ostracism
- shopping
- avoiding fighting without losing face
- accepting mistakes without having confidence destroyed

As Tricia Szirom and Sue Dyson (1986) point out, there are basically four different ways to respond to a problem situation:

1. *Passive.* Children who have an external locus of control believe that they have no control of the situation and are more likely to leave others to make the decisions. They may find it very difficult to express an opinion.
2. *Direct aggressive.* When there is a direct aggressive response, people are left in no doubt as to the feelings of the aggressor, who may use verbal or physical aggression, for example hitting out.

3. *Indirect aggressive.* When children are unable to express their feelings and anger in the appropriate place the aggression may show itself in a different situation. A child might be upset or angry with someone at home but find it safer to direct these feelings at a fellow pupil in school.
4. *Assertive.* When people are assertive, they express their opinions honestly and clearly, without damaging themselves or others. They direct what they have to say to the appropriate people.

Key skills for social confidence and assertiveness include the following:

- Body posture. Children can feel and look more confident and assertive by standing tall, with good eye contact.
- Physical closeness. This means standing near enough without crowding someone.
- Speaking clearly. This involves being able to continue speaking regardless of attempts to interrupt and without being too hesitant.
- Giving yourself positive messages, 'I can' and 'I will', replacing negative expectations such as 'she won't want to talk to me', 'I'll never be able to do that'.
- Feeling confident enough to say how you feel, and to express your opinions.
- Listening to others and accepting constructive criticism.
- Being able to say 'No' when we don't want to do something.

For specific situations like those listed earlier, practice with a script and with follow-up to ensure that the confident approach is applied successfully will be very helpful. The processes of providing models, scripts, feedback and genuine praise are effective, but need to be precisely worked out.

A reasonable level of self-esteem is necessary in order to embark on establishing good relationships with others. Teachers who wish to encourage and promote friendship and positive social interactions in school will pay attention to ways of raising and maintaining the self-esteem of their pupils.

TAKING ACTION

The aims of the activities suggested are to enable children to learn not only that they are not alone in their fears and feelings but that they are unique and special. The activities are designed to enable children to increase their awareness of themselves and to accept the possibility of change.

Some activities enable children to gain positive feedback from others. This will help them to see themselves more positively. These activities also provide safe opportunities for children to try out new ways of saying things and behaving, and develop confidence in taking risks.

Other activities have the specific aim of enabling each child to become more aware of the good and special aspects about himself and to accept himself as he is. An additional aim is to develop group awareness and acceptance.

WHAT I LIKE ABOUT ME

Ask the children to write down all the things they like about themselves and to draw pictures to illustrate this. Discussion beforehand will be useful as there may be some children who find it difficult to identify anything about themselves which is special. With encouragement every child will be able to come up with something positive, for example:

- 'I can always cheer my baby sister up and make her laugh'
- 'I can roller-skate backwards'
- 'I am tidy'
- 'I don't get cross if others can't understand what I'm saying'
- 'I'm the eldest child in my family'
- 'I'm Spanish'
- 'I can tell the time now'
- 'I'm the one who takes the dog out every day, even if it's raining'
- 'I'm learning the Koran'
- 'My new haircut!'

What the class have produced can be made into a large book for others to share.

MY LIFE-MAP

Ask pupils to draw a path and divide it into sections. In each section, write or draw good and not so good times in chronological order. Variations on this could be 'Me five years ago', 'Me now', 'Me in five years' time'. Students enjoy doing this in pairs. They could draw each other's life-map by asking questions about each other.

BODY PUZZLE

It is easier to feel comfortable with other people when you feel comfortable with yourself. We all have things about us which we like and other things that we do not like so much, but they are all part of who we are. A first step is to know the bits of the jigsaw which make up the person you are. You can only change something if you know what it is that you wish to change.

Hand out two body outlines to each pupil. Ask them to write down all the things they like about themselves on one body, and to write down things they would like to change on the other body. Ask pupils to find a partner and take it in turns to share some of the things that they have written in each body.

The preliminary discussion for this activity should ensure that pupils know that it is not only appearance that is the focus of the exercise. It may also be useful to talk about what things can be changed and what cannot. For example, we can change the fact that we are bad-tempered, but we cannot change the fact that we have size 8 feet.

IT'S A RECORD

Make an 'It's a Record!' book for the class. Ask everyone in the class to suggest a category, for example:

- has the most sisters
- travels the furthest to school
- speaks the most languages
- has the biggest number of letters in their name
- writes the longest list of words in one minute beginning with 'p'

Give out certificates when a record has been achieved.

This activity is derived from Borba and Borba (1982), Vol. 2, p. 46. See p. 37.

'I'VE DONE IT!' SCROLL

Ask the children to make scrolls or certificates listing things they are able to do. Discuss these as a group. Which are the most unusual ones? Some children will need help to be able to focus on achievements. A child with low self-esteem may answer the question 'What have you learnt to do in your life?' with 'nothing'. This must be challenged – preferably before the activity gets under way with the whole class.

Examples:

- 'put up a tent'
- 'swim 500 metres'
- 'make a pizza'
- 'speak Bengali and English'
- 'I have earned my bronze Duke of Edinburgh Award'
- 'I can play the drums'

This activity is derived from Borba, 1989, p. 285.

GOOD FEEDBACK FILE

Older pupils may like to keep a journal or file to record the positive comments of others, letters and cards from friends, notes to say congratulations or thanks. Certificates for swimming, music exams, good school reports, photographs of good times with friends could all be included. Pupils may like to share their file with others in the class from time to time, and make a positive comment in a friend's file.

FEELINGS

The aim of this activity is to enable children to recognize their own feelings in order to develop a positive self-concept. They are helped to be more aware of the various feelings we have, and how these may be shared by others. It also provides the opportunity for them to learn that it is all right to have and express feelings. This is an important part of themselves. A child's recognition of his own feelings is the first step in his realizing that he does have choices in how he responds to his feelings.

Label one sheet 'Feeling Bad' and the second sheet 'Feeling Good'. Ask the children in turn to describe times when they feel bad and times when they are happy, encouraging them to use a range of vocabulary to express emotion. It is important to distinguish between thinking words and feelings words. Ask the children to draw a picture to illustrate a feeling from each list. They could also draw a picture and write about how they are feeling today. For example:

Feeling Good	*Feeling Bad*
relaxed	uncomfortable
happy	sad
excited	angry
confident	fed up

ME, I'M FINE, GREAT – OK?

The aim of this activity, is for children to be aware of how what other people do and say can affect our feelings, how they can make us feel hurt and miserable or help us to feel good about ourselves and others.

Write on a big piece of paper or card in large letters:

'ME, I'M FINE, GREAT – OK?'

Ask the children to read this. Then tell the story of Michael. He gets up happily one morning saying to himself:

'Me, I'm fine, great, OK'

Make up a story closely reflecting children's experiences:

Michael was on his way to school; on the way he met some children who called out and teased him. 'You smell, your clothes are all torn. Scruffbag! scruffbag!'

Have one of the children tear off a piece of the card. Continue the story with other, similar events, for example:

At breaktime, one child threw Billy's new tie into a puddle of water on the field where children were not supposed to go. Michael went to retrieve it for Billy, and was shouted at by the caretaker.

Tear off another strip of card. Continue the story until all the card has gone.

Discuss situations that the children have been involved in and how it made them feel. A useful extension to this activity is to reverse the situation for Michael. Ask groups of children to make up a story about Michael's next day in which many things are said and happen to make him feel good again. 'He starts the day feeling miserable because of all the horrible things that have been said to him.' Start with a piece of card on which is written:

'I'M SAD, I'M BAD, I'M NO GOOD.'

This feeling is torn away bit by bit by all the nice and positive things that happen to him.

This activity is derived from Leech and Wooster (1986), p. 38.

WHEELS

The purpose of this activity is to develop the child's awareness of the people who are important to him.

Ask the children to think of between six and ten people who are important in their lives. They then draw a wheel with spokes of different lengths. At the end of each spoke they write the names of one of the people they thought of. The person who means the most to them is nearest the centre, and the least important is furthest out.

The children then write a sentence about why each person is important. They could imagine a sentence that each person would write about them.

The following activities are aimed at helping children to accept and value each other for their similarities and differences. They also enable children to receive positive feedback about how others see them and to provide the opportunity to practise saying positive things.

GLITTERGRAMS

In this activity, derived from Borba (1989), p. 87, the teacher has ready 'telegrams' with silver glitter on. Whenever a child is heard saying something positive about or to another child, the teacher records what has been said, adding her own positive comment, and this is then presented to the child.

THE 'FEELING GOOD' CIRCLE

The 'feeling good' circle, adapted from Settle and Wise (1986), p. 126, can be a powerful way of gaining positive feedback on how others see us. *It is an activity that enables people to say how they feel and think about another person's behaviour and qualities in a constructive way.* Such opportunities may not exist out of the group. The activity also helps children to find out how others see them. It should take place towards the end of a number of sessions once the children have got to know each other and trust has been developed.

The children form a circle. Each person takes it in turn to make a statement, speaking first as themselves:

'My name is Kate and I am proud that I work so hard at school.'

They then go on to speak as if they were each of the other members of the group.

'My name is Stephen and I am proud that I am always willing to lend my things.'

There can be discussion at the end of this. For example, 'How did you feel in the activity?' 'Were you surprised by what people said when they were speaking as if they were you?' 'What have you learnt from this?'

FEELINGS, FEARS, IDEAS AND WISHES

The aims of this activity are to share our feelings and thoughts to develop confidence in expressing feelings or our point of view, to be listened to and to accept the thoughts and feelings of others.

Ask the children to form a circle. They take it in turns to choose a card from the box and complete the sentence on the card.

- 'I'm finding it difficult to ...'
- 'I most admire ...'
- 'It's great for me when ...'
- 'My favourite place is ...'
- 'My favourite activity is ...'
- 'I used to be worried about ...'
- 'I am good at ...'
- 'I know ...'
- 'I look forward to ...'
- 'I have always wanted to ...'
- 'I wish people would ...'
- 'I wonder ...'
- 'I would like to achieve ...'
- 'I taught someone to ...'
- 'I am learning to ...'
- 'I am getting better at ...'
- 'I am happy when ...'
- 'My favourite music is ...'
- 'I am not afraid to ...'
- 'I feel important when ...'
- 'I'm scared of ...'
- 'I like it when ...', etc.

WHO SAID IT?

The children sit in a circle; one person leaves the room. The others write down positive statements about the person and put their name beside each statement. The person then comes back in and reads one statement at a time. He has to guess who said it.

The following activities focus on developing skills in being assertive. These include making eye contact, giving clear and honest statements and opinions and expressing feelings.

IT'S OBVIOUS

This activity helps children to establish eye contact and initiate conversation. It is very common for people to feel nervous about looking into other people's eyes at first, but doing so improves people's confidence in how they look and feel.

> A looks at B and says something nice about B that he's noticed: 'It's obvious that you have short hair.'
> A looks at B (makes eye contact) when this is said.
> B looks interested.
> B then says something to A: 'It's obvious that you are wearing a tie.'
> A looks at B and makes a guess about B based on what he sees. 'It seems to me . . . that you like having your hair short.'
> B then says whether or not she agrees with the statement.
> Then repeat with A and B swapped round.

Good eye contact should be kept while people are talking to each other and the questions and comments should be kept simple but friendly.

WHAT DOES 'ASSERTIVE' MEAN?

Take a large piece of paper and write 'Being Assertive' at the top. Divide the sheet into two columns headed 'What It Is' and 'What It Isn't'. Ask the pupils to list behaviours for each column.

Then in groups of four ask pupils to discuss different ways of responding to the following problem. They are asked to role-play this scene twice. In the first role play the central person is not being assertive. In the second she is.

> 'Three of your buddies are about to play a trick on someone which you know will upset them. They are calling you a killjoy and saying that you are no fun to be with. What are the options in this situation?'

Discuss these questions in a large group:

1 Was it difficult being assertive? If so, why?
2 How did you feel afterwards?
3 Did the group feel that they were able to manipulate the other person?
4 When one person in the group was being assertive did it make it easier for anybody else to be assertive?
5 Do you feel that in the end people who are assertive lose friends or lose respect?

BEING ASSERTIVE IN EVERDAY SITUATIONS

Ask the children to think of times when they need to be assertive: for example, asking a teacher for help, asking someone to return a borrowed item, returning a damaged item to a shop, etc. In small groups, role-play these situations, trying out ways of being assertive. How was assertiveness shown? (Ask the children to comment on body posture, eye contact, expressing feelings and opinions clearly, remaining calm, acknowledging the other person's feelings, etc.)

This activity can be extended by asking the children to find one situation in the week where they need to make a decision whether to be assertive or not. Ask them to share their experiences. What did they do? Did it involve making compromises?

RESOURCES

The following books and materials include useful activities which can be used to develop self-esteem and social confidence. We have referred to some of these in the chapter.

Borba, M. (1989) *Esteem Builders: A K-8 Self-Esteem Curriculum for Improving Student Achievement, Behavior and School Climate.* Rolling Hills Estates, Calif.: Jalmar Press.

Borba, M. and Borba, C. (1982) *Self Esteem: A Classroom Affair. More Ways to Help Children Like Themselves*, Vol. 2. San Francisco: Harper & Row.
Both books offer a very wide range of activities which are specifically designed to develop self-esteem in the classroom. They are generally geared towards younger children (approximately 7–9 years). Many activities, however, are easily adapted for older children.

Capacchione, L. (1989) *The Creative Journal for Children: A Guide for Parents, Teachers and Counsellors.* Boulder, Colorado: Shambala.
As the title implies, this is a guide on how to help children express feelings and thoughts and creativity through keeping a journal.

Fugitt, E. (1983) *He Hit Me Back First: Creative Visualization for Parenting and Teaching. Self Esteem through Self Discipline.* Rolling Hills Estates, Calif.: Jalmar Press.

Lawrence, D. (1987) *Enhancing Self-esteem in the Classroom.* London: Chapman.
This book gives a comprehensive and very useful account of all aspects of self-esteem. It includes chapters on assessment techniques and classroom strategies for primary- and secondary-aged children.

Leech, N. and Wooster, A. (1986) *Personal and Social Skills: A Practical Approach for the Classroom.* Oxford: Pergamon.
For children in the middle years of childhood (9–13) this contains interesting activities to develop a wide range of personal and social skills.

Long, R. (n.d.) *The Art of Self Esteem for Primary Aged Children.* South Devonshire Psychological Service.
This is a short booklet but full of good ideas.

Settle, D. and Wise, C. (1986) *Choices: Materials and Methods for Personal and Social Education.* Oxford: Blackwell.
This book was a follow-up to the 'Choices' schools television series for pupils aged 11 years and over. It contains a very wide range of activities concerned with personal and social education for teachers to use in the classroom.

REFERENCES

Bannister, D. and Fransella, F. (1971) *Inquiring Man: The Psychology of Personal Constructs.* Harmondsworth: Penguin.

Besag, V. E. (1989) *Bullies and Victims in Schools: A Guide to Understanding and Management.* Milton Keynes: Open University Press.

Blackman, S., Chisholm, L., Gordon, T. and Holland, J. (1987) *Hidden Messages.* The Girls and Occupational Choice Project. An equal opportunities pack. Oxford: Blackwell.

Carter, J. (1989) *Nasty People: How to Stop Being Hurt by One of Them.* Chicago: Contemporary Books.

Cowen, E., Pederson, A., Babigian, H., Izzo, L. D. and Trost, M. A. (1973) Long-term follow-up of early detected vulnerable children. *Journal of Consulting and Clinical Psychology* **41**, 438–46.

Gurney, P. (1987) Self-esteem in the classroom. II: Experiments in enhancement. *School Psychology International* **8** (1), 21–9. London: Sage.

Holt, J. (1964) *How Children Fail.* Harmondsworth: Pelican.

Lansdowne, G. (1993) Keynote address at the British Psychological Society, Division of Education and Child Psychology, Annual Conference, Torquay, 6–8 January 1993.

Lawrence, D. (1985) Improving reading and self-esteem. *Educational Research* **27** (3), 194–200.

Lawrence, D. (1987) *Enhancing Self Esteem in the Classroom.* London: Chapman.

Mecca, A., Smelser, N. and Vasconcellos, J. (1989) *The Social Importance of Self Esteem.* Berkeley, Calif.: University of California Press.

Milner, D. (1984) *Children and Race 10 Years On.* London: Ward Lock.

Nelson, C. (1987) *Self-esteem and the Family.* USA: Hazelden.

Reid, K. (1982) The self-concept and persistent school absenteeism. *British Journal of Educational Psychology* **52** (2), 179–87.

Robinson, G. and Maines, B. (1988) They can because … A workshop in print. *Workshop Perspectives* **3**. Birmingham: AWMC.

Rogers, C. (1967) *On Becoming a Person: A Therapists' View of Psychotherapy.* London: Constable.

Szirom, T. and Dyson, S. (1986) (British edition ed. Hazel Slavin) *Greater Expectations: A Source Book for Working with Girls and Young Women.* Wisbech, Cambridgeshire: Learning Development Aids.

Tattum, D. and Herbert, G. (1990) *Bullying: A Positive Response. Advice for Parents, Governors and Staff in Schools.* Cardiff: Cardiff Institute of Higher Education.

Tattum, D. P. and Lane, D. A. (eds) (1989) *Bullying in Schools.* Trentham Books in association with The Professional Development Foundation, Stoke-on-Trent.

Turner, J. (1980) *Made for Life: Coping, Competence and Cognition.* London: Methuen.

Yule, V. (1985) Why are parents so tough on children? *New Society* **73**, 444–6.

Chapter 3

Making Friends

A friend 'is someone who makes you feel happy'.

A friend 'is a friend to play with'.

A friend 'shares things with you'.

A friend 'is someone you can talk to and who will listen to you'.

A friend 'is someone who likes you'.

A friend 'could help you with your work'.

A friend 'should be kind to you and not bully you'.

A friend 'is someone who can have a good time with you and have a laugh'.

Ask children what a friend is and most will have no difficulty in telling you. It is clear that they recognize friendly behaviour in others when they experience it. Some, however, need help to increase their awareness of the reciprocal nature of friendship and what it involves.

A friend 'should pay for ice-cream and everything'!

WHY TEACH THE SKILLS OF FRIENDSHIP?

Many children learn the skills of friendship from an early age, and the complexities of establishing new relationships come easily and 'naturally' to them. These are usually the confident children, who believe that they have something to offer. For others, however, who are less skilled and less sure, making friends may be fraught with fear or the danger of rejection. They may be uncertain either how to initiate a friendly overture or how to respond positively to one; or they have learnt to maintain their self-esteem by behaviour that does not encourage friendship. Even for more self-confident children there comes a time, perhaps on holiday or in a new school, when they find themselves having to make a more conscious effort to make social links with others. Increased awareness of what is involved in making friends and what sort of things encourage warmth and responsiveness and what 'puts others off' can be useful information for most children. Some will be able to use the information as it is, others will

This picture is about My friend called Nimisha! I like having friends and Making friend.

need much more precise teaching to develop these social skills as well as a wide range of opportunities to practise them.

As with adult relationships there are many different levels of friendship for children. Some will be fleeting or situation-specific, others deep and long-lasting (see Chapter 1). Knowing how to be friendly ensures company if not intimacy. Having some knowledge and ability in social skills will not necessarily lead to close friendships but it will open doors to positive interactions and future possibilities.

For the practitioner in the classroom who has to deal with a wide range of ability, difficulty and differences, the direct teaching of friendship skills can supplement, if not underpin, the curriculum and aid the collaborative work that is now required in many activities. It also combats, from a less usual angle, prejudice and segregation of children for reasons of race, gender or disability. Intervention in the social curriculum, at both the individual level and the whole-class or whole-school level, can act powerfully to prevent long-term and serious problems arising both for individuals and for groups of children.

EVERYONE NEEDS TO KNOW HOW TO BE FRIENDLY

Friendship is not necessarily easier for the academically able than for the less able child. Social maturity does not always go hand in hand with high attainment. Children who are exceptionally good at lessons may find themselves cut off from social interaction, either because they live in a world of their own, often a richly imaginative world, or because they are perceived by others to be behaving in a superior or distant way. Very able children, along with others who are 'different' in some way, may need guidance in developing positive social interactions. This is also true, of course, for children who have greater difficulty in learning. They have no less need for companionship. Chapter 6 looks at ways of encouraging the incorporation of differences in the classroom and beyond, and how they can be valued within the school context.

This chapter deals primarily with what is involved in making friends, with an emphasis on individual relationships rather than joining groups. It examines which opportunities and interactions may help to establish a new friendship, and looks at ways to raise awareness about what is and is not friendly behaviour. Although it focuses primarily on tangible skills it also emphasizes that conceptions of friendship are crucial, and raising levels of interpersonal understanding needs to go hand in hand with 'training'.

SOME CHILDREN NEED MORE HELP THAN OTHERS

There is good evidence to suggest that some kinds of social skills can be taught in the classroom, both formally and informally, and that it is a rewarding enterprise for teachers as they see the real difference that it can make for some children. Although all children are likely to benefit from a focus on the social curriculum, it would be naive to suggest that increased awareness of alternative modes of interactions and specific training will necessarily lead to everyone interacting in a largely positive way. Some individuals, particularly those who have had damaging experiences with others, may have their own constructs of relationships which lead them to behave in dominant and destructive ways. They become locked in a vicious circle in which aggression and manipulation may be the only social 'skills' they find personally effective. Others may find that 'trusting' is something to avoid. As a self-preservation measure they remain aloof from others for 'safety'. There is also another group of children who, desperate for attention, behave in ways that they think may win approval but in fact lead to antagonism and avoidance by others. Research studies have shown that social skills training, without additional interventions, may have an effect in the classroom for such children, but it is often context bound and rarely generalizes to improving social relationships overall. Here we are looking at positive aspects of friendship in the classroom, the possibilities for children and teachers in changing both behaviour and the context. The more problematic aspects and difficulties that particular children experience are discussed elsewhere in this book.

CHILDREN LEARN DIFFERENT WAYS OF BEHAVING FROM AN EARLY AGE

Zick Rubin (1980), in his book *Children's Friendships*, writes about his observations of two 3-year-old children in a nursery school, one of whom is well-liked and the other of whom does not seem able to make friends however hard he tries. The first child, Ricky, has already mastered the following skills:

- gaining entry into group activities
- including others in his games
- being supportive and approving to his peers
- managing conflict in an appropriate and sensitive way

Danny, despite his eagerness to have friends, simply does not know how to interact with his peers in a way which encourages a positive response from them, and he ends up spending much of the time on his own.

This illustrates research which found that children who are regarded well by their peers are those who carry out positive or friendly acts towards others with greater frequency. Interestingly enough, there is no such correlation for negative or hostile acts. It seems that if children are nice much of the time, they can get away with being not so nice occasionally!

FRIENDSHIP AND POPULARITY ARE NOT THE SAME

All teachers of primary-age children will be able to point out which are the Rickys and the Dannys in their class, those who maintain their popularity with ease and those who, for a variety of reasons, don't ever seem to get it right. We need to be wary of making assumptions that it is best for all children to be surrounded by a large group of friends, or that the person who spends time doing her own thing is necessarily unhappy or missing out. Popularity and friendship are not the same thing. There is good evidence to suggest that it is close and reciprocal relationships that provide the most benefits for children, not a popularity which may be wide but superficial. Not all friendships are the same, and not all serve identical purposes for participants. There is, for instance, a wide gender divide in the types of friendships children have at the pre-adolescent stage, with girls typically operating within a small, intimate clique and boys in larger, more open groups (see Chapter 4). Taking into account all these individual differences, what is important is that all children know how to go about making friends and can do so when they choose.

CHANGING BEHAVIOUR

Many children, when discussing conflict or unfriendliness, will focus strongly on what the 'other kids' do. They cannot make friends because the others 'shut them out' or 'say nasty things' or 'won't let them play'. In psychologists' terms this is known as having an 'external locus of control', which simply means 'whatever happens to me, it is someone else's fault'. A fundamental aim in developing social skills is to help children to realize that the only person they are able really to change is themselves and that there is always a range of alternative reactions and responses to other people's actions. Everyone has choices all the time about what they do and what they say and it helps to have an awareness of this as well as of possible outcomes for different options. This may seem a sophisticated concept for some children but when it is reinforced regularly it can also be very empowering.

So what do children need to learn about friendly behaviour that will help them to interact more effectively?

They need to know how to:

- communicate positive messages by looks and by words
- show acceptance
- approach others appropriately
- show caring
- be increasingly aware of their own feelings
- develop and express empathy with others

EFFECTIVE COMMUNICATION

Non-verbal messages

One of the growth areas in popular psychology has been the interest in 'body language' – the messages we give about ourselves to others before we so much as open our mouths. By the way we stand, walk and sit, the expressions on our faces and the way we look at other people, we are saying something about who we are and what sort of reception someone might receive if he were to approach us. Non-verbal communication is very powerful, and if these silent messages are in conflict with the words spoken the recipient will either be very confused or will respond more readily to the non-verbal clues. A parent who reprimands a child with a smile on her face is far less likely to be taken seriously than one who also looks cross –

although the one who looks cross most of the time is also at a disadvantage, as the effect will have lost its impact.

Children often give unconscious messages about themselves especially clearly. The first thing, then, that they need to know and learn is how to *look* friendly. Although self-confidence is a great bonus, even shyer children can learn what makes them approachable and what puts others off from making the first moves.

Making contact

The child who is able to make good and appropriate eye contact with others will be off to a good start. Looking at people when they are talking shows an immediate interest in what that person is saying and therefore an interest in him. Teachers of young children will often get down on the same level as children in order to engage them more successfully. This not only makes eye contact easier but also reduces the dominance of the adult, who is showing a respect for the child by indicating a willingness to listen to what she has to say rather than talking 'down' to her.

Although looking away might be shyness it can also be interpreted as boredom or even shiftiness. Some children need help to feel comfortable in making eye contact. Teachers, however, do need to be aware that for some children, especially those from Asian families, looking directly at an adult may be construed as disrespectful and it may be wise to check with pupils as to what is culturally acceptable behaviour.

It is possible to teach subjects such as maths with considerable precision. Teaching what is good and appropriate eye contact is not so easy. As with many social skills, however, an effective way of learning is to watch what others are doing. A brief observation in a nursery class will show that for a considerable proportion of time children are intent on the activities of others – before trying them out for themselves. Older children are often expected to be 'doing' and have fewer opportunities to learn by watching their peers. Rather than explaining to children about what is appropriate eye contact, when and how much to look at others, it may be more fruitful to let them watch verbal interactions on television or video. They will discover for themselves that the active listener is one who is looking at the speaker, while the speaker actually makes eye contact less often and will look away to 'think'. It can be fun to watch programmes with the sound turned down and, if planned so that the class are making specific observations, can be a useful teaching method in raising awareness of many non-verbal aspects of social interaction.

It is also possible to give children some experiential learning of what it feels like when others do not give eye contact. This needs to be carried out with great care, however, because even socially confident adults can find it surprisingly disturbing and threatening.

A friendly face

As all new parents soon realize, it is extremely rewarding for them when their baby starts to smile. The 'cootchy-coo' efforts that some adults put in to elicit that smile are evidence themselves of the importance of the activity. Smiling continues to be a powerful ingredient in personal relationships, and showing children simply how to greet each other with a look of welcome will help those whose natural expression is less open. It would be false for children to smile when they don't feel like it, but encouraging a look of warmth and welcome, in even the shyest child, can go a long way in making others feel positive. Of course one of the best ways of eliciting this is to smile first. Even those who are feeling down are more likely to respond to a brief word of concern accompanied by a smile. While there are many and varied facial expressions which indicate aggression, genuine smiling is the universal sign of friendship and alliance.

Children are frequently not fully aware of the messages that the expression on their face is giving. Teachers will sometimes interpret a 'look' as insolence when the underlying feeling may more accurately be anxiety or simply not knowing what to say. Children who look grumpy or bad-tempered much of the time are not very rewarding companions for others and do not give the impression that they are enjoying being with them. Helping children to identify their own feelings will enable them to express them more accurately – and in a way that does not make things worse. Sometimes a child will behave quite aggressively, and a little investigation will find that she is choosing to express anger rather than to cry – perhaps because it is less painful, or maybe because she is afraid of a negative response from others. Children are often tolerant of other people's outbursts of emotion, be it anger or tears – while they are not so patient with a constant whine or wind-up. The child who consistently has a sour expression will find it hard to get over the first hurdle of establishing good relationships, whereas the one who is ready with a look of warmth and acceptance is giving the message that he is taking pleasure from the company he is in and is open to further contact.

Coming closer

Touching and distance are to some extent culturally determined. They are also regulated by context. There is no way that we would stand so close to fellow commuters on a crowded train if it was not for the needs of the journey. It is noticeable the lengths people will go to not to make eye contact with each other in such a situation. To do so would be to imply an intimacy that borders on the indecent. Knowing what distance to keep from others is, for most of us, a learnt behaviour that comes to feel automatic. When we occasionally meet someone who infringes this unspoken rule and comes too close, we are likely to take a step backwards to re-establish our 'personal space', and will back away all around the room if necessary without realizing it. These 'unspoken rules' become more established as children get older, but there are two extremes which cause some social difficulty at any age. Children who are anxious about approaching others may stand apart at a 'safe' distance and it requires a teacher's help to find an activity that bridges the gap, both figuratively and in reality. Activities in PE, games and dancing can increase these aspects of spatial awareness, and those which require children physically to support each other may be ways to build trust.

Conversely, coming too close too soon will also cause problems for the child who is 'all over' someone as soon as they have made a small overture of friendship. Making all of this explicit to a class of children and encouraging them to find out what is comfortable for themselves and others is one way of raising their awareness of what is appropriate.

Touching is an area fraught with difficulties. There are some children who regard any physical contact as an aggressive act and may react with unexpected violence to the person who accidentally bumps into them in the playground. There are also children who, starved of appropriate physical affection within their family, will either cling to adults or other children or find excuses for a good deal of physical horse-play. When it comes to touching as an expression of friendship and caring there is often a gender divide, with girls able comfortably to walk around arm in arm but the boys not so overt in such gestures of affection, unless of course it is in an acceptable context, such as the sports field.

The recent concern over abuse of children in the past decade has at least brought the whole issue into the educational arena and there are now several packages of materials for teachers which are aimed at raising children's awareness of what feels comfortable and acceptable. Some of these are given in the resources section at the end of this chapter. Extending discussions as to what sort of touching they would welcome from friends and in what circumstances might be a useful way of generalizing these materials.

Verbal messages

Getting started: what to talk about

Many children will find it a much easier task to start to communicate with each other if there is a focus for their conversation. Friendship is about sharing and about sharing experiences. The classroom is an ideal place to set up situations which children are expected to talk about with each other. For most pupils, open-ended discussions do not present problems; others will appreciate an intermediate step in which they are asked to find out something specific. Although group experiential learning is invariably a valuable teaching method, there are risks that without a clear focus for involvement, the less socially skilled child may be left out or dominated by the more outgoing – or the more extrovert and socially insensitive child may prevent others from full participation.

It is the informal situations, however, where some children may need the most help in making that initial approach towards others. Making a positive comment is hardly likely to receive a rejection. Asking a question which either shows an interest or aims to find a mutual interest is also useful. Since many children will have watched the same television programmes, 'Did you see ...?' is a good beginning and provides material for the conversation to continue. Comments about what has been going on in school also provide good conversation openers. Children will need to learn the difference between closed and open-ended questions. Whereas 'Did you see ...?' can easily have a yes or no response, a supplementary question, 'What did you think of ...?', encourages a much fuller answer as well as giving the message that what the other person thinks is worth hearing about.

Talking and listening

Verbal messages are not only about what is actually spoken. The flow of conversation is also crucial. Young children, who are not yet using spoken language but who have reached the 'babbling' stage, often indicate that they already know about the ebb and flow of conversation. They will look at someone, or even their dolls and teddies, and babble to them; they will then wait a moment before starting again. Many of these vocalizations are accompanied by a rise at the end of what might be a sentence, as if it is a question. Then there will be a pause for an answer, sometimes with the head cocked to one side in a quizzical manner. Some children either do not develop or else they lose this conversational ability, probably because their interactions with adults do not reinforce conversational rules. They need to relearn patterns of talking and listening and questioning. Interviewing others and reporting back is an excellent method of developing good listening skills and learning how to maintain a conversation.

A child who does not have the confidence to speak louder than a whisper or one who can only manage to shout may inhibit others from persevering with a verbal exchange. There are several non-threatening games and songs which draw attention to volume and tenor, and well-known stories can be adapted with loud and soft voices.

It may be that an opening remark is made by one child in an attempt to be friendly, and it is the response that will determine whether or not the interaction develops. A response which gives the message that the conversation is welcome requires at least some minimum feedback. It would be a mistake, however, to assume that all children who are friends chat away to each other non-stop. Although this is true of some, many others simply 'do' things together that they both like with a fairly limited verbal exchange, most of it around the activity itself. Working and playing with a computer can provide an excellent focus for the development of friendships in children who otherwise find social interaction difficult. There also seems to be a gender bias here, with girls finding it easier to broaden their conversation, taking thoughts and feelings into account, and boys having a much more single-minded focus to their interactions. Maybe one way of helping children to grow into more balanced adults is to provide safe opportunities and encouragement for boys to express feelings and experiences for girls in collaborating on problem-solving activities.

Listening skills are quite complex and require the smooth integration of body language and verbal responses. It would be unrealistic to expect children to acquire a level of sophisticated skills that many adults never seem to manage. Raising awareness, however, of what is involved in listening skills will enable children to take account of another person. Reciprocity is a vital ingredient in a developed friendship. The balance of give and take does not have to be entirely equal, but too great an imbalance will not foster a mutual liking or respect.

A good laugh

Sharing is the essence of friendship, and finding things in common is a powerful entry into a relationship. Sharing a joke and laughing together develops strong bonds. Not only does it give the message that individuals are enjoying themselves in the company of each other but it also gives shared experiences which may be referred to in the future. One definition of a friend at the beginning of this chapter is 'someone who can have a good time with you and have a laugh'. Teachers with a good sense of humour and the ability to take a light-hearted view, especially of themselves, can provide moments of humour for the whole class which will engender feelings of togetherness and belonging. Some teachers, however, fear that a loss of control may follow and are reluctant to encourage this in the classroom. Having a good laugh together may appear innocent, but as teachers and parents know it can be a two-edged sword. Laughing with and laughing at have very different connotations. A good giggle, though irritating to a teacher, may serve to reinforce a friendship. There are times, however, when it generates exclusivity in a way which verges on aggression. Strategies to deal with such behaviour are given in Chapter 8, which deals with bullying.

A teacher who encourages openness and positive laughter may find that it is a way of relaxing tension in a fraught classroom. Such teachers are also more likely to be able to identify when laughter is unkind and hostile rather than a healthy sharing of enjoyment between friends.

Showing you care

As was illustrated at the beginning of this chapter, children who can be empathetic to others and are able to express a concern for them are those who are well-liked by others.

To adults this may seem like stating the obvious but some children may perceive that popularity follows from the ability to dominate and manipulate. Although this may very well bring a place in the power hierarchy of the classroom it does not bring friendship in the terms that are defined here.

It is interesting that many children define a friend as 'someone who helps you'. Formal peer-tutoring has been developed in many schools to the great benefit of participants, although the social aspects of this tend to receive less comment than the academic ones. Informal help such as 'showing someone what to do' has probably always been regular practice in every school. Children who are new to a class rely on others to 'show them the ropes'. Giving a child or group of children responsibility for doing so not only raises their confidence and self-esteem but also opens possibilities of socially integrating the new child (see also Chapter 10).

Other positive, caring gestures from children might include the following:

- asking someone if she is all right when she has hurt herself
- offering to involve someone in a game or activity
- asking someone if he is better when he has been off sick
- offering to share with others: equipment, sweets, football
- making positive comments about abilities, achievements or possessions

Children who hear positive comments as a matter of course feel able to make them quite naturally. It is more difficult, if not impossible, for those who do not receive such comments to pass them to other children without a conscious effort. A class ethos which fosters positive feedback for pupils will also promote the development of the social curriculum.

TAKING ACTION

The first section of this chapter looks at what may be involved in opening doors to friendship. It makes some suggestions on how to raise awareness of friendly behaviours and ways to facilitate this in the classroom. This section provides more concrete ideas and suggestions for what teachers might do to help children both to learn and to use the skills of friendship. The ideas here should not be seen in isolation but should be taken in conjunction with those in Chapter 10. Teachers of children in their first school, where the acquisition of literacy skills is a major focus, would not dream of confining their teaching to 'reading lessons'. Early-years classrooms become a 'reading environment' where children's attention is continually focused on the written word – in books, on walls, on labels, in games. The same applies to the learning of social skills; to be effective the social curriculum needs to be an important and integral part of the day where skills of friendship are developed in numerous different contexts.

A friendly class is not only a nice place for the pupils to be, but also a pleasant environment in which to teach. A teacher who models friendly behaviour to all children, as well as setting clear boundaries, is less likely to have an unruly class.

Research has shown that social skills interventions are more likely to be maintained over time and generalized to a variety of contexts if behavioural approaches are combined with problem solving: for example, teaching appropriate eye contact together with asking questions which elicit responses from the students about why giving eye contact is important (Frederickson and Simms, 1990). Discussion and agreement among a group of students help to reinforce and give greater validation to appropriate strategies.

Within the classroom intervention can be summarized as follows:

- commentary and awareness raising
- individual and group problem-solving techniques
- providing and/or structuring opportunities for positive interactions
- modelling
- reinforcement of positive behaviour
- direct teaching, practice and generalization

From an early age, *commentary* on behaviour in terms of its social implications is useful. By middle childhood this needs to be at a more sophisticated level and to refer to perceptions of social understanding as well as behaviour itself. Wherever possible, commentary should be positive and non-judgemental. The aim is to raise *awareness* of the implications and consequences of social behaviour. It is more useful to comment freely on positive interactions (for example, 'that was a friendly thing to do') than focus on the outcome of negative behaviours. For older children, this awareness needs to extend to alternative interpretations of the behaviour of others.

Facilitating students' own *problem-solving* in social situations by encouraging them to think through possible alternative strategies in achieving their own defined outcomes is likely to increase their motivation in trying out different ideas. This is useful at a class level when students are presenting a difficulty which it is within their power to resolve – such as bullying. It is also useful for individual situations, although admittedly time-consuming. Problem-solving techniques involve defining what is contributing to a difficulty, looking for the positives in the situation and deciding what is the desired outcome. This information is then used to plan actions.

Friendship, either for companionship or for more intimate relationships, cannot develop in a vacuum. Children need *opportunities* to interact with each other, both in structured and unstructured settings. Grouping children for activities is common practice in most elementary classrooms. But how each group actually works together, how the individuals within it interact and how much opportunity there is for each child to take an active role in any collaborative activity are not always considered. Sharing experiences and activities, as we have seen, is an important element of friendship. Sitting watching others can be a useful learning technique, but it does not involve sharing. When a group is supposed to be doing something together it can be detrimental both to learning and to self-esteem for anyone who does not fully participate. Grouping and pairing children and giving each a specific role and function will lead to greater collaboration and a more shared experience. Children also need less formal opportunities to get to know each other and to find what they have in common.

The teacher who wants the children in her class to know how to be friendly must be consistent in *modelling* such behaviour. A warm and welcoming greeting every morning, looking at children and smiling at them, making positive comments and showing an interest, not only will have benefits for social interaction between peers but also will help greatly in class management and control. Children will benefit by having as many positive models as possible.

Attention and praise from teachers are very effective in shaping and reinforcing behaviour. *Positive reinforcement* for friendly behaviour not only helps to establish good practice for individuals, but also raises awareness about the nature of friendly behaviour. If comments are heard by others without being overtly public it can also enable children themselves to act as models for each other. Too much public attention and praise, especially for children in middle childhood and above, can make them feel uncomfortable. For children who are having particular difficulty it is often very useful to explain to parents exactly what is happening in school to reinforce positive social behaviours and to suggest that they can help by carrying out similar strategies at home.

Ideas for the *direct teaching* of social skills are to be found in the following section.

ACTIVITIES

All the following activities provide opportunities to learn and practise social skills in a relaxed, non-threatening and, it is hoped, enjoyable atmosphere. This is important if children are to feel able to try out new ways of communicating. It is equally important that opportunities are provided in the classroom to build on and generalize these skills.

Some of these activities can be slotted in during tutorial time, others within the personal and social curriculum. There are those which can meet curricular demands in other subjects such as physical education, English and drama.

There should be some discussion before the children take part in the activities. They need to be aware that while the games are fun they also have a serious purpose.

Follow-up discussions may also form a valuable part of the sessions, to encourage reflection on what has been experienced.

Many of these activities have the added bonus of being easily adaptable to work with children who have a limited knowledge of English, and in fact will help develop social relationships in the process of learning the language.

BEGINNINGS

Ways of initiating contact: raising awareness of others.
This activity needs a large space, such as the hall.

1   Children walk around and greet each other as they pass, using as many different expressions of greeting as they can. These can be written up on the board afterwards.

2   For children who are familiar with each other. They walk around and stop in front of each other and have a short conversation which is based on their knowledge, for example:

'Did you have a good birthday last week?'
'Are you feeling better now?'
'How is your new baby sister?'

3   For children who do not know each other. They walk around and stop in front of each other and have a short conversation which begins with a question that could be asked of anyone, for example:

'How are you today?'
'What do you think of the weather/this school/class/any major topical event?'

4   When this short interchange is complete the children say goodbye to each other. Ways of saying goodbye can also be written up on the board.

For classes with bilingual children, walking around in pairs may be a useful variation.

LINK THE WORD

This game is to develop listening and responding skills. It ensures that all children actively participate with a verbal response and is useful as a 'warm-up' activity.
Children sit in a circle. The game is played to a clapping rhythm. Everyone claps twice, and on the third clap a child says a word, for example:

clap, clap, 'key'

Everyone continues to clap and the child sitting next to the first one says a word on the third clap associated with the first word, for example:

clap, clap, 'lock'

If there is any repetition of words or the child cannot think of a link, he is out (or loses a life).

KILLER

The aim of this exercise is to raise awareness of eye contact and to have fun together without talking. The groups will need some supervision at first to ensure that the rules are kept. For some reason this game is immensely popular!

The teacher hands out playing cards to a group of five or six children. One of these cards must be the ace of spades. The children must not see each other's cards. The child who has the ace of spades is the 'killer'. She 'kills' her victims by winking at them. When a child is winked at, he must count to ten and then 'die' dramatically. The killer wins if she manages to 'kill' everyone without being identified. If someone thinks he knows the name of the 'killer' he can call out the name. If he is wrong he is also considered to be 'killed'.

INTERVIEWS

The aim is to give children the chance to ask questions and to listen in non-threatening situations with younger children or familiar adults.

Children are given the task of finding out information from members of other groups. This could be asking younger children about games they play in the playground or older relations about what school was like in days gone past. Deciding what questions to ask beforehand and perhaps taping the answers takes some of the anxiety out of the interactions. This activity could, of course, be part of a much larger project in which the social curriculum is an integral part of other curriculum objectives.

Follow-up discussions of interviews are particularly valuable in eliciting what sorts of questions were the most useful, how the interviewee felt about the experience and what would have made it even better.

DISCOVERIES

The aim of this exercise is to find points of shared interest and experience on which friendships may be built.

Every morning for ten minutes children get together in pairs. Each individual must pair up with someone different each day. During that ten minutes they must try to discover things that they have in common. These could be ordinary shared experiences such as having two older sisters or having the same kind of pet or having travelled to the same country, but the aim would be to discover something 'special' in common. The more unusual shared experiences can be fed back to the whole group. This could be followed up by their writing their discoveries down, making this a more academic collaborative activity.

READING FACES

Recognizing expressions of emotion on faces.

The children, in a group of up to eight, are each presented with a picture of someone with a clear expression on his face. These pictures can be collected either from magazines, from photographs or from commercially produced materials. The child looks at the face and, without showing the picture to others, attempts to copy the expression. The other children try to guess what feeling is being conveyed. After a moment, they are also shown the picture and encouraged to comment on it and on whether the 'actor' conveyed a similar expression to the picture. It is also possible to use the same materials in a written exercise in pairs.

BODY LANGUAGE

Recognizing the messages that different body postures might give.

Children are divided into pairs. Each pair is given a collection of outline postures and a list of 'feelings'. As far as possible they match the figure with the feelings. When the exercise is complete they are given a checklist. They discuss whether or not they agree with the checklist because it is not a question of right or wrong but of interpretation.

Children could also be asked to imagine an appropriate situation for each figure; for example, winning a match for the picture of someone with their arms in the air or having lost something for the person with their head down and shoulders slumped.

Social Skills Training, by Sue Spence, listed in the Resources section at the end of this chapter, contains some excellent materials for use in these last two activities.

IN THE MANNER OF THE WORD

Focuses on how emotions may be conveyed by body movements and facial expression.

This game can be played with a whole class of children, but may be more successful in smaller groups.

1   One child leaves the room and the others choose an adverb from a list – happily, sadly, cheerfully, crossly, angrily, fearfully and so on. The list will need to be adjusted according to the age and ability of the group.
2   The child returns to the room and asks group members to act out certain tasks 'in the manner of the word'. The tasks may be chosen from a list or generated by the child. Riding a bike or cleaning your teeth are among the more straightforward ideas; washing an elephant, walking a tightrope or playing the drums can perhaps be more fun!

The aim is for the child to identify the emotion portrayed in these activities and find the word that the other children have chosen to act out.

SPEECHLESS

The aim of this exercise is to focus both on body language and on tone, volume and tenor of voice.

A small group of two or three children is given a scenario in which they each take a role. These scenarios are written down and not made known to the rest of the class. The group acts out the scenario using body language, mime and sound – but no words. The rest of the class have to try to work out what is going on.

Examples of scenarios:

●   returning a pair of jeans to a shop because they are too tight
●   checking in at an airport and discovering that the plane went yesterday
●   waking up one morning to find a horse grazing in the back garden
●   walking through deep snow to school and getting there to find it's shut
●   burning toast and trying to conceal the fact from a parent

YOU NEVER CAN TELL!

The aim of this role-play activity is to help children to realize that there may be a hidden agenda for other people and that they should not jump to conclusions about the way people behave.

Children are divided into small groups. The same scenario is given to each group to role-play, the only difference being that there is an additional piece of information about one person.

For example, the scene is a shoe mender's stall in the covered market. One individual plays the customer, one the customer's partner and the other the shoe mender. The scene is always the same. The customer comes, with her husband, to the shoe mender's with a pair of shoes that need mending. The shoe mender looks at them and says that they are not worth mending and she would be better off buying another pair.

The customer and her husband try to persuade the shoe mender to mend the shoes. Then they leave.

> *Version One:* The customer was hoping that the shoes could not be mended so that she could go and get a new pair.
> *Version Two:* The shoe mender's car has just broken down, and his home team have not won a game for a month.
> *Version Three:* The customer's husband had been walking around for ages in the shops and wants to go home for a cup of tea.
> *Version Four:* The shoe mender has just won the pools!
> *Version Five:* The customer does not have enough money for another pair of shoes and to buy her husband a surprise birthday present.

The rest of the class have to decide what they think is going on by the way the people behave. This can be done in the groups and the group which gets nearest to the right answer 'wins'. It is possible to get the class to devise a whole range of similar scenarios. A useful follow-up to this activity may be to ask children to think of situations that they have experienced when they have jumped to conclusions about the message someone was giving.

POINTS

An activity in the PE lesson to encourage contact and 'bridge-building'.

Children are divided into groups of four or five. A 'point' is a point of contact on the floor. The children are asked to arrange themselves so that they have ten points in their group and hold that arrangement for a count of five. In a group of five children this may mean that they can stand in a circle with all of them having both feet on the floor. The next arrangement may have eight points, the next six and so on until children are having to support each other in some way. Groups that cannot maintain their 'arrangement' for a count of five are 'out'.

It is important to bear in mind the following:

1 The activity should be carried out on a soft surface.
2 The number of points takes into account the age and ability of the children.
3 No one is made to participate if he does not feel comfortable.

OTHER SUGGESTIONS

Non-verbal activities

Learn sign language.
Send messages in code, invisible ink, Morse code.
Design a cartoon story with no words.
Find out how the body sends and receives messages.
Choose a photograph of a person from a magazine. Write a description of what their personality might be like.
Choose a story from a comic and blank out the words. Can you retell the story using only the pictures?

Verbal activities

Make a telephone and find out how it works.
Write and produce a radio play — with sound effects.
A school or class newsletter.

Making friends

Link up with another class in Britain or abroad.
Exchange letters, stories, tapes, newsletters.
Draw a picture of yourself and your friend(s) and write about it.
What is a friend? Write down what friendship means.

RESOURCES

Bond, T. (1986) *Games for Social and Life Skills.* London: Hutchinson.
   Tim Bond is a social worker rather than an educationalist and many of the games are for adult groups. Nevertheless, a good number of them are adaptable for use in the classroom.

Brandes, D. and Phillips, H. (1979) *The Gamester's Handbook.* London: Hutchinson.
   There are now two of these and there have been several reprints since the original. Again, although some of the games are aimed at adults there are also many which are intended to be used in school. The book is usefully divided into games for social development, games for personal development and games to improve concentration. There are also introductory games.

Jackson, D., Jackson, N. and Monroe, C. (1983) *Getting Along with Others: Teaching Social Effectiveness to Children.* Champaign, Ill.: Research Press.
   This is as much a book about promoting positive behaviour in the classroom as it is about generating friendship. It is highly structured and basically teacher led.

McConnon, S. (1989) *The Skills of Friendship.* Basingstoke: Macmillan.
   This is an excellent book which contains a number of photocopy masters for friendship-building activities. Strategies addressed are those developing empathy, looking at ways of making others feel valued, developing interpersonal communication skills and self-assessment.

Spence, S. (1980) *Social Skills Training with Children and Adolescents.* Windsor: NFER – Nelson.
   This is the classic text in social skill training and contains an excellent section on assessment as well as training techniques and activities.

Kidscape has materials to generate awareness and discussion about appropriate touching. Its programmes for schools on personal safety are available for various age groups. Kidscape can be contacted at: World Trade Centre, Europe House, London E1 9AA, England.

REFERENCES

Frederickson, N. and Simms, J. (1990) Teaching social skills to children: towards an integrated approach. *Educational and Child Psychology* 7 (1).

Frosch, S. (1983) Children and teachers in schools. In S. Spence and G. Shepherd (eds) *Developments in Social Skills Training*. London: Academic Press.

Maxwell, W. (1990) The nature of friendship in the primary school. In C. Rogers and P. Kutnick (eds) *Social Psychology of the Primary School*. London and New York: Routledge.

Richardson, A. and Ritchie, J. (1989) *Developing Friendships*. London: Policy Studies Institute.

Rubin, Z. (1980) *Children's Friendships*. (The Developing Child Series.) London: Open Books.

Spivak, G., Platt, J. and Shure, M. B. (1976) *The Problem Solving Approach to Adjustment*. London: Academic Press.

Chapter 4

Part of the Group or Out in the Cold?

'They all *have* to have the same trainers, and the ones they *have* to have are always the most expensive.'

'None of the others will be my friend, they won't play with me.'

'We like hanging round together.'

'This record is for Gemma, Barbara, Angela, Ruth, Micky, Simon [26 others] and any of my other friends.'

'A strong group identity may make it more likely that those who do not conform to it are bullied.' (La Fontaine, 1991, p. 26)

'Alcoholics Anonymous saved my life; without the group I'd be dead.'

GROUPS IN SCHOOL

Working in groups can help children to learn about social skills and try these out in real situations. Being part of various groups in school can help all children to develop socially, can help to maintain positive behaviour and to promote effective and successful learning. Groups can contribute to a happy working atmosphere and build the self-esteem of children who are otherwise vulnerable. They can create a sense of belonging, rights and responsibilities. School grouping can bring together children whom society might otherwise divide. Supportive groups can sustain motivation in spite of disappointment, and can help children take part in activities that are wide-ranging, demanding and fulfilling. Many schools organize children to work in groups; others have groupwork sessions backed up with clear expectations of working collaboratively and flexibly throughout the day.

Structured groupwork can have many benefits. John Thacker and Gillian Feest describe how twenty children were interviewed in high school, a year after doing such work in primary school. The children reported that the groupwork helped them with:

- ' ... getting on with each other.'
- Sharing ideas and working 'even with people you don't get on with'.

- Speaking out: ' ... groupwork makes it possible for you to say something, not keep it to yourself'; ' ... saying how you feel'.
- Problem solving: ' ... take the best ideas and get on with it'.

(Thacker and Feest, 1991, pp. 146–7)

Important benefits were seen as:

- learning to mix without shyness and embarrassment
- looking at concerns and problems in an atmosphere of trust and calmness
- adjustment to high school
- increased confidence and better skills to make friends
- the ability to work in mixed-gender groups
- being able to speak out and ask more.

None of these may happen, however, without school intervention. Group formation will occur otherwise according to personal, community and traditional influences. How a group comes together and functions can either support children or exclude them. There can be harmful effects both for children who are part of the group and those who are left out. The formation of groups is a fact of school life; whether they prove to be largely positive or significantly negative depends partly, but not exclusively, on the school and its ethos. The importance, nature and outcome of group influence can be different in different cultures and situations, reflecting school, home, community and developmental factors.

As children grow, their relationships change, usually moving towards the intimate relationships of adult life. In the middle years of childhood and adolescence, the importance of group relationships can be intense. Children have grown out of the relationships of playing together into a new intimacy but have yet to apply this to one-to-one relationships. As they begin to question the rules and procedures determined by adults, developing group loyalties and identity is a way of legitimizing their maturity and independence from adults.

What is also important for children and young people is the ease and confidence with which they can enter groups, leave them or resist their pressures. They will also feel better if they have the skills and assertiveness to support, passively or actively, those who are under pressure or threat from others.

For teachers and parents the issues are, first, the extent to which adults lose control over children and young people, especially when not under direct supervision; and, secondly, how the power that young people usually gain over themselves and each other is used. Teachers also seek to establish groupings of various kinds which promote the school's learning and social objectives and to deal with those groups which undermine them. They know that two kinds of interventions involving groupwork have been used and argued over by researchers: class organization of working groups in which seating plans and joint tasks are important, and specific activities to build co-operative groups.

For children and young people, the issue is stated clearly by Shelley Hymel and Sylvia Franke: 'a substantial number of children express dissatisfaction with their own peer relations and extreme feelings of loneliness' (Hymel and Franke, 1985, p. 79).

If children have the skills and confidence to be accepted as part of one or more groups, they are less likely to be dissatisfied or lonely.

THE POWER OF THE GROUP

Young children play alongside others. Beginning to play co-operatively is welcomed as a sign of development. By the time they are teenagers they can do many things individually, but usually have a strong urge to spend time as part of a group; this can vary according to cultural, personal and other influences. Spending time with others usually is not enough; being seen by others to be with and in the group can be vital. Clothes, symbols, badges, habits, locations and rituals of group membership become important. Adults can find it amusing when teenagers say they want independence but demonstrate conformity to a fine level of detail. They find it less amusing if teenagers are strongly influenced by a group leader; the follower role is one they feel may lead, literally, to difficulties.

If adults try to prevent or question attempts to identify with a group they may meet fierce resistance. Adult attempts to do so can trigger significant conflict with young people. For both it can be important to win these confrontations and to be seen to do so. Usually, parents and teachers are able to recognize adolescent rebellion and view it with a degree of good humour; some of the forms it takes can be unacceptable to them. What is also uncomfortable for adults is the knowledge that the power relationship they have had with a child is changing; the adult and the group may be competing for the allegiance of the young person. The adults and young people concerned may or may not see allegiance as something that it is possible to share. If they do they may accept difference and the growth of independence as a productive and fascinating process. If they do not, then each party may be setting trials, asking for specific things to be done or not done and seeing the outcome in terms of loyalty or betrayal.

Group influence can be dramatic. The fear of being excluded from a group is great, and the pay-off from being included and given a prestigious rank in a group can be substantial. Where group identity is strong, children who are not seen as suitable for group membership may be seen as targets for bullying. Group pressure is strong across a wide range of ages but is especially powerful for teenagers and older children. Younger children, however, do demonstrate strong group influences, and advertisers are keen to start trends where children feel a strong need for a particular product.

GROUPS OR GANGS?

A major worry for adults is that groups of adolescents are often associated with crimes that would not occur without group pressures. Theft and vandalism of cars and other property, fights, verbal aggression and rudeness are all more common when a group is present than with individuals. At some stage most young people begin to assert the teenage 'right' to have and sometimes to abuse independence. While almost everyone commits what can be described as a criminal act in the teenage years, persistent offending is a predictor of later problems. Teenage offending often is promoted by pressure from 'friends'. Sexual and racial taunting can involve 'decent' young people who lack the assertion skills and confidence to stand up to group pressures.

Parents' anxieties and dreams for their children often centre around their group competence at this age. Will their children be bullied, isolated, led into wrongdoing by influential group leaders? Will they become part of a 'bored' group of loungers, made fun of as swots, or, worst of all, will they be isolated and sad, aggressive and lonely?

More positively, will they begin to show the older generation what friendliness and real friendship are? Perhaps they will demonstrate that it is possible and desirable to build strong group loyalties yet respect the rights of others; that it is possible to have a good time, yet be responsible and achieve educational and other success.

YOUNG PEOPLE, YOUNG ADULTS

For parents this process offers predictions of how their teenagers may begin to cope in adult life. While there are disputes in the research, and the links are not simple or direct, isolation, dependence and unassertiveness are associated with stress. Belonging and social acceptance are part of psychological health, which in turn supports physical health.

Teachers, too, begin to predict what might happen as children become teenagers. There may be a widening communication gap and distance between some adults and young people, while others begin to participate in adult discussions and actions. Many become involved in voluntary work and begin to assert an influence for inclusion and responsibility to others in the community, class and school. This is promoted by school arrangements for community work or collaborative learning.

For some children and young people, the transition from child to adolescent is relatively smooth and uneventful. They find ways of meeting the need for group membership and acceptance within structures that have high levels of adult supervision and approval. It is more difficult if the expectations of the various parts of a young person's life are discordant; perhaps a little dull and unchallenging if they are very consistent.

GROUP INFLUENCES

Michael lives in a troubled housing estate and attends the local school. There is a high rate of teenage crime and vandalism locally. Michael is invited and encouraged to be a spectator to or to participate in these crimes. He has been questioned by local police and sometimes stopped by them in the street. The police are suspicious that he is involved to some extent.

Michael's school has some problems with managing pupil behaviour. Examination results are disappointing and there is an attendance and truancy problem. The school finds it hard to recruit and retain the most capable teachers; there is, however, a core of competent and dedicated teachers.

Michael is under some pressure from other pupils to truant, to resist work expectations and to behave in a casual, arrogant and sexist manner. Yet he is also aware of older teenagers who attend the local college; they are ambitious and are seen as fashionable and popular. They are accepted by the local teenagers as OK and as having some prestige.

Which group influence will have the greater effect on Michael? How influential will adults be and which adults will he take most notice of? Which influences will he seek out? How will he see himself? Will he have had the opportunity to develop the skills and confidence to resist pressures and work out what his preferences are?

Razia is 12, comes from a happy, prosperous home and does well at school. She is regarded as a delightful and cheerful child by the school and by others who know her. Razia's parents are proud of her. She is liked by most young people of her age. She works hard and is successful at school; her parents see her as an 'all-rounder', good at sports, involved in all kinds of activities: music, dance, drama. She has excellent social skills for her age.

What is less clear is how successful Razia is in dealing with group pressures. Does she do many things because she wants to or because she cannot say no to these pressures? Has she joined drama activities because she wants to or in response to others who persuaded her to join, because she would always help out? She views herself as fat, because there is group pressure to diet, although she is slightly under-weight for her age.

POSITIVE GROUPS

Issues of group influence are relevant at any age. 'Groupthink' is a process by which poor and sometimes disastrous shared decision making occurs. Each member of a group can feel obliged to assert or accept an aggressive or polarized view; moderation or ambiguity may be seen as a sign of weakness or betrayal. The pressure to conform not only reduces questioning but can also produce extreme decisions – more so than any individual's original view. Group pressures on individuals to agree to and implement actions they would not otherwise accept create stress, guilt and uncertainty. By contrast, positive group pressures promote individual well-being and fulfilment. The ability to contribute to and draw on positive group processes is relevant at all ages but especially important for children and young people. Children benefit from their own social skills and from group support when they are facing stress and new situations.

Groups can help young people to change and develop, to see themselves as worth-while and in control of their own futures. They can help in problem solving and can provide individuals with support in reaching sensible and useful solutions to life's difficulties. The strength and influence of groups for the good of members is well known and has often been the focus of research and study. Support and treatment groups have value in helping with some of the difficult problems we can experience, including alcohol and substance abuse, eating disorders and dieting. How therapy groups are run is critical both ethically and for the success of the clients. Teachers are not equipped to run such groups, although they can be run in schools by other professionals. Teachers can have an important role, however, in promoting the development of groups within the school, rather than merely letting it happen. Social skills are usually taught in groups because they are the skills of interacting with other people, and because this is efficient in terms of use of time. There are often individual teachers within a school, especially a high school, who have knowledge of and skills in groupwork, for example in drama. There are also useful source materials for running groups as part of the personal development programme for all students.

Setting up and running social skills groups in school is something teachers often do jointly with other professionals in the first instance. There are good manuals for running social skills groups in schools, but the purpose and operation of the group need to be coherent, and planned to meet the particular needs of the students. This type of group is specific and structured, but can be very effective if it remains an extension of school work.

A SOCIAL SKILLS GROUP

Luke is withdrawn and isolated in school. The school is aware of a number of significant family stresses, including parental illness and discord. A counselling strategy is devised for Luke, but he is also selected by the school to be one of eight students in a social skills group run each school year for his age group. This is run jointly by the school and by the psychologist. The children selected are between 12 and 14 and are withdrawn and quiet to various degrees. They all have good school attendance, for the school wants to build group cohesion with ever-present members. Although no individual records will be kept, parental consent is obtained. The school discusses with each pupil what is involved and ensures they are all happy to be included.

There are four sessions, which cover the non-verbal skills of friendship, the verbal skills of friendship, assertion, specific situations and talking about problems. There is also a discussion of what social skills are, why they are important, emphasis on the fact that they can be taught and learnt, and an outline of the rules and procedures of the group.

The group leaders work from a script and each session has a similar structure. This involves whole-group activities as well as paired and individual work. The sessions begin and end with a group item. Each session starts with an outline of the topic and schedule for the session; the leaders act out the skills or situations before the students do; there is discussion, role play and homework. When the students have been guided in their role play to a good level of competence, they are videoed and shown the video of each of them demonstrating the skill or dealing with the particular type of situation effectively. There is group encouragement and celebration of success. Each student has homework where they practise the particular skill for real. They are encouraged to practise their skills in two situations if possible, one in school and one out of school.

Luke and the other students join in easily, somewhat to the surprise of the other teachers in the school. An important skill that they needed and learnt was finding what to say to start a conversation; another was the use of eye contact. The group also seemed to benefit a great deal from discussing what to say and what not to say in specific situations: for example, approaching a teacher for advice, or joining a group already involved in a game or activity.

The school is delighted with the outcomes. All the students are reported to be much less withdrawn in school and not isolated. They form something of a group themselves, although they are included in other groups. Luke is doing particularly well. When his teacher asks why the groupwork has been helpful, Luke says that when his family began to have problems he decided to be quiet in school, because he worried about being made fun of and he did not want to risk any problems in school. But this led to his becoming lonely and left out; the groupwork helped him to change this. In his written homework, Luke describes how he made a friend out of school, too:

> 'There was a boy of my age living a few doors away but I had never spoken to him or looked at him in the eye as though to speak. He was often out fixing his bike and riding it around. Because of the group I went up to him and asked him about his bike, and what else he was interested in, and computers. Now we talk a lot and we are friendly. When I told this back to the others in the group they thought it was great.'

For the group leaders, choosing what to do and how to do it needed clear planning and aims. Many social skills groups run in clinical settings have fifteen sessions or more. For the group in which Luke took part, only four sessions were run. It did address specific skills and types of situations but was not intensive or hard. It linked with what the school was doing in its ongoing personal development work. This added something powerful and valuable to what the school contributed, and made sense to the students and the school as an extension of their work. It became something the school could repeat or extend in the future without outside help.

SCHOOL TRANSFER AND GROUPWORK

There is a particular need for this kind of work when children change school. When children transfer into high school, many changes take place in their lives, and new social demands are made of them. These include finding their way to and around a new and larger campus, meeting new pupils and teachers, and increased responsibility for their own learning. The change of school may take them away from their local neighbourhood and local friendship network. The unfamiliarity of the layout of the building, and learning how to go from one place to another and where to find things, can be stressful. This can be especially so for children who find it difficult to ask for help or who feel vulnerable and insecure. Many children combine concern about unfamiliarity with worries about being bullied. How well an individual copes with this will depend partly on how well certain skills have been learnt at an earlier age, especially skills of joining and forming groups.

At secondary school parents have much less direct contact with the teachers and less direct knowledge of what is happening than at primary school. David Smith and Sally Tomlinson (1989), for example, reported that the usual number of contacts between parents and secondary school teachers was 1 per year, and approximately 25 per cent of parents had no contact at all with their children's secondary school. Parents are not routinely told of school events by young people; even serious bullying may not be mentioned. Whether or not an individual is welcomed into groups or isolated from them may well not be something a parent will know or easily be able to identify from discussions with teachers. Children can move to the new situation to face increased social demands, with less immediate teacher responsibility or parental involvement.

GROUP STRENGTH

Schools have an important role in helping children and young people to join and participate in group activities. This places the teaching emphasis on working in groups, on welcoming others to be part of groups and to leave and allow others to leave without stress or rancour. It is prudent to teach young children to leave groups as well as join and be part of them and to continue this through adolescence. Young people benefit most from a situation where there is a choice of and variety of groups meeting different needs and interests. Group membership needs to be flexible, so that young people can choose to be included or to look for something else. Rigid group identity can act to exclude others, depict those not in the groups as inferior and exert damaging pressures on marginal or low-status group members.

Flexible grouping is helpful in preventing the domination of the school environment, especially shared and unsupervised space. A school that allows strong groups to form, gain power over members and lay claim to parts of the school or neighbourhood is taking a considerable risk. One of the risks is the proliferation of graffiti, especially when the school tries to claim back territory it has lost. Schools are places where pupils have equal rights to resources; giving space away denies rights. Care for the school environment, with groups of different membership working on different parts at different times, is a necessary strategy. This helps to build an ethos of common responsibilities and rights, both by ensuring that space is shared, and by improving the environment through group tasks.

Groups that are clearly task oriented are easy for children to relate to. The greater the social difficulty a child has, the greater the need for precision in defining what to do and how to do it in a group activity.

Danielle, aged 9, moved school, and found it hard to mix with the children in her new class. They already had patterns of working and playing. While they were friendly enough, Danielle did not seem to fit easily into these groupings. One issue was that she was highly intelligent, the most able child in the school by far, and was diffident about displaying her talents, preferring to remain quiet. She was not disliked or excluded; rather the inclusion had not taken place as might have been hoped.

Because of her talents, Danielle's teacher wanted her to be the editor of a class newspaper. This would involve interviewing children and adults, writing much of the newspaper, organizing the layout and helping to publicize it. It would also involve leading a team of pupils, organizing work and meetings. Clearly this was not possible until Danielle was better integrated into the class and confident in going from group to group. Her teacher began by working out a written questionnaire and helping Danielle to go through it with other children. Danielle then used the questionnaire without teacher supervision. In two weeks she no longer needed the structure of the questionnaire to interview her class colleagues, and had become a full and active class member. She was able to join, influence and leave groups easily; she had a recognized and positive role.

The next step was to talk through with Danielle and her team how meetings would work. The teacher gave guidelines and supervision until it was clear that the meetings were successful. She checked regularly and observed as part of the class routine. The outcomes of these meetings for the class included better displays in the classroom organized by pupils, and efficient production of a high-quality class newspaper. The class had begun to benefit from Danielle's talents through groupwork; the alternative would have been for her to work on her own tasks, coincidentally in the same room. When Danielle had moved into the class, it had rather strong and rigid group habits, and she did not have the skills and confidence to gain acceptance. Because of these two factors, the clear structure of the questionnaire and the precision in how the meetings should be run were necessary.

RULES AND STRUCTURE

A significant aspect of being an accepted member of the group involves knowing and using the 'rules' of the group. This becomes more important for older children and young people. Andy Sluckin (1981) gives examples of how this develops. Children under the age of 3 will play with marbles freely. At the age of 3 or 4 they are beginning to imitate the rules used by the older children for marble games, although they may break the rules all the time. By the age of 7 or 8 children will play according to an agreed set of rules. At a later stage the rules are understood thoroughly with most children adhering to them. Andy Sluckin outlines some of the 'rules' for group games and rituals:

Joining a game:

- ask whose game it is
- ask this person if you can play

He observes that just joining in is not permitted or accepted, unless you are a close friend of the person whose game it is.

Choosing roles:

- dipping and counting
- assertion of choice or direction

Dipping and counting is a method often used to allocate turns, for example:

'Ip, dip, sky blue,
Who's it, not you!'

Excluding others from the game:

- it's not my game
- you're not my friend
- we're in the middle of the game

● there shouldn't be too many in a game

Andy Sluckin notes that children usually accept these reasons for exclusion.

David and Frank Johnson emphasize the importance of clearly understood goals for effective groups as the basis for reasonable and fair rules which can be honoured:

> Group goals must be clearly understood, be relevant to the needs of group members, highlight the positive interdependence of members, and evoke from every member a high level of commitment to their accomplishment.
>
> (Johnson and Johnson, 1991, p. 21)

They also see an effective group as having three core activities:

1. accomplishing its goals,
2. maintaining good working relationships among members,
3. developing and adapting to changing conditions in ways that improve its effectiveness.

> (Johnson and Johnson, 1991, p. 21)

Children benefit by learning what rules are and how to follow them; young people expect rules to be clear and followed. The use of grouping in class work and groupwork is best done with clear guidance and rules about group functioning, and firm behaviour management. Working and discussion in groups are important in building friendly relationships and as preparation for adult life. For adults, 'job satisfaction is high and absenteeism and labour turnover low in work teams that are small and cohesive' (Argyle and Henderson, 1985, p. 242). There are rules and expectations of social behaviour at work and in other aspects of adult life. Children will benefit from knowing that successful groupwork is governed by rules and from following those rules to manage group experiences successfully.

Because children devise rules for games and other group activities, as noted above, coming new to a game or established group can be expected to present challenges. This is what Kenneth Dodge (1985) found when he analysed children's ratings of problem social situations using TOPS (Taxonomy of Problematic Social Situations for Children) and identified problem issues involving groups as:

● trying to join groups when they are playing
● dealing with the norms and expectations of groups

There is no need for membership of a group or team to be in conflict with individual aims if these respect the rights of others. If children are involved in a group activity or game, however, including a new person may not be convenient. The activity may have to be adapted and rules, norms and expectations conveyed to the newcomer. The newcomer may have to ask for acceptance as a favour, and find out and learn rules and norms efficiently. It is like being the new person at work; you have to ask about everything and worry whether the staff will accept and welcome you. Kenneth Dodge does advise teachers to intervene to promote the behaviour and language skills for tasks and group access, and notes the success of these interventions. These are parallel to induction programmes into new posts for adults at work.

There is debate about the most effective group activities and structures in the classroom. Maurice Galton, for example, reports on pupil perceptions of class organization into working groups. The research suggested that if children have responsibilities for working in groups they may worry about failure, about the quality of their work, and may interpret teacher comments as applying mainly to behaviour. This emphasizes a need for clarity in teacher discussion with pupils about grouping in class and any specific groupwork. Clarity is required to establish exactly who is responsible for what in the task, where there may be risks of failure for the children, and how the work will be evaluated. It also needs to be specified when teacher comments relate to learning and the task and when they relate to discipline (Galton, 1992).

Neville Bennett contrasts practices of group organization in the United States with those in Britain. In Britain:

> Primary teachers appear to have taken on board the prescription to seat children in groups, and most often in homogeneous ability groups, but are organizing them within a framework of individual, rather than co-operative groups, goals ... Simply putting pupils near each other and allowing interaction to take place is no guarantee that intended outcomes will occur, even if those intended outcomes are clear.
>
> In America, on the other hand, where classroom groups are not part of teachers' ideologies, models of co-operative group work have been imposed which are highly structured and prescriptive, yet appear to work successfully with different kinds of pupils, including those with special educational needs, in both cognitive and affective areas.
>
> (Bennett, 1987, pp. 15–16)

Clear rules and procedures for class work in groups can be combined effectively with specific group activities, and there is evidence that the greater precision is of benefit.

GROUPS AND FRIENDSHIP

Group membership and access are not the same as having friends. Friendship relates to a degree of intimacy which is different from the play- and activity-based nature of groups. For teenagers, some confusion may occur. Some may not have the social skills or self-confidence to go beyond group membership to seek and build friendships. They may see the group as meeting all their needs, rather than asserting their personal needs for friendship. Where such groups act as substitutes for deeper relationships there are likely to be unduly strong group identities and adherence. If this occurs, group acceptance can be determined by what happens in the playground and who decides what happens in the playground. Planning, training and supervision for friendly break-time will reduce the likelihood of strong groups dominating space, dominating others and dominating the social agenda of group members.

Rejection from group membership is a very negative experience, more extreme than choosing not to become friends. It is a public process, with the rejected individual being separated from opportunities for play, sharing and discussion. It can signal that if that child is bullied, nobody will intervene to support and protect them. It can signal to the individual and to others that they are worthless. The loss of self-esteem that can follow this is exceptionally difficult to recover. Becoming part of a group or groups needs skills and attitudes both for the individual and for the others in the group, although one committed and skilled individual can do wonders for group building. Important group skills are: following group or task rules; encouragement and helping others; relevance in conversation; resisting group pressures and assertion; including others; seeking inclusion; organizing games and work; asking for help; and avoiding the disruption of group activities.

When children are changing schools or school situations they need actively to seek acceptance with skill and confidence. They need to be able to project themselves into a new situation without taking too much time to work out what that situation is.

It is the first lesson on the first day of high school. Martha is going into the class for the first time and sees the layout of the desks. The teacher tells the class to go in and sit down. Because they are all new there is no talking, in fact an unnatural silence, which does not help Martha in having the courage to suggest that she sits next to somebody or at a table where four can share. Some of the others went to the same first schools and form groups easily.

If Martha is able to join a group straight away, then she will be with others at break-time and stronger group ties can form both from the work in lessons and from discussion later. If she is not then the others will set about the processes of group building without her. There will be three factors operating: what Martha brings to the situation; what the adults do; and what the other children do. These will determine whether or not children who are already vulnerable will be supported or made more vulnerable, whether they will be accepted as part of groups or rejected.

TAKING ACTION

Teachers are well used to devising and implementing 'inclusion' activities, especially early-years teachers. They try hard to make sure every child takes part in all activities, that all children work together. In early-years classes, each child takes a turn in a group and activities are set up with clear functions for each member and mutual support. In classes with older children and young people, some children do not know the names of every pupil in the class and have not spoken to everyone there. Hence these early-years activities and rules can be extended.

Useful rules include:

- all children will work with all other children
- all children work next with children whom they haven't worked with much
- all children take responsibility for any child who is alone and invite that child to join their group

These and other rules and expectations can be acknowledged by stars and other systems of recognition or reward. The rationale for the rules could be explained to the class as follows:

- the class will work best if everyone joins in and is helped to join in
- everyone has an equal right to join a class group
- nobody should be left out
- everyone needs encouragement to join in
- nobody should feel anxious about joining a group; they should know they will be made welcome

Going from whole-class management to groupwork allows for precise attention to skills and situations. John Thacker and Gillian Feest (1991) give clear guidance about the teacher skills and organization needed to run group sessions, together with basic rules for all sessions and useful points about planning sessions. The final teacher skill they list is given particular emphasis:

> above all, acting in the session and outside, according to the belief that each person is important, of real value, and is to be listened to and cared for by each other.
>
> (Thacker and Feest, 1991, p. 141)

ACTIVITIES

In choosing activities for any particular groupwork, a central issue is whether the objective to be reached is one which the whole group needs to reach before any individual can be successful, or whether the individual goals are reached through group processes. Adapting the bean jar activity is a good way of starting.

THE BEAN JAR

The aim of this activity is to demonstrate that different ways of running groups produce different results.

In this activity, adapted from Johnson and Johnson (1991), the teacher divides the class into groups and sets up a large jar of beans. The task is to estimate how many beans there are in the jar. Each group, except one, is given a different way of going about the task. Some examples are:

- Democratic: the group estimate is the average of the individual estimates.
- Leaders and followers: the group picks a leader who makes the estimate.
- Majority vote: the group votes until a majority agree on an estimate.
- Consensual: the group discusses the issue until all the members are agreed on one estimate.
- Random: each estimate is put into a hat and a draw is made.

The other group goes round the class observing. After the estimates have been finalized, discussion covers:

- How accurate the estimates were.
- How did group members feel? Were they involved and contributing, satisfied or dissatisfied?
- Finding words to describe their feelings in the group.

ROLE PLAY

Role play can be threatening, but can be used where a clear script for the situation has been supplied and where the teacher plays the role first. When the participants have gone through the script, discussion of exactly what to say and do is productive. Once the specific situation has been role-played well, the group will be asked to apply the same skills in a real situation. Useful situations to role-play include:

- inviting somebody to join a group
- joining a group

- assertiveness skills; refusing to do what the group wants
- prompting others to speak
- listening to others and showing interest

WHAT WE LIKE

The aim is to practise finding positive interests in common in group situations.

The group sits in a circle. Each person has a whispered conversation to find out at least four or five things that other people in the group like. They have to be truthful about what they like. Then the group as a whole works out what everyone in the group likes. The teacher can set titles and limits for topics: for example, books we like, games we like, what we like to do in the playground.

WORDS AND MUSIC

Each person is assigned to a group of four to six people. Each person in each group has to be taught how to sing a new song: by their family, for example. That person teaches the others in the group so that everyone in the group knows all the songs. Then each group sings them for the rest of the class.

BIRTHDAYS

Each child in the class is given membership of a 'birthday group' at the start of the year. This means that four to six children with birthdays at the same time of the year form a group. The group has to work out how to celebrate each person's birthday with a small and pleasant surprise.

SOUND EFFECTS

Groups are given the script for a radio play. They not only do the play but also work out how to do sound effects. This is easy and good fun for older children, and works well for younger ones too and for young children in mixed age groups.

THE TEAM MACHINE

Groups of four to six are set up in class. The activity is to decide on a piece of equipment which they will act out together, each member being a part of the machine. It can be simplified by giving suggestions of machines and how to enact them (Rustin and Kuhr, 1989, p. 59).

PLAYGROUND SURVEYS

A committee of children of different ages across the school is formed to discuss what happens at break-time and how best to help children to play together in various groups. The committee is supported in carrying out a survey into how children can join in and form groups in the playground. It can evaluate and guide a rota of playground monitors who will encourage children to join groups and to accept others, and to play with children who are alone or hovering on the fringe of groups.

RESOURCES

Leif Fearn and Robert E. McCabe (1975) *Magic Circle: the Human Development Program. Supplementary Idea Guide.* San Diego, Calif.: Human Development Training Institute.

Possibly the most useful source there is, with ideas that can form part of every teacher's week. (See Chapter 10.)

Nancy F. Jackson, Donald A. Jackson and Cathy Monroe (1983) *Getting Along with Others: Teaching Social Effectiveness to Children. Program Guide.* Champaign, Ill.: Research Press.
Thirty-three activities with outline of structure, record formats and guidance, linking social effectiveness with positive behaviour management.

David W. Johnson and Frank P. Johnson (1991) *Joining Together: Group Theory and Group Skills.* Englewood Cliffs, NJ: Prentice-Hall, 4th edn.
Possibly the most influential text on groupwork with situations and exercises. Some of these need adaptation as they do not apply specifically to children and young people.

Michelson, L., Sugai, D.P., Kazdin, A.E. and Wood, R.P. (1983) *Social Skills Assessment and Training with Children: An Empirically Based Handbook.* New York: Plenum Press.
Gives background, principles and sample scripts for social skills groups. Especially appropriate for older children and young people.

REFERENCES

Argyle, M. and Henderson, M. (1985) *The Anatomy of Relationships.* London: Heinemann.
Aronson, E., Blaney, B., Stephan, C., Sikes, J. and Snapp, M. (1978) *The Jigsaw Classroom,* Beverly Hills, Calif.: Sage.
Bennett, N. (ed. J. Thacker) (1987) Co-operative learning: children do it in groups – or do they? *Educational and Child Psychology* 4 (3, 4), 7–18.
Corsaro, W. (1984) *Friendships and Culture in the Early Years.* Norwood, NJ: Ablex.
Dodge, K. (1985) Facets of social interaction and the assessment of social competence in children. In B. H. Schneider, K. H. Rubin and J. E. Ledingham (eds) *Children's Peer Relations: Issues in Assessment and Intervention.* New York: Springer-Verlag.
Fearn, L. and McCabe, R. E. (1975) *Magic Circle: Supplementary Idea Guide.* Human Development Program. San Diego, Calif.: Human Development Training Institute.
Frederickson, N. (1991) Children can be so cruel: helping the rejected child. In G. Lindsay and A. Miller (eds) *Psychological Services for Primary Schools.* Harlow: Longman.
Galton, M. (1992) Grouping and group work. In C. Rogers and P. Kutnick (eds) *The Social Psychology of the Primary School.* London: Routledge.
Hymel, S. and Franke, S. (1985) Children's peer relations: assessing self-perceptions. In B. H. Schneider, K. H. Rubin and J. E. Ledingham (eds) *Children's Peer Relations: Issues in Assessment and Intervention.* New York: Springer-Verlag.
Johnson, D. W. and Johnson, F. P. (1991) *Joining Together: Group Theory and Group Skills.* Englewood Cliffs, NJ: Prentice-Hall, 4th edn.
Kutnick, P. (1988) *Relationships in the Primary School Classroom.* London: Paul Chapman.
La Fontaine, J. (1991) *Bullying: The Pupil's Perspective.* London: Calouste Gulbenkian Foundation.
Perry, K. and Firmin, C. (1991) *Feeling Left Out: Playgrounds.* Hauppauge, NY: Barrons.
Rizzo, T. A. (1988) *Friendship Development among Children in School.* Norwood, NJ: Ablex.
Rogers, A. and Kutnick, P. (1992) Individuals, groups and interventions. In C. Rogers and P. Kutnick (eds), *The Social Psychology of the Primary School.* London: Routledge.
Rustin, L. and Kuhr, A. (1989) *Social Skills and the Speech Impaired.* London: Taylor & Francis.
Schneider, B. H. (1993) *Children's Social Competence in Context: The Contributions of Family, School and Culture.* Oxford: Pergamon.
Schneider, B. H., Rubin, K. H. and Ledingham, J. E. (eds) (1985) *Children's Peer Relations: Issues in Assessment and Intervention.* New York: Springer-Verlag.
Slavin, R. E. (1987) *Cooperative Learning.* Washington, DC: National Education Association.
Sluckin, A. (1981) *Growing Up in the Playground: The Social Development of Children.* New York: Plenum Press.

Smith, D. and Tomlinson, S. (1989) *The School Effect: A Study of Multi-racial Comprehensives*. London: Policy Studies Institute.

Tann, S. (1988) Grouping and the integrated classroom. In G. Thomas and A. Feiler (eds) *Planning for Special Needs*. Oxford: Blackwell.

Thacker, J. (ed.) (1987) Working with groups. *Educational and Child Psychology* 4 (3, 4).

Thacker, J. and Feest, G. (1991) Groupwork in the primary school. In G. Lindsay and A. Miller (eds) *Psychological Services for Primary Schools*. Harlow: Longman.

Zander, A. (1985) *The Purposes of Groups and Organizations*. San Francisco: Jossey-Bass.

These 2 People are my very Best friend Me and lisa Just Started talking to each other und I knew Carin for a long time we dident yoose To Talk but know we are always talking to one and another

Chapter 5

Communication for Friendship

'Nobody understands me.'

'If only we'd realized that she was being bullied.'

'We've talked about it in class. Other children said that children cussed their mum. They said it made them feel angry. I feel angry too. It's better now we've talked about it.'

'Our phone bill is ridiculous.'

'Michael said to me that he was going to beat John up, maybe, so I told John's friend Simon and he said that John could handle Michael and he'd make sure he was waiting for him.'

'We told her not to talk to Mary; they'll cause trouble if they play together.'

WHAT IS COMMUNICATION?

In this chapter we look at the social importance of speech and language skills. Then we look more widely at communication skills and their application. Other chapters also relate closely to communication skills, especially Chapters 3, 7 and 10.

Within any society, the complexities of relationships are reflected in the amount and type of communication between people. Language nuances and codes express difference, similarity, liking and distance, power and influence. Children have to learn not only to communicate, but also to go beyond basic messages to express their own feelings and recognize those of others.

When Mark first attended school, he was unhappy and difficult to manage. He had been slow to talk, and this had been associated with temper tantrums, difficulties in concentration and fights over toys with other children. At school, Mark's problems were reported to be unacceptable. At story-time and assembly, he was often in trouble, standing up and walking about, calling out, talking to himself and others and not listening. In class he wandered around, and would upset other children, pushing and pinching them, interfering with their work and equipment and throwing objects at them. Mark was making little progress and had little to show for his time in class. At playtime other children did not want him in their games;

Mark would force his way in anyway, but after he did this the games broke up into arguments.

Eventually, Mark moved to another school. His parents were glad to move him and, to be truthful, his first school was pleased to see him leave. His new teacher was firm but also worked through the skills necessary to help him to speak and listen to children and adults. This included increasing the time he was expected to listen and concentrate, and helping him to remember instructions by repeating them. It also included encouraging him to ask questions and to speak in sentences. Mark was reminded to speak more slowly and clearly and at the right volume. He was taught to ask to join in games, to find friendly things to say to the other children and to respond pleasantly when other children spoke to him. He practised these skills with the teacher and helper and was encouraged to try them out with the other children.

Slowly Mark's behaviour and work improved and he began to mix with other children more successfully. He began to join in some of the group activities which involved language, singing and rhymes. This helped keep up the progress with his language development while needing less direct attention from the teacher. By the end of the year he was speaking in correct sentences of eight or nine words regularly and had conversations with other children in which they took turns three or four times each. His tantrums took place less often and were less serious; Mark would settle down to read or to work in groups. He was still not an easy child to teach, but there had been great progress.

Effective communication begins in infancy, building up patterns of social life. When a parent responds to a baby's smile and the baby gurgles in pleasure at this, expectations of responses between the two are being established. Both understand that they take it forward and then wait for the other person; it is a social process in which each has a place and a role.

Communication is the exchange of meanings, finding out and sharing, the expression of needs and feelings. It is our way of knowing what is happening in our world, and gives us clarity and security, especially at difficult or confusing times. It is the way we find out about other people, find out how they view us, and exchange ideas and opinions. It gives opportunities for pleasure and passing the time pleasantly, learning formally or informally or helping others to learn.

Adults and children need a number of basic social and language skills for effective communication. Key skills include:

- suitable vocabulary
- clear sequences within and between sentences
- appropriate modulation and volume of speech
- starting, sustaining and ending conversations
- relevance in content of speech
- eye contact
- a range of active listening skills
- assertiveness skills

For friendship and good relationships, we need to communicate ideas, thoughts, and ways of solving problems, and also feelings, needs and emotions. Friendship also requires listening, the expression of personal support and honest comment provided in ways that will be seen as helpful.

The meaning of friendship develops as children grow. The required communication skills become much more complex for older children and young people. For younger age groups, Hyman Hops and Melissa Finch list the following verbal skills used by socially competent children: need statements, commands, requests, suggestions, conditionals, statements, questions, claims, play noise, calling (Hops and Finch, 1985, p. 64). The same skills can also be used at an advanced and complex level:

> Pupils should be able to listen and respond, in complex, detailed discussion, demonstrating a full and perceptive understanding of what has been said and making significant constructive contributions.
>
> (DFE, 1993, p. 23)

Communication skills for friendship can be improved. Doing so makes a huge difference. Going beyond basic skills to much more complex communication competence is valuable for individuals and those with whom they develop relationships. These high-level skills help the development and expression of sensitivity and the exploration of feelings.

Across different age groups there are common themes which need to be addressed in communication for friendship and for friendly relations in school. Communicating friendly intentions, giving and receiving compliments, active listening skills, encouraging others to confide and confiding in others are all important. Other key skills are coherence and relevance of speech, speech quantity and quality, giving positive feedback, the skills of joining groups, encouraging others to join in. A friend will be somebody who tells you the truth, even if it hurts, but the truth will hurt less if told to you by a friend. A friend will find out how you feel and you will want to find out how the friend feels, so that you can help each other. Teachers can bring these basic themes in communication together with specific speech and language skills to help children and young people to apply them in real situations.

SAY THE OBVIOUS AND MAKE IT MATTER

People who have good communication and social skills are clear and unambiguous in what they say and how they respond. Good communication means leaving little to the imagination, because until we communicate, we cannot be sure of shared understanding or feelings. Going through and taking others through processes which make positive feelings, questions, doubts and pleasures obvious is necessary to achieve satisfying relationships. At the most basic level, it means speaking clearly, without room for misunderstanding, sharing ownership of the conversation and expressing positives about the other person and the situation which are true and specific. Many adults and young people find this difficult, especially when dealing with feelings, and try other ways, for example to 'say it with flowers'.

Practice in the communication of friendship and relationships is essential. It cannot be taken for granted. We are amazed that others may see us differently from how we see and hear ourselves. We are surprised when we hear a tape of our speech at how it is less resonant than we think it is, and hear all the slips, vagueness and hard to understand slang that we edit out of our consciousness when we are speaking. A similar experience can happen with video when we notice just how we do or usually do not assert a point of view clearly or coherently. That others fail to respond as we think they might is easier to understand and accept as something we can influence. Video and audio taping are important parts of teaching communication skills.

The style of communication skills that is effective is a rather explicit, clear style. A similar style is now common for written communication, where short, direct sentences with no spare words are friendly to the reader. Reading our own letters from the perspective of the reader improves their quality and effectiveness. The other style of communication which is effective is the use of skills to encourage others to have their full role in the interaction, to listen to them carefully, to help them to talk about more difficult issues and to help them be clear and to the point. These skills need to be combined with the appropriate eye contact, touch and distance, postures and expression (see Chapter 3). Most people benefit from seeing what they do on a video for the final few practices. These are not skills that can be taken for granted; even giving directions to a place we know well is an exercise most of us find hard to do well enough for the stranger to follow them correctly.

We also need to ensure that children have the vocabulary to develop social skills. Children can learn the vocabulary of emotions, feelings, hopes and fears by direct teaching, word games, groupwork, and from literature and other media. The teacher can introduce more structure and more opportunities to learn for those children who have not mastered this and other relevant vocabularies. In school, almost every situation gives opportunities to develop, practise and guide these communication skills. The situations do need to be used to help children practise these skills to a very high level of clarity, so it is obvious what they are communicating, and to take these skills once learnt and apply them to different situations. Each school has its own social world and can build opportunities to practise and apply these skills (see Chapter 10).

COMMUNICATION FOR LIFE

Teachers and parents are aware of how important communication skills are in social competence, and hence for overall development, success and happiness. This applies both to adults and to children. Effective communication is essential for individuals, families and organizations. Poor communication is associated with conflict, poor relationships and underperformance.

Research has emphasized just how critical the development of effective communication skills is for social competence. It is one of the core areas. In their survey of research into children's social behaviour, for example, Joseph Strayhorn and Phillip Strain give three main goals for social competence. Two of the goals relate to kind and co-operative behaviour and showing an outgoing interest in people. The third is the 'ability to use language well, to have a command of a wide range of vocabulary and syntax such that ideas may be both comprehended and expressed with facility' (Strayhorn and Strain, 1986, p. 286).

For children or young persons at a particular level of development, it is necessary to look not only at how they apply the speech and language skills they have to social situations, but also at the speech and language skills they have and need to acquire. Strategies to help a child may focus either on basic speech and language skills or on how these are used, or both. For children who have difficulties with communication for friendship, looking at both will almost always be necessary. As with other social skills for friendship, the development of basic skills needs to be backed up by practice in real-life settings.

There are valuable skills and resources which teachers have and use to help children to develop communication skills. Early-years teachers combine the use of a curriculum of communication skills which can be listed in a very clear way with the use of activities and room design to promote the application of speech and language skills. For example, teaching a specific aspect of spoken vocabulary is combined with a 'shopping' activity. There is a great deal of early-years teaching which relates to friendship, playing and working together, sharing, helping, even though teachers may not have consciously stated objectives. This teaching is likely to involve a high level of reference to the items on the relevant curriculum, especially those in detailed checklist form, amending them to relate specifically to friendship. For Mark, this meant taking the objective of using a wider range of adjectives, and ensuring that adjectives he learnt and used helped to build his relationships. Where children have difficulties with communication skills and/or friendship, precision is important in identifying either the communication skills they next need to learn, or which skills they need to apply.

Teachers are aware that language skills develop spontaneously within a supportive and language-rich environment. Those who have young children are frequently astonished by what they hear, as toddlers take the language around them and transform it into original and personal contributions. Language and speech development, including written language, can change to a shorter and simpler form before a more complex form is generated, so adults can be surprised both by complexity and by simplicity. Teachers will need to consider the learning and social situations they are setting up in school, the speech and language skills that are essential for these situations and how the children who manage these situations best use specific communication skills. Formal curriculum documents and resources address the communication skills of academic progress but the language of feelings also needs to be addressed. While teachers may elicit and teach these in safe tasks they have to be practised in real situations. Social skills courses for young people usually involve practice, role play, discussion and homework to bring together necessary skills.

Teaching the communication skills of friendship helps children with all aspects of their learning as well as overall social development. Communication skills are enmeshed with general social development and the learning of all kinds of skills. Children learn specific communication skills which they can apply generally and creatively; they benefit if the creativity and complexity of using communication skills are built into the learning of those skills. This can be easy for some children and for their teachers and parents; for others it can be harder to focus on specific skills without sacrificing the living nature of communication. Douglas Cooper and Lynne Anderson-Inman express this clearly and effectively:

> the study of language and socialization is an attempt to study processes that in everyday experiences are inseparable. To be socialized is to learn the language of the surrounding society.
>
> (Cooper and Anderson-Inman, 1988, p. 226)

To fail to learn that language is to be vulnerable in all everyday experiences.

COMMUNICATION DIFFICULTIES AND QUALITY OF LIFE

Research confirms how important it is to help children who experience problems with learning and communication. Those who have significant difficulties with communication are vulnerable to wider problems which can threaten their quality of life. Those who are close to children with communication problems know how these can lead to general social difficulties, setting up a vicious circle. This is partly because of the attitudes and resources of the world in which children try to cope. We give some examples from research, relating to a range of language and learning problems.

For children with specific developmental language difficulties (SDLD), Michael Rutter, Lynne Mawhood and Patricia Howlin conclude that the difficulties 'extend well beyond language and often include substantial problems in social relationships' (Rutter *et al.*, 1992, p. 76).

Joseph Strayhorn and Phillip Strain take up this point from their survey of research, noting 'a direct relationship between ratings of language difficulty and the label of psychiatric disturbance' (Strayhorn and Strain, 1986, p. 292). Society can isolate those with language difficulties. The outcome can be problems arising from loneliness, such as depression.

For children with a range of speech and language problems, Lena Rustin and Armin Kuhr conclude as follows:

> If children are unable to communicate verbally in the normal way, their chances of participating in satisfying interactions and forming good relations are reduced. Young children normally seek out those peers with whom they are able to communicate verbally.
>
> (Rustin and Kuhr, 1989, p. 11)

In the case of children with hearing impairments, others in society may assume that they are unintelligent and/or have little of worth to communicate (McCracken and Sutherland, 1991).

Where children are aggressive or overactive, when they are seen by children as demanding, annoying, intrusive or intimidating, the others may not want to mix with them. The communication from other children becomes more negative in comparison with the positive interactions experienced by more popular children (Whalen and Henker, 1985).

For many children and young people with learning and communication problems, the language competence of the other children is used to remind them of the low status they have. This is a problem which children with learning difficulties face every day at school. Children can use complex vocabulary and other communication skills to highlight the difficulties others may have, making jokes and comments they do not understand. At its worst, children use their language competence to generate a huge negative vocabulary to describe their classmates who have learning difficulties. David Galloway gives an example:

On an INSET training course, a group of 70 teachers took less than five minutes to produce a list of more than 70 derogatory labels in current use in their own schools when pupils were referring to peers regarded as slow learners (for example, 'divvy', 'remmo', 'spas').

(Galloway, 1992, p. 215)

As well as the medical and/or developmental problem itself, the assumptions we can make can be set against the child. People with communication problems typically are trying very hard to communicate; children need to learn this. Quite apart from the benefits for the child with the difficulty, being actively interested in others is one of the three key areas we cited above, and all children will benefit from making the effort to communicate where communication takes an effort.

There are four main reasons for looking closely at the social and teaching needs of children with speech and language problems:

- Their problems may be hard to solve.
- They may find it hard to make much response at first so people can reduce their attempts to communicate.
- Communication skills are central to social success and quality of life.
- Our society frequently has negative attitudes towards people with learning and language problems and takes negative actions against them.

There is a great need to do this. A large number of people, adults and children, have serious problems with communication, making up a substantial percentage of the overall population. Far more people would benefit from speech and language therapy than receive it. They also need help with the use of skills in real-life situations away from the clinic, not only with the communication skills but also with the social situations in which they need to be applied successfully (Rustin and Kuhr, 1989). For children with serious speech and language problems both therapeutic and everyday help are required.

Sasha, aged 4, has experienced delay in speech and language development. Recent progress has been good, and Sasha can now say three-word phrases and understand more complex sentences said by others. He has always been interested in other children, and even when he could not speak he would watch what they were doing, point and make noises if it was interesting or exciting. He has always been a cheerful child but silent for long periods, smiling but not speaking. He was a quiet baby with little or no babble. His nursery worker has been teaching him phrases that he can use to start conversations and express friendship:

'Sasha play too'
'You [name] play'
'Sasha help'
'What you doing?'

She encourages him to use them throughout the day, and she and the other children are delighted when he uses something similar he made up himself. If it is not correct, and often it is not, they praise him and say a correct sentence for him to repeat. He uses words such as 'happy', 'sad', 'help', 'play'. Sasha uses children's names, makes eye contact and smiles. He knows that what others say is important and, on the whole, listens better than he used to.

Sasha still has much to learn about the skills of friendship but has friendly relationships with the other children in the nursery and is liked by the adults. He is fortunate that he reached two of the three main goals identified in research: he is interested in other people, especially children, and he is co-operative and kind. He seems to have reached these goals at a good level for his age without any formal or planned help. The help he is having in nursery with the third goal of language competence is planned carefully although it is easy to carry out. It has had positive results not only in his speech and language development but also in the way other children help him, play with him and give him encouragement. It is not clear how quickly or how far Sasha will progress with his speech and language skills, but his good relationships in nursery are helping with his language, and his use of language is helping with making friends.

Peter, aged 9, is currently making good progress with his reading and writing skills. He has always found maths easier than language-related skills. His parents and the class teacher are pleased with the progress made, but they continue to be concerned about Peter's language and social skills. While Peter has interesting things he wishes to talk about, it is difficult to communicate with him. He becomes excited about what he has to tell you, his thoughts rushing ahead of what he says, with the result that he produces disjointed sentences, and his articulation deteriorates so that it is hard to understand what he is saying. Peter does not make much eye contact when he is speaking to you and looks out of the window, while tugging at your sleeve to tell you something. The result is frustration on both sides about communication.

A plan of action is agreed. Adults will ask Peter for eye contact before they start to talk and praise him if he responds: 'That's good. We're both looking at each other. Now we'll be able to talk.' They will also remind Peter if eye contact begins to be lost: 'Oh. Can you look at me when you're talking to me? – it's much easier for me to follow what you're saying.' Peter will also be given prompts and praise for speaking slowly and clearly: 'You explained the first part really well, then you started to rush it and I missed the last part. Can you tell me again?' So far this is working well. The next step will be to make up a story with two other pupils to tape-record with an adult, to give practice in listening and speaking with others.

BEYOND BASIC SKILLS

The examples given above indicate the importance of basic communication skills, and how they influence and are influenced by wider social processes and skills. Developing both specific and general communication skills that are effective and teaching children to apply them will help them socially, academically and emotionally.

Helping children develop high-level skills in speech and language will give them more opportunities to develop and enrich relationships. They will also be able to explore more demanding situations which take them into social competence for adult life more smoothly and successfully. These high-level skills are a feature of close relationships in adulthood, which are based on shared understanding and explorations of personal values and needs. Just as the complexity and depth of children's friendships develop as they grow older, so does the language competence which communicates much of this process.

The development of shared understanding both reflects and assists the deepening of a relationship. This can include secrets, jokes, talking about difficulties and stresses. Talking through a problem with a friend who respects the confidence and is supportive is a skill that is currently better exercised by women than men. The subtleties of communication in a relationship can go further so that the friends understand the meaning of a slight change of tone of voice, of the choice of a word. In older childhood and teenage years, individuals can develop skills in using a variety of speech and language styles for the closest friends, the others and for the classroom. Usually we can tell whether people are friends or not by the greeting they give each other.

Such high-level skills can be applied to help problem-solve with others, to generate alternatives, to discuss options and to express and share support. Identifying, expressing value for, drawing on the skills and support of others and providing support in turn are effective in dealing with difficult situations and also in planning positive paths forward. These skills and attributes can be helpful both in social situations and work or leisure circumstances. The opposite approach is to use language skills to make others feel inferior and left out, to use language as a way of excluding others from communication.

Paula has had problems with learning and language throughout her life. She has struggled to make progress, having particular problems with reading and writing in high schools. She is now 15, trying her best and hoping to achieve some formal results for her efforts. She is working hard and finding it very difficult. Paula is quiet but liked by others in her class. They can help her but in the end she has to do the work herself.

One of the boys has been taking an interest in Paula and she feels he wants her to go out with him and be his regular girlfriend. Paula does not know him very well and thinks he is probably quite nice but does not know what to say if he asks her out. She talks to her friend who suggests that she sees what happens and, if he does, say that she likes him but wants to concentrate on the work for now. Paula knows that this is what she does want to say and is happy that this is the way to say it. Paula was fortunate in the school she went to and the attitude of the other young people.

The development of communication skills and confidence helps children to assert their own rights and the rights of other children. There is a need for more research into bullying involving children with special educational needs and into the role of language in this. It is thought that children with learning difficulties may be more at risk of bullying than other children. These potential victims may have low status and self-esteem because of their learning difficulties; it may also be hard for them to find the words to express how they feel to assert their own needs and to help others empathize with them. Improving the situation can be done through the development of verbal and non-verbal assertion skills and listening skills, to promote an awareness and understanding of the needs and feelings of others.

Andrea is 14 and is having a successful and enjoyable time in school and with her friends locally. She is popular and admired partly because of the way she refuses to be defeated by a serious stammer. She works hard but also is cheerful and jokes a lot. Sometimes she has been able to make a good joke better by selecting exactly the right word and after the others have had to wait; they have had to wait but the wait has been worthwhile for them.

She tells others that one way she manages her stammering is by thinking ahead to what she would like to say and devising a sentence that starts with a word she will find easier and continues with a flow she feels she can manage. Andrea has read at assembly and says she is unconcerned that people have to wait until she can say something; she feels that they are supporting her in trying to produce the words. Because of her smiling, cheerful nature, nobody has considered making fun of her and she has told her classmates and the teachers they must not put in words for her. They must wait for her to decide if she can complete a sentence as chosen or change what she says.

There are many situations that Andrea finds very difficult – shopping, for example. She will ask for somebody to come with her and she gives that person clear instructions on what she wants them to do and not to do. She makes it clear to people who are new to her how she manages her problem and what kind of support is helpful. Andrea or her friends tell people that stammering is a very difficult problem, which makes her feel terrible. She dreams that one morning she will wake up and will be able to chatter without fear or risk. Andrea has a serious communication problem, but this is not made worse by loneliness, teasing or other social problems. With encouragement and patience she can manage.

For children who are experiencing any of a range of problems including anxiety, stress, abuse and failure, communication problems develop along with the basic problem (see Chapter 7). Improving communication is part of the process of dealing with the basic problem.

TAKING ACTION

THE FEELINGS BEAR

The aims are to generate the vocabulary of feelings and to link this correctly with non-verbal signals, especially facial expression.

There are different ways to use this activity, partly depending on the age of the children. It can be used successfully with children of 10 or 11, although they can be introduced to it by saying they will be doing this with younger children and the session is for practice.

The children sit in a circle and one of them has a toy bear. The teacher explains that the bear has feelings just like us but needs to show how it feels. The first child then makes an expression and the other children call out what they think this means about how the bear is feeling. When the feeling has been guessed, the first child throws the bear to another and they express the bear's feelings.

This activity helps in a number of ways: by having the children look closely for facial expression, by their practising appropriate facial expressions for emotions, and by their generating vocabulary for emotions.

JUST A MINUTE

The aim of this activity is to have children focus on coherence in speech.

This radio game has each participant in turn try to speak for a minute on a topic given to her. She has to speak without hesitation, deviation or repetition. Others can challenge her if they think she has failed to do so; if the challenge is ruled to be successful, the child who has challenged takes over. Whoever is speaking at the end of the minute is the winner of that round.

CALL MY BLUFF

The purposes of this activity include raising awareness of the importance of how we say things. It also shows that in communication we need to interpret what somebody else is saying, to assess if it is plausible, to see if it makes sense.

Each group has up to five members. They are given unusual words which occur in the dictionary. They then have to think up false definitions which sound convincing. Each group pairs up with another; they take turns to present their definitions for the word. The other group has to try to guess which was the accurate definition. Repeat this process for several words per team. Each team scores a point for guessing correctly from what the other team says and for each correct bluff themselves.

DIRECTIONS

This aims to raise awareness of the need to be explicit and clear in speech to achieve the understanding of others. A version can be found in Michelson *et al.* (1983).

Older children and teenagers give directions to a motorist to a destination that requires several twists and turns. The motorist has to repeat them back accurately. One variant of this is to address also the personal safety issues of talking to a stranger, and have the young people role-play, making it clear that they are keeping a social and physical distance, being brief and business-like, while not being rude, and still giving accurate directions.

WHAT HAVE WE HERE?

In an activity suggested by Rustin and Kuhr (1989), one group member leaves the room while the rest arrange themselves in a scene; for example, involving two cars which have collided. The member is then invited back into the room to guess what the scene shows. This can be simplified by using pictures to help.

PHOTOS

Discuss a series of photographs of faces with a range of expressions. In a more structured version, specific photos are made which express particular emotions and the emotions have to be matched up with the photos (Spence, 1980). Making your own photos to show expressions is a useful activity in itself and can also be used with groups to demonstrate and discuss expressions in a specific situation.

SILENT MOVIES

Show a video of a scene or two with the sound down. In groups, children devise and record a soundtrack according to instructions about character or style; this can mean the characters are being very obvious in the way they express themselves, or have particular ways of speaking.

THOUGHT BUBBLES

Stop a video at intervals and ask the children either to say or to write down what one or more characters are thinking or feeling at these times. This helps to teach recognition of both verbal and non-verbal communication of emotion or thought and can give rise to interesting and amusing discussions. Alternatively, cartoons with the script taken out can be used; the children write in thought bubbles. For younger children speech bubbles can be used instead.

JUST ENOUGH

This is a variant on a basic social skills activity in which the young person is helped to communicate a feeling. The teacher acts out the verbal and non-verbal skills of the feeling as applied to a particular situation, for example confidence in asking for help in a shop. Then the teacher rehearses (with video if possible) until the young people can all express confidence in their communication in the shop. The next stage is to work through the same process to define and act out more precisely the level of confidence appropriate to the situation, with practice in 'not quite confident enough' and 'just a little too confident'. This helps to fine-tune the use of communication skills.

TELEPHONES

Small children like to use the telephone and will play with a toy telephone. It gives many opportunities for speech and language development activities. These are especially helpful for children with communication problems. It is important for all children to learn the appropriate use of the telephone, for emergency, social conversations, etc. In schools where there is an answerphone, have the message recorded by a child and rotate the message regularly so that many children have a chance to record.

For verbally competent young people, rather more testing scenarios can be devised, looking forward either to work situations or to more amusing ones. For example, you and your friend are in their house when his parents are out. You both try to move the television and drop it. The following day you phone your friend to find out what the response of his parents was — and the parent answers the phone.

SCHOOL RECEPTIONS

Many high schools have a reception area staffed by students. There is rotation of staffing and the students are rehearsed in how to greet visitors and deal with enquiries.

FRIENDLY SITUATIONS

The importance of compliments was outlined in the chapter on self-esteem. One way of developing this across an age range is to take a part of a story or scene from a play and have children change it to make it more friendly. This can be great fun (for example, in Charles Dickens's *A Christmas Carol,* Scrooge is just as mean with his money but a great deal easier to like) and focuses on the details of communicating friendliness and/or friendship in a variety of situations.

BEHIND THE SCREEN

This aims to help the use and interpretation of tone of voice.

One person is given a list of adjectives or adverbs and is asked to count from nought to ten out loud from behind a screen in the manner of the word. The rest of the group has to guess what the word might be. An alternative is to have pupils in pairs counting nought to ten. They have a 'tone' conversation; that is, one pupils starts and the other responds to his tone of voice. There can be discussion of the way in which tone of voice invites a particular response.

RADIO SHOW

A group of children or young people devise, script and deliver a radio show. It can be almost any kind of show, although chat shows and phone-ins work well, and the degree of teacher support varies accordingly. This can be useful in teaching intonation and expression of mood.

RESOURCE

Lena Rustin and Armin Kuhr (1989) *Social Skills and the Speech Impaired.* London: Taylor & Francis.
   This gives over ninety activities cross-referenced to aspects of communication difficulty. It applies to adults as well as children and is primarily for use by therapists.

REFERENCES

Asher, S. and Gottman, J. (1981) *The Development of Children's Friendships.* Cambridge: Cambridge University Press.
Cooper, D. C. and Anderson-Inman, L. (1988) Language and socialization. In M. A. Nippold (ed.) (1988) *Later Language Development: Ages Nine through Nineteen.* Boston, Mass.: College Hill Press.
Cromer, R. (1991) *Language and Thought in Normal and Handicapped Children.* Oxford: Blackwell.
Department for Education and the Welsh Office (1993) *English for Ages 5 to 16.* London: HMSO.
Galloway, D. (1992) Children with special needs. In C. Rogers and P. Kutnick (eds) *The Social Psychology of the Primary School.* London: Routledge.
Garbarino, J., Stott, F. and the Faculty of the Erikson Institute (1989) *What Children Can Tell Us.* San Francisco: Jossey-Bass.
Honey, P. (1988) *Face to Face: A Practical Guide to Interactive Skills,* 2nd edn. Aldershot: Gower.
Hops, H. and Finch, M. (1985) Social competence and skill: a reassessment. In B. H. Schneider, K. H. Rubin and J. E. Ledingham (eds) *Children's Peer Relations: Issues in Assessment and Intervention.* New York: Springer-Verlag.
McCracken, W. and Sutherland, H. (1991) *Deaf-Ability, Not Disability: A Guide for the Parents of Hearing Impaired Children.* Clevedon, Avon: Multilingual Matters.
Michelson, L., Sugai, D. P. Kazdin, A. E. and Wood, R. P. (1983) *Social Skills Assessment and Training with Children: An Empirically Based Handbook.* New York: Plenum Press.
Rustin, L. and Kuhr, A. (1989) *Social Skills and the Speech Impaired.* London: Taylor & Francis.
Rutter, M., Mawhood, L. and Howlin, P. (1992) Language delay and social development. In P. Fletcher and D. Hall (eds) *Speech and Language Disorders in Children.* London: Whurr Publications.

Spence, S. (1980) *Social Skills Training with Children and Young People.* Windsor: NFER – Nelson.

Spitzberg, B. H. and Cupach, W. R. (1984) *Interpersonal Communication Competence.* Beverly Hills, Calif.: Sage.

Spitzberg, B. H. and Cupach, W. R. (1989) *Handbook of Interpersonal Competence Research.* New York: Springer-Verlag.

Strayhorn, J. M. and Strain, P. S. (1986) Social and language skills for preventive mental health: what, how, who and when. In P. S. Strain, M. J. Guralnick and H. M. Walker (eds) *Children's Social Behavior: Development, Assessment and Modification.* Orlando, Fla: Academic Press.

Tann, S. (1991) *Developing Language in the Primary Classroom.* London: Cassell.

Thomas, D. (1978) *The Social Psychology of Childhood Disability.* London: Methuen.

Whalen, C. K. and Henker, B. (1985) The social worlds of hyperactive (ADDH) children. *Clinical Psychology Review* **5**, 447–78.

Chapter 6

A Celebration of Differences

'I was very grateful that this man was so different from me; without knowing it he was an enrichment to me.' (Brian Keenan about fellow hostage John McCarthy, 1992)

'The boys used to mess up all our games.'

'I'd really like to be friends but their dad doesn't like us.'

'No one wants to play with her — she smells funny.'

'She may be very tiny but she's great ... there's always some way she can join in.'

'Mark was very upset when a group of boys shouted abuse at Alan because of his colour; they'd been mates since starting school. He wanted to defend his friend but wasn't sure what to do for the best.'

INFLUENCES FROM BEYOND THE SCHOOL GATES

Children in junior and senior schools are making choices in their friendships. They are choosing who to sit next to, talk to and play with. How are these choices made? At first sight the answer appears obvious: older children make friends with others who are friendly and like the same things. They and adults tend to like others who are perceived as being similar to themselves. This raises the question of what the possibilities are for friendship for those who appear to be different. This question concerns complex issues and reflects attitudes of society towards gender, race, class, culture and ability.

Children's friendships and friendship choices are influenced by society and cultural values. For example, children identify with their own gender, so that girls and boys mostly choose same-sex friendships. Girls may be reluctant to allow boys to join their games; likewise boys may show reluctance to play with 'girls' toys'. Often this is in direct contrast to the attempts of adults to encourage non-sexist and non-racist behaviour; the children are responding to adults' and society's powerful 'hidden messages'. While we may say we want all our children to have the same opportunities, we may continue to have different expectations of behaviour. For example, a parent may

become concerned about an older boy who continues to enjoy playing with dolls and may try to discourage him.

This chapter looks at how society's attitudes to differences influence children's friendships, and suggests ways forward to maximize every child's opportunities for friendship.

DOES EQUAL MEAN EQUALLY LIKELY TO BE FRIENDS?

Equality of opportunity is still a long way off, especially for some groups. There may be a good deal of lip service in the direction of equal opportunities, but how much does this convert to action? Schools may feel that they have effective policies and practices, but the formation of friendship may still take place according to race, gender, class, or ability. Children may be friendly towards each other and celebrate differences, but may not go on to form deeper friendships across society's divides.

Because social behaviour can be used with subtlety it can be a secret and deadly weapon in exaggerating social distance. This can involve use of 'invisible' differences like class and learning as well as the visible differences of race, gender and physical disability. Children can feel, and be, left out and considered unworthy of friendship. Children whom society defines as 'normal' can learn attitudes of suspicion and avoidance of those society defines as 'different'. These children can be harshly treated and ostracized. Yet if social behaviour can be used negatively to isolate vulnerable children, it can also be used positively to include them. A first step is the creation of a friendly classroom in which celebration of and interest in difference has been established.

MEETING NEEDS INCLUDES THE NEED FOR FRIENDSHIP

Rahina, aged 10, has cerebral palsy. This has affected all her limbs, although she is an 'indoor walker', managing up to a hundred metres or so with her frame. She drops objects and finds writing very hard. Her pronunciation of speech is also affected and she needs time and a patient listener to make herself understood. She has problems chewing and swallowing.

She has been to a special school, where there are 40 children. Three of the children there are of a similar culture to Rahina and their families share a first language. However, the families do not live very near to each other so there is not much social contact apart from school-related events. Although Rahina is socially isolated from school friends she does meet relatives and is with children every week. The neighbourhood children call in and play with her.

Rahina is intelligent and works to a high standard, using personally adapted computers to help access the curriculum. Transfer to a local mainstream school has been suggested and discussed in some detail. The work there would be demanding and meet her intellectual needs; moving about could be assisted by the use of a powered wheelchair for longer distances; and arrangements could be made so that she would be able to have her regular physiotherapy.

But how might such a move affect Rahina socially? Will she make friends in the new school? Will she be respected and admired for the way she struggles to speak clearly and walk further? Will she be given due credit for the excellent work she does? If she has an adult helper, will this isolate her from classroom discussions with other children? Will she join in playground games? Will she go to other children's homes and they to hers?

WHAT DO WE MEAN BY 'SUCCESSFUL' INTEGRATION?

These questions begin to illustrate how central relationships are in equal opportunities. Making friendships and friendly relationships can take equality of opportunity forward. Isolation, insult, making 'fun', refusal to play or work with someone are ways of expressing prejudice, inequality and discrimination.

For Rahina, how integration works out will depend partly on her own friendship skills and attitudes and partly on those of others in the new school. It will also depend on how much teachers are prepared to plan for her social as well as academic integration. We all hope it goes well.

EQUAL OR GRATEFUL?

Yet some interesting and important issues remain even if it does go well. Will Rahina feel sufficiently accepted and confident to disagree with other children and adults in school? To fall out with them and still feel confident of being accepted again as a friend when the issue is resolved?

Perhaps the school she attends does help children to express pride in their culture. Will she feel confident about doing this and will she know how to do this in a school context? Will she be able to express her religious opinions knowing that they are a minority view and that strong religious beliefs are not shared by most of the class?

Will her exercise programme be seen as interesting and her determination and progress be celebrated? Will she be left out when her classmates' interest in their own appearance becomes very important to them?

Will Rahina have the choice of making friends and being friendly across the whole of the class if she wishes? To do so, will she have to fit or be compatible with the stereotype of a quiet and docile Asian girl, or can she be loud, boisterous and bossy? Will she be able to express dissatisfaction over any problems or is she bound into the role of being grateful for acceptance?

The traditional role of the disabled is to go 'cap in hand' for charity rather than to demand and obtain full human rights. Can she achieve attainment of her rights without positive role models, and will these be available?

MAKING ASSUMPTIONS

Even if Rahina has excellent social skills and confidence she might have to deal with all kinds of assumptions by others. Many of these promote social distance and limit opportunities to develop friendships.

Often the reasons given for the lack of integration are superficially positive in that they appear to be for the benefit of the child with special needs. Not playing or working together might be planned to prevent her being at risk. She may find herself not eating with the other children because she needs help with feeding. Other examples might be going out of school for physiotherapy rather than using school-based programmes and having her computer set up in a separate area. With the best of intentions, adults can organize situations which create many barriers to personal growth where only one exists. The outcome for the child, despite these good intentions, is likely to be separation, loneliness and a feeling of being second best.

SOCIAL STEREOTYPES, PREJUDICE AND PREJUDGING

Adults do not mean to isolate vulnerable children, but often their own assumptions are based on stereotyped thinking. These assumptions lead to planning what should happen to children on the basis of how they are different, rather than on the basis of how they are similar. Planning for 'differentness' can lead to social distance and reduced social opportunities.

The prejudging by adults assumes that children who have differences of race, disability, etc. will neither become nor wish to become friends. One assumption, for example, is that only children of similar ability and school performance will want to be friends with each other. This goes far beyond the reasonable view that children will seek at least one friendly relationship with somebody with whom they can share and compare work but may well make friends across a wider range who meet different personal needs.

For children with disabilities, it is the prejudging that becomes the major handicap, particularly in terms of restricted opportunities for social contact (Furnham and Gibbs, 1984).

Margaret was about to have a year's intensive tuition in a special class for children with specific reading difficulties. She was pleased about this but anxious about travelling on the bus with 'handicapped' children. She had only once come into contact with someone with disabilities and had been frightened by his behaviour, a feeling unfortunately reinforced by her parents' reaction. She was reassured by the notion that just as the children in her class didn't all look or behave in the same way, so people with disabilities were different — each an individual. She hadn't really thought like this before.

LIMITING CATEGORIES

It is common practice that in order to make sense of others, we learn to place and describe people in terms of categories and groups. The following descriptions of children, for example, are well-known:

- 'pre-school child'
- 'Asian child'

- 'hyperactive child'
- 'child with a visual impairment'
- 'gifted child'

Use of groups and categories can appear to simplify and ease communication. These labels and categories have meaning because they are based on shared assumptions. The problem with the use of any label or category is that it focuses on one specific attribute at the expense of everything else about an individual. Even 'positive' labels are gross distortions. Tessa Cohn puts this very succinctly:

> Proper names allow specific differentiation but more general categories limit the possibility for discreteness and encourage us to learn how to fit our experiences into a relatively small number of categories. Placing an individual into one of these general categories, whether or not it has a derogatory label, diminishes the person, ignores their idiosyncrasies, denies them those very attributes which distinguish them from their neighbours. In focussing on just one attribute, whether physical or mental, related to gender or ethnicity, all others are obliterated, at least temporarily. The recipient of the label may well be unable to establish his or her individual identity in interaction with the group ...
>
> (Cohn, 1988, p. 35)

NAME-CALLING

Other ways of labelling and categorizing include name-calling. This may be trivial or serious, depending on intent and effect. An example of trivial name-calling is when a child will call out a minor insult in order to get another child to chase him. Serious name-calling has the effect of making a child feel angry or miserable. Elinor Kelly's study (1988) found that 66 per cent of pupils reported name-calling in this category. Tessa Cohn's study revealed the following:

- Name-calling referred to physical and mental attributes, race and ethnicity, sex and gender.
- Girls reported more sexist name-calling than boys, 45 per cent compared with 12 per cent.
- The proportion of racist name-calling, in relation to that of sexist insults and names based on physical and mental characteristics, steadily increased with age:
  31 per cent of name-calling among 10−13-year-olds;
  53 per cent of name-calling among 13−17-year-olds.
- Name-calling regarding race and family was seen as the most hurtful. This is likely to relate to the fact that name-calling regarding family and race makes reference 'not only to the child but also by extension to their family and indeed more broadly their ethnic community as a whole' (DES, 1985).

Serious name-calling involves the labelling and stereotyping of individuals and groups of people in a discriminatory way, and can significantly affect self-esteem and identity. Pupils interviewed in Cohn's study often did not report incidents of name-calling to teachers.

We do not see schools as having the responsibility for solving all of society's problems. We do, however, see schools as aiming to be part of the solution rather

than part of the problem. As friendship formation is critical in equality of opportunity, this is a priority area. It also seems that some schools are using effective
strategies while others may not be. David Smith and Sally Tomlinson, for example,
looked at the factors that help to explain the friends chosen by children aged 12–13
in a school setting and concluded as follows:

> There are some large differences between schools in the way that friends are chosen.
> Most important, while there is a strong tendency in some schools for children to choose
> friends within their own ethnic group, this pattern is either much weaker or completely
> absent in a number of other schools. The pattern of variation cannot be explained by dif-
> ferences in ethnic composition; it probably springs from different approaches or methods
> of organisation.
>
> (Smith and Tomlinson, 1989, p. 108)

A THRESHOLD FOR FRIENDSHIP

There has been a lot of interest in social psychology as to whether like seeks out like
in relationships. It would appear that people who are similar do meet, make friends,
and sometimes become lifelong partners; and that similarity of race, class and occu-
pation do contribute to mutual interest and the building of a relationship. People like
others who hold the same attitudes as themselves. The liking is increased if these attitudes are held for similar reasons (Duck, 1986). Yet in one study, a group of people
who were paired first with strangers who were similar to themselves, and then with
strangers who were dissimilar, gave higher ratings to dissimilar strangers, even after a
brief interaction (Sunnafrank, 1983). Duck concludes that 'interaction has a positive
effect on liking and it modifies the effect of similarity on its own' (p. 78).

WHAT DOES THIS MEAN IN EVERYDAY TERMS?

It appears that we can like people who are different from us, so long as we have
the contact. It's a bit like saying, 'I don't like people from big cities, except all the
ones I've met.' We are likely to overcome differences if we are in an environment
in which this is encouraged. At various points in this book we refer to a threshold
for friendship. This means that we need to reach the stage where we know someone
well enough to decide whether or not we would like her to be a friend. We cannot be
close friends with everyone, but if children have friendly behaviour and attitudes, the
range and number of individuals with whom they can explore possible deeper friendships will increase.

INTEGRATION AND FRIENDSHIP

The positive social effects of integration are very much borne out by the numerous
projects which have sought to integrate and bring together children attending mainstream and special schools, and have successfully included children with the most
severe learning difficulties. One effect of even relatively brief part-time integration
is that children learn to see beyond a disability to a person. Children in mainstream
schools learn how to greet and make someone feel welcome, how to include someone

so that he can join in activities. They also learn not to do things for 'special' children who need to learn to do things themselves and be challenged to do so. For the integrated children, there is often a reduction of inappropriate social behaviour, such as rocking and messy eating. All children learn how to play and enjoy games together.

Children who attend even the best special schools will have a smaller number of children of similar age with whom to interact than in mainstream schools, fewer to play with, and fewer positive role models in play and friendship.

A review of the literature yields a wealth of publications giving descriptive accounts of specific integration projects (e.g. Surkes, 1987; Bartlett and Dean, 1988; Luckett and Luckett, 1988). These report benefits for both integrated and mainstream children. Indeed there is little or no research which suggests that integration is not mutually beneficial.

The benefits of integration programmes were seen in terms of social opportunities for all children. It also appears that children will respond positively to opportunities for meeting, play and friendship without a great need for adult guidance. Studies report that children do communicate and show friendly behaviour with minimum unacceptable behaviour (Ellis, 1985).

One junior school we know was approached by the local special school for children with severe learning difficulties to ask if a class could join them regularly. The proposed activity was country dancing sessions. Aspects of country dancing that were considered useful in this context were:

- everyone dances with everyone else
- no one is left out
- the sequences can be complex so there is a need to listen closely to instructions
- co-operation is necessary
- some controlled physical contact occurs

There was a concern that country dancing would not be seen as fashionable and children (and adults) who see themselves as fashion leaders would have the initial attitude of seeing themselves as too superior to participate!

In this instance, as is usual, children were initially wary of each other. Some of the mainstream children were reluctant at first to make physical contact by joining hands. After several weeks, however, there was a marked improvement in communication and attitudes. The class cheered when children from the special school came down to join them. They exchanged personal greetings and even small gifts: for example, one child had bought stickers for another who liked the same soccer team. While it cannot be said that firm friendships developed in the limited time of the project, many positive effects were seen. Certainly the prejudicial responses of fear and avoidance were eliminated. Children were seen showing accepting and friendly behaviour, opening up channels of communication to provide opportunities for further friendship. Here was clear evidence that interaction did have a positive effect on liking.

ADULTS MAKING THE LINK

In many respects the children described above were very different from each other. Nevertheless, communication and contact arising from structured activities worked well. Some important similarities were revealed and children showed interest in each other, which developed over time into greater understanding and acceptance.

Perhaps it is not always 'sameness' that is sought and found reassuring, rather the possibility of establishing common ground or some link. Both adults and children spend time doing this when they first meet each other – for example, finding out about which schools they went to, or whether they have mutual friends or experiences.

Adults can either help children who are different to make links with each other or they can hinder the process. Parents have a valuable role to play, not just by 'letting it happen' but by promoting and encouraging friendliness. Taking and collecting children from the houses of others, speaking about other children positively, and so on, give messages about integration which are important for children.

FEAR AND AVOIDANCE

The attitudes of fear and avoidance that our segregated society unconsciously fosters have negative consequences for all children. It is clearly damaging to the children who are seen as 'different' to suffer isolation, to be seen as too unworthy or dangerous to be befriended. It is also unhelpful for 'normal' children to be burdened with fantastic fears. It is unhelpful for them for a range of reasons.

- Fearfulness in itself limits confidence and self-esteem, socially and more generally.
- Avoidance is not generally a useful response to social situations that are seen as potentially difficult; assertion skills and attitudes of positive challenge are much more productive.
- A child who learns to be anxious and/or aggressive about difference is likely to limit her social opportunities.
- Children experience self-doubt over the 'different' characteristics they might have themselves, even though these might not be very visible. Thus a child who learns that being 'normal' is highly desirable and being 'different' is something to fear and avoid may suffer greatly if he has learning difficulties, is visibly overweight or has some other 'undesirable' feature. He may suffer because of the responses of other children and adults, but above all he will suffer because his internal view of what is required of him is not consistent with what he actually is. This has great effects on his self-esteem and social confidence.

ACCEPTANCE OF SELF, ACCEPTANCE OF OTHERS

For psychological health, young children need to learn how valuable they and others are. They also need to learn that they and others have responsibilities. This means linking self-esteem with esteem for others.

Acceptance of self and others is a necessary step to celebrating differences as part of friendship. It goes beyond the short-term curiosity that diversity naturally produces and promotes. This initial curiosity, however, can be used in many activities which will start the process of valuing one's own and others' diversity. Children love to find out about themselves and others: how tall are they, who has a brother and sister, what kind of games they like, etc.

There are benefits in such activities for children of all ages, partly to encourage the natural curiosity of children about themselves and others, but also because of the need to build in pride in a sense of self that will not be so easily destroyed by hostility.

Nicola, a pupil in a secondary school, told us about Fatima, a Somalian refugee who joined the class last year:

> 'When Fatima came she was introduced to the class. Later on, she told us about her experiences, and why she had come here. She also told us about her family. She had lost contact with some of her relatives and she didn't know what had happened to them. She's very interesting. Fatima has lots of friends here. We hope she stays.'

In this school, the focus on creating a friendly and accepting ethos, helping children from very different backgrounds to share experiences, was an enriching experience for all concerned and created the threshold for friendship, which enabled several deeper friendships to be made.

Friendships can be a complementary process in which a degree of difference brings an additional asset to each person in a relationship.

SOCIAL SKILLS, POWER AND EQUAL OPPORTUNITIES

The power relationships of social development are learnt at an early stage and can be hard to shift. To feel 'king of the castle' or 'top dog' at an early age can seem inoffensive and trivial. And so it is, unless it is the first step to behaving as if others are followers, or inferior. Unfortunately, patterns of social inequality can often be traced back to the nursery where racist and sexist attitudes and negative responses to disability have been left unchecked. Children can learn about power at a very early age. They also need to learn about equality.

Many studies have looked in more detail at the ways in which inequality links with learning and friendship in school, especially in the classroom. Examples which relate to gender and/or race include:

- aggression and violence against girls, or the use of ridicule as a means of dominance of girls by boys (Shaw, 1977; Spender and Sarah, 1980)
- exposure to racist and/or sexist name-calling (Kelly and Cohn, 1988)
- dominance of space and the creation of territory by boys at the expense of girls (Clarricoates, 1987)
- Barbara Tizard and her associates followed the progress of children from thirty-three inner city schools and concluded that the experiences of black and white first-school girls and boys were different in important ways: 'not only the attainments, but also the experience of infant school tended to be different for these four groups of children, e.g. white boys (top infants) spent a greater proportion of time doing maths – apparently because the teacher had given more maths tasks' (Tizard *et al.*, 1988, pp. 167–76, 181–3)

This is consistent with findings that a disproportionate amount of teacher time is directed towards boys. It requires effort and a high level of self-monitoring to reverse this, as well as to deal with the complaints from boys that they are being treated unfairly when they get less attention than they are used to! (Ebbeck, 1985).

DO PARENTS INFLUENCE FRIENDSHIP CHOICE?

Teachers can feel confident about their work in building friendships among children but worried about what parents might think. Research is at a relatively early stage into the respective influences of family, school and culture (Schneider, 1993). Awareness of where the school stands in respect of the community is necessary. If the school is ahead of the community then what the school does will need to be tightly planned and a support network will be useful. Some parents may object to interracial or intercultural friendships but they have no right to make their children aloof or unfriendly to others, nor to determine how groupings for class tasks are determined. If they try to do so they will make the school's task harder, not simply in the social development of children but by limiting the flexibility of work arrangements. Parents are pleased with good order, good work and friendly behaviours among children generally and in their own child's class in particular. Children will accept that schools want them to be friendly and helpful and to accept help and friendliness when it is offered; they have choice over friendship development beyond this threshold.

CHILDREN CAN ALSO INFLUENCE PARENTS

Children are very good at reading unspoken messages from adults. Children who are friendly in school may not greet each other if they are out with their respective parents; they may wait and see if their parents greet each other. Whatever the adults do, the children will make eye contact with each other, giving the message of acknowledgement together with the message that they are waiting for the adults to decide. Yet children can give a lead and the school can be influential in this, partly by discussing this situation with the children, or even acting it out. Parents who might not automatically greet certain other parents because of difference may well be influenced to help or at least to tolerate the children's friendly behaviour. The rituals of friendship are important in establishing this acknowledgement and influence. Birthdays and other key days, visits, arrangements to go out together, adult – child events in school, joint work and productions are useful in helping to generalize and maintain friendly behaviour and friendship. Where parents acknowledge this in situations away from the school by their actions, the school's work becomes easier.

In opening the door to friendship across society's barriers, parental influence is important but not critical in most instances. What is critical is the extent to which the teacher is able to foster behaviours and attitudes of friendliness. This will allow children to discover whether they have the compatibility and contrast to make deeper friendships without being bound by society's disapproval. If they are able to explore this then appropriate and unforced friendships will develop.

ARE CHILDREN JUDGED ON THEIR FRIENDSHIPS?

The concept that people can be known by their choice of friends is an ancient one, biblical at least. Samuel Pepys frequently deplored the friends chosen by Charles II. Pepys could not understand why the king selected such unsuitable friends. He felt that the king had many admirable qualities but that his unsuitable friendships would be the ruin of him and the monarchy. Basing drama and fiction on the adult view of suitable/unsuitable relationships is so frequent as to be unremarkable, from *Romeo and Juliet* to *To Kill a Mockingbird*. We expect children to be judged on their friendships. This not only is almost inevitable but also need not be something of concern in itself. What is of concern to us is if these judgements are based on stereotyped beliefs and actions.

This issue can be explored with great effect and enthusiasm through consideration of real-life as well as fictional situations. Children of most ages are well able to explore the concepts of adult approval and disapproval. They may find it harder, however, to turn their understanding into behaviour. For example, a child may recognize that an adult is right in suggesting that a friendship is unsuitable because stealing is a central activity of the friendship but this may not necessarily lead to the child's making different friends or stopping stealing with the same friends.

MAKING CHOICES IN FRIENDSHIP AND LEAVING OPTIONS OPEN

Children can make judgements about other children but do not need to do so from stereotyped assumptions. They can be helped to understand how to identify positives in others, how to be friendly, but also how to keep a degree of distance if that is what they wish. It is critical that adults make explicit the notion of choice in friendship. They also need to ensure that children know that friendliness to everyone is necessary so that they are able to make those choices when they wish to do so.

In Chapter 5 we note the importance of an interest in and curiosity about other people as one of three key goals for social competence. Crossing this threshold is important for every child.

FRIENDLY BEHAVIOUR WHERE DIFFERENCES OCCUR

Friendships can sometimes be described in negative terms, usually by adults, with judgements of the child implicit. 'She plays with younger children' seems to have the hidden implication that the child has to play with younger children because she and they share a developmental level. 'He plays with older boys' may imply that the child is drifting towards delinquency.

The friendships that these children have been able to make provide them with opportunities to gain acceptance and to practise and further develop friendship-making skills. In a sense these are things which everyone needs to do. Steve Duck (1991) argues that many of us are not making the most of our friendships and are therefore missing out as a result. Most of us could do either with more friends or with better-quality friendships. We all benefit from friendly neighbour-hoods and workplaces. Perhaps we should be slow to criticize the friends children have, although we can criticize specific behaviours.

TAKING ACTION

What will be effective?

In this chapter, we have put forward the view that children's friendship choices are influenced by school, family and society values. Where stereotyped and prejudicial assumptions are made about individuals and groups, opportunities for friendship are denied and discrimination and social inequality are perpetuated. This affects educational opportunities, relationships, and the quality of life.

Celebration of difference is an important part of whole-school and community initiatives for equality of opportunity. It is positive and productive to address issues of friendliness, friendship and effective working partnerships. It is vital that these are worked on in a school context where staff are developing policies and practice regarding equal opportunities and seen as part of those initiatives. By these means some of the implications for teaching can be addressed effectively and in a collaborative way.

Factors affecting the success of any policy for developing equal opportunities

General structural conditions for equal opportunities are critical, and Matthews (1989) provides a useful checklist:

- the way intelligence is defined and interpreted
- creating a warm and child-centred environment
- democratic teacher – pupil relationships
- emphasis on co-operation
- discussion of ambiguities
- validity given to a wide range of views
- background of the child held in esteem
- process learning model of education
- informal assessment, including groupwork, discussion and problem solving

(Matthews, 1989, p. 210)

From issues to action

The strategies for friendship building proposed throughout this book create a positive climate towards equal opportunities, but teachers also need to manage immediate challenges.

Following a problem-solving sequence gives a structure to the development of strategies to address these potentially complex issues.

Start by brainstorming possible factors which negatively affect relationships and contribute to unequal opportunities between children. These might include:

- racist or sexist name-calling
- integration links with special school(s) not successful
- bullying
- cliques or exclusive groups at school
- inadequate introduction for refugee children
- unequal use of space in the school grounds

Identify other areas where there is inequality of opportunity in the school. This is essential. Although you may feel that these factors do not directly affect the relationships between children they give powerful 'hidden messages' regarding attitudes and treatment of individuals and groups. For example:

- school staff do not reflect the racial and cultural make-up of the community
- meetings with parents only take place in school time, when some parents can't attend
- library and displays contain old stock and do not reflect a multicultural community
- the school building is inaccessible to anyone with physical difficulties
- there is no access to professional interpreters when teachers meet with bilingual parents
- differentiated curriculum is not provided
- male staff are rapidly promoted

For each factor listed in the above two brainstorms, think of reasons why it might be happening and indicate whether you think action can be taken by the school or the community or both.

Then list strategies at both individual and organization levels to help solve the school-based problems. For example, for racist name-calling:

- staff training on equal opportunities issues including racial awareness
- developing a procedure for racial incidents – for example, making clear that racial name-calling will not be tolerated, explaining why, recording the incident and writing to parents if further incidents occur
- strategies to increase collaborative working in the classroom
- activities which explicitly value different ethnic groups, for example cooking sessions which involve parents
- social skills sessions to develop friendship skills, which include challenging activities regarding racism

These first steps in a problem-solving process will help to indicate some priority areas for action, and specific target objectives.

Starting from basic principles when working directly with pupils

All of the above will be useful in devising and developing policies and strategies, but there are general issues to consider when working directly with children to promote equal opportunities for friendship. With pupils we need to address the following:

- Self-concept. Who are we? In what ways are we similar and different?
- How do others see us and why? How can we be effective in our relations with others?
- When something happens to us why does it happen?
- Identification of rights. What do we have the right to? What do others have the right to?
- Strategies to assert rights. How can I ensure I receive what I am entitled to? What strategies can I use to respect and uphold the rights of others?

Of the items listed above we believe the most important is the first, because a celebration of difference depends on self-concept. Here we explore paths to celebrate difference. The opposite path is to propose strategies to create similarity.

Processes of implementing an equal opportunities policy

At this point you may well discover that you want to find out more about what is happening in your school and devise a process which involves the commitment of everyone towards further development of policies. This could be carried out by the following:

- behavioural observation of what is happening, especially perhaps in the classroom
- action research, finding out what is happening in and out of school
- collaboration with students, colleagues and parents
- use of groupwork and teamwork procedures
- exploration of self-concept and values
- specific definition of objectives and responsibilities

ACTIVITIES

School and class actions

- Teach skills to raise interest and awareness and acceptance of different groups, for example sign language – then invite a person from the community to come and sign with the class.
- Invite other community members to the class, so that children can ask questions and find out about different life-styles. Usually these sessions benefit from a preparatory activity with children where they discuss what questions would be interesting to ask. Speaking and questioning skills are also addressed by this.
- Welcoming practices. For example: displaying clear and friendly messages in community languages; displaying posters (e.g. of women explorers and male nurses) which challenge stereotypes and discussing them.
- Ensuring physical access, using it and discussing it.

- Staff greeting children and expressing expectations.
- Exploration of rights and responsibilities in curriculum and delivery.
- Empathy exercises.
- Assertiveness exercises.

Specific activities with pupils

CLUSTERS

This is a good activity with which to start to explore similarities and differences. Children become aware that there are many ways in which we are similar and different, and that it is acceptable to be different. The activity is adapted from Settle and Wise (1986).

Clear a large space in the hall or classroom. Ask the class to get into groups according to different criteria, for example colour of shoes, eyes, hair (the latter can facilitate discussion about degrees of similarity and difference), number of younger brothers and/or sisters, way of getting to school (walking, bus), etc.

One criterion is given at a time, moving at a swift pace. Children will need either to observe carefully or to ask questions.

Can they suggest other criteria?

CLASS TREES

The aims of this activity are to help the class see themselves as a group and to compare similarities and differences in the group. The activity is adapted from Settle and Wise (1986).

Ask the class to think of ways in which they are all similar; for example, they are all in class 5J. If several suggestions are made, ask the class to choose one of these. Write this down on a large piece of paper.

Ask the class to think of ways to divide the class into two groups. Choose one. Ask the children to get into these two groups. Write this as a question on the paper – for example, are you a girl or a boy?

Ask the two groups for a further question which would divide the groups up further (into sub-groups); for example, musical/not musical.

Further divide each subgroup. Ask the subgroups to think of another question. If several suggestions are made, ask the groups to vote on which question will be selected. Carry on until five or six questions have been asked.

Ask individuals if they can remember the different groups to which they belong. For example, 'I'm in class 5J, I'm a boy, I'm not musical, I'm good at drawing, I speak two languages, I don't have any sisters.'

Reflect on the activity by asking children to say who was most similar to or different from them, and what they can say about their class, etc.

PEOPLE BINGO

Design a bingo sheet with statements such as 'vegetarian', 'travelled to India', 'plays chess', etc. Give out copies to the class. The idea is that individuals go round the room asking questions to find out a person who fits the description. When they have found a person they write that person's name in the appropriate box. The game ends when someone has completed the sheet. Players may only put the name of the person in the box when they have spoken to that person directly.

PARCELS

Most of us will have possessions which are very special to us. They express our individuality and uniqueness and also the social group to which we belong. *This activity gives children the opportunity to share stories which may surround these objects and helps trust to develop. Listening and language skills are also involved. The activity also helps pupils to become more aware of themselves, thus developing a sense of self.* It is adapted from Settle and Wise (1986).

The pupils are asked to bring an object which has a special meaning to them to school wrapped up. The objects are put into a bag. Each child then takes a parcel and unwraps it. The children then have to identify who the owner is by careful questioning. Direct questions such as 'Is this yours?' are not allowed.

Possible questions might be:

'I know you belong to a tennis club, have you ever won a trophy like this?'

'This shell might be part of a collection; are you the sort of person to collect things?'

If the person giving the questions feels that she can identify the owner, she approaches this person, stating that she thinks this item belongs to him. She must give a reason, for example:

'I think this trophy belongs to you because you're good at tennis, and you tell me your club has won a competition recently.'

If this is correct, the person who owns the object sits out while the game continues. The game ends when all possessions have been matched with their owners.

If, towards the end of the game, there are several people who have not been identified, the group is asked to help the questioner with questions. If they are still unable to identify the owner, the owner is asked to step forward to claim their possession and explain why it is important to them.

An additional activity would be reflective. Form one large or several small groups. Individuals share with the group why their possessions are special.

Was it difficult to identify the owners? Why was this? What did everyone learn about other people in the group today?

LOOKING FOR FRIENDS

Make a list of statements about yourself. Include likes, dislikes, views, opinions, activities, star sign, music, what makes you angry/happy, etc. Go around the class and interview others.

Reflect on the activity: What did you find out about others? Who held similar views? Who interested you and why?

JUMPING TO THE WRONG CONCLUSIONS

The aim of this activity is to develop awareness that placing people into categories is limiting and doesn't allow us to find out the full details of an individual situation. Making judgements based on this limited information can lead to wrong conclusions.

This activity, which is derived from Blackman *et al.* (1987), p. 60, is most appropriate for older children.

Make up a *WRONG CONCLUSIONS* sheet like this one:

THIS IS TRUE	AND THIS	BUT IS THIS TRUE?
I can spell	I'm short	Short people can spell
I can't swim	I'm brown-eyed	Brown-eyed people can't swim
I can cook well	I'm in Year 7	People in Year 7 cook well
I can't dance well	I'm a boy	Boys can't dance well
I'm not good at sport	I'm a girl	Girls are not good at sport

Ask children to discuss the conclusions in groups. Which are false and which are true? How do you know? Point out that some of the conclusions above seem ridiculous, while others may seem to be convincing. Ask the children to devise wrong conclusions that sound ridiculous, and others that sound quite feasible. Why are the conclusions false? This activity can be followed up by asking children to think of wrong conclusions in real life. Why were the wrong conclusions drawn? What can be done to avoid jumping to wrong conclusions?

CULTURAL EXCHANGES
The aim is to give children an opportunity to experience being strangers in an environment where values and expectations of behaviour are unfamiliar.

Children are placed in groups of about twelve. Each group is given a name such as the 'Rockies' and the 'Terrians'. Each group is given (or devises) a set of expectations and values. For example:

- Rockies only smile at someone when he has smiled at them first.
- In the Terrian community it is regarded as insolent to disagree with anyone about anything.
- Terrian people are very generous and put a lot of effort into giving things away.
- Rockies greet each other very enthusiastically.

Older students may devise cultural norms for themselves or build on those that have been given by the teacher. There need to be enough to make it interesting but not so many that the children cannot remember them.

In the second part of the activity the groups interact with each other and 'practise' being a 'Rockie' or a 'Terrian'.

When the groups are well into 'role' — after about five minutes — a small 'exploration' party from each group 'visits' the other and brings back accounts to inform their own group. Every child should have a turn at 'visiting'. By the time the last 'visiting party' has come back there should be a good understanding of what to expect.

Findings could be written up during the process and then exchanged to see how accurately each group has understood the other(s).

Challenging activities

Activities can be devised in order to raise awareness of prejudicial attitudes towards individuals and groups, and to practise strategies to cope with these situations.

WHAT WOULD YOU DO

Present various scenarios to groups of children, where a person or group of people are or have been subjected to a discriminatory behaviour, for example racial name-calling, bullying, sexist remarks. Ask the children to brainstorm strategies to challenge the perpetrator. Challenges can be made by observers, friends and/or the individual.

Ask the group to reflect on the activity by asking these questions:

- How did the perpetrator feel initially?
- Did this change after the challenge?
- How did the victim feel?
- Did this change?
- How did the person making the challenge feel?
- Was the challenge effective?
- Discuss reasons for the effectiveness or otherwise of the challenge and identify other strategies which could be tried.

Possible scenarios:

1. Natasha is a talented pianist, a friendly pupil who is very overweight and self-conscious about this. Natasha and her two friends are walking home from school. Two older girls from a different school walk towards Natasha making rude comments about Natasha's weight.

2. Barry and Mark spend a lot of time together in the classroom and usually mix well. However, just recently, when having 'pretend' fights, Barry has been calling Mark names referring to his race. Mark does like Barry; however, he feels very hurt and angry when this happens and is thinking of breaking his friendship with Barry.

Empathy with disability

This can be done in a number of ways. Blindfolding and trust-related exercises are common. Perhaps the best way to do this is to play games where one person is blindfolded and the others are not, and then taking turns to be blindfolded.

Another such activity is to have children cover up their mouths with their hands and try to communicate with each other where there is a lot of noise. This could be provided by a tape of loud music or by a recording of playground noise played at high volume. This is what it is like for a hearing-impaired child with auditory aids when she cannot see the person who is speaking to her. Children trying to communicate under these conditions will quickly understand some of the needs of such a child.

The following activity gives an understanding of the difficulties that children experience when they do not have the ability to express themselves in the language that others are using.

Children are in pairs. They are not to use verbal language to communicate with each other but can use gesture, facial expression and noises.

The teacher has a number of cards on which are written messages that one child is to communicate with the other. Examples could be:

'My cat has had kittens.'

'I like two spoonfuls of sugar in my tea.'

'Someone bumped into me in the playground and I have hurt my arm.'

RESOURCES

Szirom, T. and Dyson, S. (1986) (British edition ed. Hazel Slavin) *Greater Expectations: A Source Book for Working with Girls and Young Women*. Wisbech, Cambridgeshire: Learning Development Aids.
This is a comprehensive resource and contains many activities on a range of issues regarding gender, including self-concept, being assertive, life-styles, work opportunities. The book is primarily designed for older girls and women's groups. Quite a few activities could easily be adapted for younger boys and girls. It could also be adapted and used for staff training to develop awareness of gender issues.

Blackman, S., Chisholm, L., Gordon, T. and Holland, J. (1987). *Hidden Messages: The Girls and Occupational Choice Project. An Equal Opportunities Pack*. Oxford: Blackwell.
This is one of the products of a schools-based action research project. It is aimed at 11–14-year-olds and contains interesting activities to challenge beliefs related to traditional gender roles, especially in occupational choice.

J. Maximé (1987, 1991) *Black Identity*. (Workbook 1 of Black Like Me Series.) Beckenham, Kent: Emani Publications.

J. Maximé (1987, 1991) *Black Pioneers*. (Workbook 2 of Black Like Me Series.) Beckenham, Kent: Emani Publications.
These two workbooks aim to help black children develop awareness and pride in their racial and social identity.

Longman Tutorial Resources (1989) Harlow: Longman. Book 1: Chris Watkins, *Your New School*. Book 2: Linda Marsh, *Take a Look at You*. Book 3: Anna Dolezal, *Making Choices*.
These three pupil books are part of a series for older children and young people (one for each year). The books contain activities and assignments covering a wide range of issues for young people. These include children's rights, self-awareness and friendships. The books have been designed so that they can be used as part of school programmes.

REFERENCES

Bartlett, R. and Dean, M. (1988) Parents' views on an integration scheme for children with severe learning difficulties. *Educational Psychology in Practice* 3 (4), 40.

Blackman, S., Chisholm, L., Gordon, T. and Holland, J. (1987). *Hidden Messages: The Girls and Occupational Choice Project. An Equal Opportunities Pack*. Oxford: Blackwell.

Bugental, D., Kaswan, J. and Love, L. (1970). Perception of contradictory meanings conveyed by verbal and nonverbal channels. *Journal of Personality and Social Psychology* 16, 647–55.

Clarricoates, K. (1987) Child culture at school: a clash between gendered worlds. In A. Pollard (ed.) *Children and Their Primary Schools*. Lewes: Falmer.

Cohn, T. (1988) Sambo — a study in name calling. In E. Kelly and T. Cohn (eds) *Racism in Schools: New Research Evidence*. Stoke-on-Trent: Trentham Books.

Cole, M. (ed.) (1989) *The Social Contexts of Schooling*. Lewes: Falmer.

Commission for Racial Equality (1988) *Learning in Terror: A Survey of Racial Harassment in Schools and Colleges*. London: CRE.

Dadds, M. with Lofthouse, B. (eds) (1990) *The Study of Primary Education: A Source Book.* (Classroom and Teaching Studies, Vol. 4.) Lewes: Falmer.

Department of Education and Science (1985) *Race Relations in Schools: A Summary of Discussions at Meetings in Five Local Education Authorities.* London: HMSO.

Duck, S. (1986) *Human Relationships: An Introduction to Social Psychology.* London: Sage.

Duck, S. (1991) *Friends for Life: The Psychology of Personal Relationships.* Hemel Hempstead: Harvester Wheatsheaf.

Ebbeck, M. (1985) Teachers' behaviour towards boys and girls. *UPDATE Current Issues in Early Childhood.* London: World Organization for Early Childhood Education. UK National Committee.

Ellis, B. (1985) Integration in action: an evaluation of an integration project. Unpublished MSc dissertation, University of Southampton.

French, J. (1986) Gender in the classroom. *New Society* 7, 404–6, March.

Furnham, A. and Gibbs, M. (1984) School children's attitudes towards the handicapped. *Journal of Adolescence* 7, 99–117.

Kelly, E. (1988) Pupils, racial groups and behaviour in schools. In E. Kelly and T. Cohn (eds) *Racism in Schools: New Research Evidence.* Stoke-on-Trent: Trentham Books.

Luckett, E. and Luckett, N. (1988) Success for Abigail. *Special Children* 20, 20.

Matthews, B. (1989) Chaining the brain: structural discrimination in testing. In M. Cole (ed.) *The Social Contexts of Schooling.* Lewes: Falmer.

Maximé, J. (1993) The ethnographic dimension of race and its mental health and educational implications. Paper presented at the British Psychological Society, Annual Course of the Division of Educational and Child Psychologists, 5–8 January 1993, Torquay.

Pollard, A. (1985) *The Social World of the Primary School.* Eastbourne: Holt, Rinehart & Winston.

Pollard, A. (ed.) (1987) *Children and Their Primary Schools.* Lewes: Falmer Press.

Schneider, B. H. (1993) *Children's Social Competence in Context: The Contributions of Family, School and Culture.* Oxford: Pergamon.

Settle, D. and Wise, C. (1986) *Choices: Materials and Methods for Personal and Social Education.* Oxford: Blackwell.

Shaw, J. (1977) Sexual divisions in the classroom. Paper given at the Teaching Girls to Be Women Conference, Essex, April.

Smith, D. and Tomlinson, S. (1989) *The School Effect: A Study of Multiracial Comprehensives.* London: Policy Studies Institute.

Spender, D. and Sarah, E. (1980) *Learning to Lose: Sexism and Education.* London: The Women's Press.

Sunnafrank, M. (1983) Attitude similarity and interpersonal attraction in communication processes in pursuit of an ephemeral influence. *Communication Monographs.*

Surkes, S. (1987) Integration in practice: making contact. *Times Educational Supplement,* 18 September.

Tizard, B., Blatchford, P., Burke, J., Farquehar, C. and Plewis, I. (1988) *Young Children at School in the Inner City.* Hove: Lawrence Erlbaum Associates.

Chapter 7

Crisis and Conflict in Friendship

'It's the kids she hangs around with — they're a bad influence.'

'One minute she's saying "We're best friends, aren't we?" and the next she's calling me all sorts of horrible names.'

'When Gavin moved away to another town Brian was completely at a loss. He didn't want to do anything for a while — even go to school.'

'Julie arrived at my school and now she's Mandy's best friend instead of me.'

'Kenton wants friends but he just winds people up all the time.'

The course of friendship does not run any more smoothly than other aspects of life and most children will find themselves at one time or another having to deal with painful or difficult situations. Conflicts and crises can arise as a result of friendship difficulties or they can be a cause of them, sometimes both. This chapter deals predominantly with situations which involve conflict and loss.

WHAT TEACHERS ALREADY DO TO HELP

Teachers can feel helpless in actively meeting the needs of children who are troubled. They underestimate the importance of what they are already doing in providing consistency and positive messages for pupils. There are some individuals for whom school is the only place where they have some security, where their strengths are being acknowledged and where they are experiencing a supportive environment. For the purposes of this chapter a supportive environment can be defined as somewhere where emotions are not dismissed or denied, where children are encouraged to think through alternative perspectives on situations, and where they have positive relationships with significant adults in their lives who treat them in a consistent way. If confidence and self-esteem are being supported by adults it helps children both to cope with distressing situations and to make what may be risky changes in social interactions with peers.

WHEN TO INTERVENE ACTIVELY AND WHEN NOT

There is a strong urge in most adults to protect the children in their care and to shield them from hurt of any kind. This sometimes includes acting for them and intervening in their social life to 'sort out the problems'. When there is nothing to be done, such as a close friend moving away, some adults are at a loss to know what to do so end up making comments they know are not very helpful, such as 'you'll soon find someone else to team up with'. Children experiencing difficulties in relationships, however, need to be encouraged and supported in exploring a range of strategies for coping. This lays the foundations for dealing with future interactions. The young person who reaches adulthood without ever having had any practice at the downs as well as the ups of friendships will be poorly equipped to manage the intricacies and demands of adult relationships.

CONFLICT

Conflict between friends and equals

Jennie, an 11-year-old middle school student, has been friends with Natalie for over two years. Last week Natalie borrowed Jennie's personal stereo without asking and then forgot to give it straight back. When Jennie found out she immediately felt angry and phoned Natalie at home and said that she was not going to come over to her house at the weekend as they had arranged. Natalie was defensive and they ended up having a fierce row. On Monday morning Natalie took the personal stereo into school and returned it to Jennie saying rather grumpily, 'I didn't mean to take it for long, I just forgot.' Jennie took this as an apology and replied that she hadn't needed it anyway. By break-time all signs of hostility had vanished.

In conflict situations such as this adults may see their role as intervening directly to prevent a potential escalation. Sometimes, however, intervention may not be helpful. If the relationship is an equal one it may be better to leave some time for a 'natural' resolution of the situation. James Youniss (1980) carried out some interesting research which indicates that there is an understanding by middle childhood about the nature of friendship which includes not only supportive interactions but also occasionally selfish or insensitive behaviour. Children accept that the norms of co-operation in friendship are bound to be violated from time to time simply because friends have personalities of their own.

There are clear patterns of responses to 'offences' by peers. Between equal friends there exists the right to some sort of retaliation for an insult. This can lead to negative chaining in which there is further retaliation. Often, between friends, there is an arbitrary breaking of this chain so that the initial offender makes some positive overture which is accepted, perhaps with a mutual apology or positive act. Older children may also obviously ignore or walk away, which draws attention to the displeasure but does not embark on the same kind of tit-for-tat behaviour. The resolution of the conflict between Jennie and Natalie includes elements of both these strategies.

Children who have frequent conflicts with friends for which there is no such resolution may not have learnt ways of going about re-establishing the balance in a relationship. Providing some examples of similar problems within a group and using role play may encourage them to develop. Children are interested in face-saving measures and will see the procedure of offence/response/resolution as basically fair and equitable. 'Hit them back' is an injunction that some parents offer their children as a solution which teachers are forever countering with 'Tell a teacher instead'. The pupils themselves need to know that there are other ways of dealing with conflict which will maintain their self-esteem but not destroy the relationship.

Conflict and imbalance of power

Most people have a range of relationships, not just a couple of close friends. There are different individuals in their lives who fulfil different roles and meet different needs. You do not necessarily tell your troubles to the person with whom you go swimming every weekend. It is the same for children. Some friends may enjoy shared interests and feel secure within an equal relationship. But they might also want to be associates with those who may be appear to be more exciting and appeal to their sense of daring and rebellion. The balance of power in these different relationships will differ from one to another. This will have implications for the maintenance of friendship and dealing with conflicts.

The Youniss research showed that it is only when there is a clear inequality in the relationship that the more powerful offender sees no need to make retribution to maintain the friendship. If only one person perceives she has a need to go to any effort to continue the liaison then it is that person alone who will be the one to make way to the demands of the other.

Jason is the best football player in the fifth grade. He is not physically aggressive but he is bossy and wields considerable personal power. Derek is one of the gang who hang around with Jason and accepts as his lot the fact that he is sometimes treated with a degree of contempt because he is not so good at sports and is not confident generally.

Both of these boys are fortunate in having other relationships in which they can build better foundations for future successful relationships. Derek does not have the confidence in his relationship with Jason to express his feelings at being insulted and it would benefit his self-esteem if he could learn to be a little more assertive here. He does, however, have friendships with children who share his interest in computers and with whom he can display his own strengths. In these relationships his self-esteem is not under threat and he feels confident and safe enough to make his views heard. Jason also has friends who win his respect. To keep these friends he has had to learn how to make amends if he offends them in any way. Without these sorts of experiences Jason would only know how to be dominant in relationships, not how to repair them or to support others.

Conflict and confrontation

Conflict and disagreement are part of normal behaviour. It is inevitable, therefore, that there will be times in every school when, despite all the efforts to foster a positive social climate and a high level of co-operation, confrontation between pupils erupts.

Continual or extreme behaviour, however, causes serious concern and requires action to be taken. There are many books on behaviour management and classroom control that are helpful in offering effective strategies. Some of these are listed at the end of this chapter.

We have taken the view that someone who is socially competent is less likely to behave in ways that cause difficulties in school. He will be in touch with his own feelings; be better able to make accurate judgements about the feelings and intentions of others, have a repertoire of social behaviours that enable appropriate responses to be made and have the confidence to carry them out. These skills need as much input as any other to be learnt successfully. Focusing on the personal and social learning aspects of behaviour, ensuring that specific needs are identified and addressed, will help children who behave in 'anti-social' ways to handle conflict in less disruptive and damaging ways.

Teachers can do only a certain amount to address the underlying reasons for difficult behaviour as these are often historical, deep-rooted and outside their remit to change. They can, however, create an environment in which students are valued and can learn behaviour which is ultimately more rewarding. Where pupils are having difficulty they need to be provided with structured opportunities for positive social interactions. This means that the social behaviour of all students needs to be challenged, such as the way they give verbal and non-verbal feedback to each other. In an interactive situation attention needs to focus on all involved, not just an individual.

Wind-ups and inappropriate attention-seeking

On one level Marvin has some good social skills. When he is with adults he is outgoing and polite, asks relevant questions and comes out with some socially useful stock phrases such as 'Did you have a nice week-end, sir? The weather wasn't too good, was it?' He is, however, the one boy in his year who is regularly avoided by the others. Marvin has not yet understood the finer subtleties of positive interactions. He is truthful to a painful degree and has not learnt when it is better to keep quiet. He repeatedly tells the same joke which once got a laugh and if he knows it will tell the punchline of someone else's joke. If, by any chance, Marvin is included in a game in the school yard, he is the one who will run off with the ball for a laugh. He is not aggressive and not devious but the fury that he arouses in others results in angry confrontations time and time again. Most of the time Marvin has no idea why he's in such trouble.

All behaviour has an appropriate context. Yelling at the top of one's voice at a baseball game or football match is virtually mandatory. Yelling in a court of law might see you fined for contempt. Much inappropriate behaviour is intended to attract attention and usually succeeds in doing this very well. One reason that straightforward social skills training programmes are not always successful is that children's aims and goals in social interactions are not addressed at the outset (Renshaw and Asher, 1983). It may be that the immediate, maybe unconscious, aim for an individual is to gain maximum attention from a situation, or to be seen as the 'strongest' person who can dominate others. This will be in conflict with that person's ultimate goal, which may be to be thought of well by his peers or to establish himself as part of a group. For Marvin to begin to behave in ways that are more acceptable to the group he needs help:

1. To raise his awareness of his immediate and end goals and to understand the conflict between them.
2. To raise his awareness of the signals that others are giving out, especially the non-verbal messages.
3. To increase his awareness of what is and is not appropriate behaviour.
4. To learn behaviours that will give him positive attention and have opportunities to practise them.
5. To know that he has choices in what he says and what he does and that each of his choices has a different consequence.

Fights and feuds

All teachers will have been in situations when aggression between pupils replaces co-operation and fists begin to fly, either figuratively or for real. It is often possible to see these confrontations coming in time to take some preventive action. Children who lose control in social situations are usually already in a state of heightened emotion. Sometimes they come into school in a 'mood' and it is no surprise to anyone when they have an outburst. Often it doesn't much matter who the other person is: he is simply a safer target for anger which has been generated elsewhere.

Although it is essential to be clear with students what boundaries there are for acceptable behaviour it is also useful to focus on feelings. Acknowledgement by teachers of a pupil's emotional state gives validity to the pupil's feelings and perhaps helps the pupil to understand them better. Then it will be possible to discuss the link between emotion and action and explore acceptable ways of expressing these feelings which take into account the needs of others.

It may be frightening for some individuals to 'lose control', and the focus of inter-vention could be to look at ways of recognizing how that situation builds up so that preventive action can be taken.

Jo-Anne, an intelligent 13-year-old, was usually well-behaved in school. Occasionally, however, she would react violently in situations where she perceived that she or her family were being criticized. She had thrown chairs, banged a girl's head against a wall and had lashed out at boys twice her size. Unsurprisingly, there were few individuals prepared to associate with her and she was on the point of being expelled from school because teachers were rightly worried about the safety of the other pupils. Weekly counselling sessions with Jo-Anne helped her to be in touch with her own feelings and to learn what physical signs would indicate that she was becoming distressed. The teachers also looked at how she was jumping to conclusions about people's intentions rather than checking them out. Jo-Anne worked out several strategies to help herself which included giving herself time to think. If she was having a day when she felt particularly vulnerable she would ask to stay in the classroom at break-times. She was also given permission to walk away from situations at any time if she felt that her control was about to go. There were whole-class discussions about respect for each other's families as well as other strategies to raise Jo-Anne's self-esteem and give her opportunities to interact positively with her peers. Over a period of about eight weeks Jo-Anne became more confident that she could control her own behaviour and other young people became less wary of her.

For other young people, a confrontation gives a real 'buzz'. They seem to enjoy the energy and drama that fights and conflicts engender. The focus here needs to be on the conflict between the feelings at the time and the feelings afterwards, together with an exploration of other more acceptable, less damaging ways of having excitement without pain – for themselves and for other people. How much individuals will respond to this will depend on many things, including the value systems they have internalized, the level of their moral development, and the extent to which they have an internal locus of control and can feel they can personally effect change.

A bad influence?

In some classrooms there may be a small group of children who cluster around a leader who has been identified as having behaviour problems. This 'leader' is influential but not generally popular with other children because of a tendency to be aggressive. Others are wary rather than friendly. The children who make up the entourage around this individual are likely to be others who have been rejected by peers because of their inability to handle social situations positively or because they do not command a high enough status in the class on other measures, such as academic or sporting success. Research suggests that there is a potential pattern of development for some children starting with negative experiences in infancy and a lack of good models for interactions with others. These children tend to throw their weight around and disrupt rather than join in games and activities. This leads to rejection by peers and an increasing commitment to a deviant peer group in late childhood and adolescence (Patterson *et al.*, 1989).

What happens in middle childhood, therefore, can be important in preventing the escalation of social and behavioural difficulties. It is not the province of this book to deal with more serious problems, but for those young people who have been caught up in a peer group which seems to be leading them into worrying situations there are ways to weaken the child's commitment to the group which teachers and parents might like to try. Overt attempts to do this such as saying 'That Julie is no good, I won't let you have anything to do with her' may only strengthen loyalties. For some children, however, especially younger ones, parental injunctions may give them the strength to dissociate themselves from individuals who wield uncomfortable amounts of power. 'My mum says ...' is safer than 'I don't want to ...'. It will be easier for a child to accept parental 'interference' in her friendships if parents do not condemn the other child but talk about the behaviour that is causing the concern, for example:

'Julie seems to be always using bad language – I don't think I like you playing with her while she's doing that.'

It may be that the 'problem' child is going through a particularly hard time and that his behaviour is reflecting this. Labelling children rather than their behaviour as 'bad' makes it much more difficult for them to leave a reputation behind when their circumstances improve.

Where it appears that a child is being manipulated by others it is useful to think of ways which will increase his sense of his own individuality and control so that he begins to acknowledge that he does make his own choices and perhaps begins to question them. The child who is the 'bad influence' is also likely to be in great need of genuine friendship. Working more intensively with a small group of children to develop more positive relationships may be worthwhile, although time-consuming. Alternatively, collaborating with parents to encourage more supportive and positive friendships will ensure that their child is not left alone and without support should that child move out of the more deviant group.

It is unwise to deny children, at any age, their own choice of friends. Most parents, however, will provide the settings in which their offspring will meet others and this in itself will be highly influential. By middle childhood children can be encouraged to think through the consequences of the choices they make. Asking questions, rather than stating opinions about the actions of others, can be helpful in beginning to talk things through.

Instead of
'I think that was a dreadful thing to do'
ask
'What did you think of that?'

Instead of
'I don't think you should be playing with him'
ask
'Are you happy playing with him? What do you like about it?'

Instead of
'I think you ought to ...'
ask
'What do you think you might do about it?'

Inner conflict

Erica, aged 12, had become increasingly distressed by teasing that was intimidating others in her class. The girls who were central to this had been part of her circle of friends for a long time but she eventually decided that she was going to distance herself from it even though she risked no longer being part of the 'in-crowd'. She worried about this decision for days and talked it over with her elder sister but eventually came to the conclusion that she needed to do what she felt most comfortable with. She could no longer feel at ease with herself silently colluding with the behaviour of

her group. She let her views be known and walked home on her own for two days.
It was a brave step to take but by the third day several others had joined her and
not only did she not find herself isolated, she discovered that her own status in the
group had risen.

Taking risks may be part of building friendships and building self-esteem. Children
need to learn to judge how 'comfortable' they are with certain other people and with
situations in order to help them make difficult friendship decisions. We need to think
how we can encourage and support those who need a safety net if they are going to
put themselves on the line. Some of the circle work described in Chapter 10 may be
valuable in this context.

Conflict between friends and family

Conformity to group norms increases with age until it peaks at about age 14 (Berndt,
1979). This is especially true for anti-social behaviour and for boys. There is a contrasting decrease in conformity to the values and standards of parents, so that by
mid-adolescence friends and family are given equal weight in their influence. Other
studies have shown that those individuals most likely to conform to group pressures
are those who are most anxious to be accepted by the group and have most to lose
from alienating others. This tends to be those individuals with intermediate status.
The leaders tend to set the trends and makes the 'rules'; those with least status have
least to gain from behaving in accordance with them.

Disapproval of an individual's choice of friends can lead to considerable conflict
within the family. Dealing with such concerns is difficult and more so as children
become older. Parents of adolescents who disapprove of their friends may have battles
on their hands as those young people become increasingly rooted in their loyalty to
their peers. It is worth remembering that for the majority of young people this stage
of friendship is simply that − a phase. Parents of teenagers frequently think that it
is only their child who is rebellious, difficult and being led astray. This is far from
the truth; most families will have their own stories of adolescent turmoil and trauma.
Dealing with this on its own is wearing and parents should seek support where they can
find it. Teenagers will be inclined to say that everyone else's parents are more lenient.
It is worth checking what others are doing but parents need to be clear about their
own boundaries and make these clear. Teenagers will be more able to accept these
if they know that they will be able to 'win' independence steadily by showing that
they can handle situations well.

Parents need to be primarily concerned with the behaviour of their own child rather
than the way others are behaving. How well can she resist 'going along with' her
friends when it is not in her best interests?

Parents do need to be honest with themselves about why they disapprove of their
child's choice of friends. The very term 'deviant peer group' implies a value judgement
on the part of adults. Although they may justify their view as being in their own
child's best interests it may be that simple prejudice is at the root of their unease.
What exactly is it that they consider to be a 'bad influence'? Is it the way they
dress, the language they use, the music they like? Children, especially older ones,

tend to associate with those individuals with whom they have things in common and who in some ways meet their needs. Adults are not always aware of what these things are and may focus only on the obvious and possibly more superficial aspects of an individual. To undermine a friendship may be doing the child a disservice as there may be elements of sharing within that relationship which fulfil a need that is not met elsewhere. It would be better to explore with the child why someone is a good friend and try to understand and support the friendship, perhaps by welcoming the child into the family home. This will both maintain good parent – child relationships and provide opportunities for a degree of oversight and positive influence.

That said, there will be times when a young person continues to belong to a group whose behaviour and values are becoming damaging in terms of dangerous behaviour, and possibly law-breaking and truancy. Parents/carers and teachers need to ask how this group meets the needs of the children within it and whether these needs could be met in other ways. There may be a case, particularly with younger children, for actively removing them from a clique which is undoubtedly doing them harm, but not without clear explanation and considerable forethought, particularly about providing opportunities to re-establish relationships with others.

LOSS

Friends who grow apart

Friendships have a beginning and are maintained for a varying length of time at different levels of intensity, and many also have an ending. How they end is important, and different endings require different responses from others. Some friendships simply weaken over time, or come to a natural conclusion with equanimity. In others, one partner becomes disenchanted or matures at a different pace and is the one who recognizes that the friendship is lacking. Inevitably there will be a sense of rejection, a temporary sense of loss and threat to self-esteem to the partner who is 'left behind'. Both partners need to find ways of dealing with this which will give them skills that they will find useful as they develop into adulthood. The child who is outgrowing the friendship may very well feel guilty, especially if she is making other friends whose company she enjoys more. This emotion need not determine her actions but might help her to be more sensitive to the needs of her old friend and find ways of 'letting her down gently' or perhaps more slowly. Unfortunately the opposite often happens and arguments and disagreements are fostered to justify an eventual parting of the ways.

The 'rejected' child needs to understand that people change and that it is not necessarily a fault within her. It may be useful to explore with her how much she still wanted that friendship and whether others might be more compatible at the moment. For anyone undergoing relationship difficulties the adults around should be paying extra attention to maintaining her self-esteem and giving her encouragement and confidence to explore other social situations. Providing opportunities to talk things through may also be useful, although giving 'good advice' may not.

Friends who move away

There are times when friends are lost because family circumstances lead to a move away from the area. The child who is changing her school has particular difficulties which need to be addressed by the new teachers. Many schools now realize that an active intervention which welcomes new entrants into the school and enables them to find their way about also helps them to settle into a friendship group. Nevertheless, it takes a while not to feel like a stranger and feelings of confusion, disorientation and isolation may exist for some weeks. For children in middle childhood and beyond, transfers to other schools may be more difficult as friendship groups have been established and integration into them may require more sophisticated skills.

The child who is left behind may also suffer the loss of her friend more than may be realized. If the friend was a special long-time companion and confidante then the loss can be akin to a 'little death' and it will take time before adjustments can be made. This may involve a mild version of the grief process in which there will be a pattern of behaviour which is perhaps not characteristic of the child. Anger and frustration may be followed by a period of quiet unhappiness. Most children, however, are highly resilient and their distress is most likely to be short-lived, especially if they have the means to keep in touch with old friends. After a time new patterns of friendship will begin to be established.

Loss in the family

For some children there will be events such as the death of a parent or loss due to family breakdown which inevitably affect their emotional lives and needs for quite some time. Friends may be especially important during such a crisis for a number of reasons. The parent who is left may be distressed himself and find it difficult to provide the emotional support the child needs. The child himself may feel unable to seek help from this source because of fear of inflicting additional demands. It is possible that no one in the family is talking with the children, in the misguided fear that 'talking about it might upset them'. Children at any age need to know what is going on at a level at which they can understand. Not knowing simply leads to fantasies and imaginings. Unless children know what the reality of a situation is they cannot come to terms with it and learn to adjust.

For children in middle childhood a major function of friendship is having someone to talk to and with whom to share secrets and problems. It may be worth guiding children to others who have shared similar experiences of family breakdown or loss so that they do not feel isolated. It is useful for adults to know what might be the emotional responses and needs of children whose families are in crisis, and there is a resource list at the end of this chapter which may help. Friends themselves need to know how best to support someone in difficulty and grief, and that just listening to and accepting the person and 'being there' is a powerful way of doing that. If someone behaves in a way which is out of character others need to know how to deal with that and support each other in being more tolerant for a while. Children need to know that anger is not necessarily directed at them but might be expressed in some way by the individual who is distressed. Being able to 'not take things personally' at these times is a step towards real maturity in relationships.

The most useful function that friends fulfil at stressful periods, however, is to give a strong focus for 'normality'. Whereas adults may focus on the 'problem', children are much more likely to encourage a return to the everyday and ordinary. This provides a healthy contrast to the attention given by adults which may unintentionally prolong difficulties.

A loss of trust

On the one hand being let down by someone is a fact of life − it is bound to happen to everyone at some point or another. On the other hand it is difficult to maintain friendships where there is a poor sense of trust and reliability. However much fun someone is and however well you get on together, a relationship will run into serious trouble if one person persistently does not follow through with agreements, does not keep confidences or does not tell the truth.

By middle childhood trust is a vital element in a flourishing relationship. If and when that trust is broken it can be very painful and limit the degree of intimacy to which future friendships are allowed to go.

One important intervention that teachers can make is to clarify for children the meaning of trust and look at how it is interlinked with honesty and integrity. Some children have learnt to lie because they might get into trouble if they are truthful; others lie because they don't want to hurt people. Learning to be truthful with kindness is a sophisticated social skill which is part of assertiveness training.

Knowing when to keep silent is also something that perhaps needs to be made explicit. This includes keeping silent in order not to undermine someone or to prevent feelings being hurt, such as not publicly pointing out that he has a large spot on his nose. It also applies to keeping confidences and keeping secrets.

When children have been let down it is important that they are able to make judgements about the event in a way that has a positive, rather than negative, influence on future friendships. They can be encouraged to think through their own behaviour in relation to others and work out for themselves what are reasonable expectations of friendship. They can set their own boundaries for the way others behave towards them so they will be able to let someone know clearly when that person has overstepped the mark. It is most worrying for children who have had many such experiences because it leads them to expect that this is what will continue to happen to them. This has consequences for their ability to form close relationships and strengthens their view of the world as being inconsistent and unsafe.

REJECTED AND REJECTING CHILDREN

Some children are friendless for reasons which have emanated from their early childhood where their basic emotional needs have not been met. This leads them to have expectations of others which are predominantly negative. Where children have learnt to expect either hostility or indifference from others they are unlikely to be open and friendly. They still have the basic needs of love and care but reject overtures of friendship because such behaviour does not fit in with the world as they think it is. Many teachers will be able to identify such individuals as those who seem to be desperate for affection one minute and hostile and destructive the next. This behaviour means that although they may have a series of superficial alliances these never last long enough to become real friendships. They may manipulate rather than co-operate and are so needy that they are unable to take account of the needs of others in a relationship.

Other children, like Marvin, have not learnt the skills which endear them to their fellows; they disrupt ongoing activities, make negative comments about others and may not have an awareness of what is appropriate behaviour within their social group.

Short-term behavioural strategies alone are unlikely to be successful in helping such children to form proper friendships. It takes time to help someone to readjust her concept of the world. Not only do such children require many positive experiences, they also need these to be 'mediated' for them so that they do not distort their perception of events to fit in with their own negative constructs. Teachers cannot be substitutes for parents but they can challenge perceptions, raise awareness and structure positive experiences for children. This, together with more specific interventions, can make real life a therapeutic experience. Within this framework other children can be 'effective therapeutic agents' (Furman, 1984).

For this to happen perceptions need to be open to change and, if necessary, challenge. Someone who is viewed negatively by others, for whatever reason, may very well continue to be so viewed, and even positive changes in his own behaviour may be construed within a negative framework. If you expect someone to be warm and friendly and then one day he is cold and distant you wonder what is bothering him or if it is something you have done. If, however, he is always cold and distant then suddenly he is all smiles you may be a bit suspicious about his motivations. It is the same for children. They need to have ways of interpreting the behaviour of others which increase the possibilities of children being accepted, even if this is at a neutral rather than a positive level.

It is worth having some way of monitoring the success of any programme by taking a measure of social acceptance at the outset (ways of doing this can be found in Chapter 1), at the end of the intervention and again in a few months. Asking parents whether skills and attitudes have also changed at home is also a valuable indication of success.

The importance of acceptance in school

There is good reason to be concerned about children who are not socially accepted by their peers. The evidence suggests that rejection by classmates in primary or elementary school is related not only to poor achievement and attendance in high school but also delinquency and mental health problems in later life (Cowen *et al.*, 1973). What happens in school really does matter and teachers can make a difference.

TAKING ACTION

All children benefit from clarity and consistency from those around them. This is especially so for those who are having difficulties. Any strategy to improve interactions will need to be positively reinforced in a number of contexts so that new behaviours generalize to different situations.

Drama lessons can be used to good effect to raise awareness and develop positive interactive skills, especially in the first instance. For some pupils it helps to put activities in a context which is non-threatening and does not single them out.

Dealing with inappropriate social behaviour

Children who are still at a stage of social development which does not take the perceptions of others into account may have difficulty in understanding what is or is not appropriate. It is helpful, therefore, to focus generally on developing conceptual understanding which promotes 'decentralization' and the ability to look at things from other points of view.

1. **Reducing behaviour that is unhelpful**
    Start by raising awareness of the outcomes of inappropriate behaviour and contrasting these with chosen end goals. Ask whether the consequence of the behaviour was wanted or intended.

    It may be useful to ask children 'Was that friendly?' after an incident. It takes away reinforcement if minimal attention is given for inappropriate behaviour. Other students may find that it helps them to control their anger or irritation if they have something to say before they turn away, such as 'This is a wind-up' or 'We've heard this before' or 'That's not funny'.

2. **Learning new behaviour that will help in making friends**
    a. *With a group*
    Scenarios for role-play activities focus a discussion.
    Pupils are encouraged to think what they might do in a given situation.
    The role play could be recorded and played back on video.
    There will be feedback and further discussion about how friendly different ways of behaving in a situation were and about the feelings that were generated for all the participants.
    b. *With individuals*
    A discussion with the pupil identifies the difficulties she is having and changes that could be made.
    The pupil agrees to focus on developing one behaviour.
    This could be a 'thinking' behaviour which applies in many situations, for example 'Is this a friendly thing to do?' or 'Would I like this?'
    The behaviour change is likely to need supporting by teachers in the first instance to remind and encourage.
    It could be an actual behaviour such as passing the ball in a game quickly.
    Taking small steps slowly is better than expecting major changes overnight.

3.   **Positive behaviours need to be reinforced**
     Regular attention for improved behaviour is useful, especially at first.
     A smile and a nod from the teacher may be all that is needed.
     A regular, initially daily, review of how things have been is even better. Five
     minutes at lunchtime or at the end of the day for the first week would make
     a big difference. The number of reviews can be reduced over time.
     Discussions of situations and alternative possible behaviours help pupils to choose
     the most friendly response next time.
     Pupils could later be encouraged to monitor their own progress with less fre-
     quent reviews with a teacher.

4.   **The class needs to be given fresh perspectives**
     Reputations and labels take a long time to live down and even longer to wear
     off.
     Other children should be given opportunities to reinforce more appropriate
     behaviour.
     It will depend on the child in question and the teacher how overt the
     reinforcement can be.

Resisting peer group pressure

NO THANKS

'No thanks'

This is simply a straightforward group exercise in practising saying 'no'.

1.   Students select behaviours which they might want to resist, such as truanting
     from lessons or smoking.
2.   They make a list of the reasons why they might not want to do this, for
     example:

> might be caught
>
> in enough trouble already
>
> my mum would keep me in for a month
>
> I quite like the lesson as it happens
>
> tried it – made me sick

3.   The students devise as many ways as they can of saying 'no' to peer pressure
     and these are written on large pieces of paper, for example:

     'no thanks'

     'no chance'

     'not likely'

     'don't fancy it'

     'no way'

     'don't let me stop you'

     and so on.

Each student in the group takes turns to be the one 'under pressure'. While the group tries all means of persuasion and pressure the individual goes into the 'broken record' routine of repeating the statements saying 'no' – especially those she feels most comfortable with. The activity needs to be time limited and each individual praised for her strength of will in resisting.

Different situations can be tried and the statements rehearsed so that the written cues are not needed.

Reducing negative peer influence by increasing the internal locus of control

This is a longer-term procedure which is based on cognitive strategies and changing perceptions rather than directly intervening with behaviour.

Those individuals who believe that everyone else is responsible for what happens to them have an external locus of control. They genuinely believe that little they do changes or affects things. Unfortunately, people like this are also unable to accept that they are also at the centre of their successes and achievements – it is all due to luck. Teachers will have come across children who habitually reject praise, and they are bewildered by this as most children love it. This is often because they have come to believe that their actions are not self-propelled and that they are directed by others and by fate. Praise, therefore, has no real meaning and does not fit in with their own constructs of the world and how it is. When others try to change that view, even in a positive way, they may become irritated and cross rather than be pleased.

These are some ideas for increasing children's perspectives of themselves as having some control over events rather than being under the influence of others.

- Encourage children to evaluate their own performance rather than do it for them. If, as is often the case with such students, when looking at their academic performance they say that what they have done is 'rubbish', it may be an idea to generate comparisons with previous efforts so that there is an acknowledgement of progress.
- In dealing with specific incidents it is useful to ask questions not only about actual behaviour but also about intent. For example:

    'When you said to Daniel, "Throw Martin's bag in the river," what did you want to happen?' 'What did you want to happen after that?' 'Was the end result of the incident something that you meant to happen?' 'What could you have done instead?' 'What would have been the problems in doing that?'

- This approach makes the individual child see that there might be alternatives and that 'joining in' is one option and that she chooses it – along with the consequences.

Encourage alternatives

It is also important that attention is paid to how individuals can be helped to make more positive social links with others who will give them the sense of belonging and personal support they need.

Conflict among equals

PARTNERS IN CRIME

When conflicts occur in school between individuals who seem to be roughly equally involved it may be useful to use the old strategem of fostering unity by providing an outside 'enemy'. Placing the two contenders together for a period of time saying, 'You are both in deep trouble, but I haven't time to deal with you now' may well result in the conflict resolving itself. The teacher on her return can simply ask each child how he intends to behave to the other now, which will focus on future action rather than spend time discussing the detail of a past incident.

FACESAVERS

Someone has upset someone else – who feels she must do something but can't retaliate by taking aggressive action. What can she do to make the situation equitable and 'save face'? The following suggestions should be followed by leaving the situation.

1.   State feelings calmly:

'I think that was a really nasty thing to do.'

2.   Active ignoring:

'I am not going to stay here and listen to you talking rubbish.'

3.   State future action:

'You might think you've got away with this but don't be so sure.'

4.   Be heavily dismissive:

'I just hope you're happy with yourself.'

Face and friendship savers for those who might have cause to apologize might be:

'OK, so perhaps I overreacted.'

'I wouldn't have done it if I'd thought you were going to be so upset.'

'I didn't mean to be unfriendly.'

'I wasn't thinking straight.'

'I'd like to make up friends with you.'

'I wonder if we can sort this out.'

'I guess we see things differently but I still enjoy your company.'

Other possibilities might be brainstormed. There will of course be differences according to age and level of maturity. For young children simply saying sorry is not very meaningful; finding some sort of action to 'make it up' to the 'offended' child can be structured to strengthen good social interactions.

REAL-LIFE PROBLEM SOLVING

The aim of this activity is to encourage pupils to think about their perceptions of behaviour and to devise alternative ways of dealing with difficulties.

This might be considered time-consuming but can in fact save time in the long run. The idea is to re-enact incidents a little while after they have occurred and when the emotional content has subsided. The teacher takes each member of the group involved in an incident and asks him to act out exactly what happened, with the exception of making physical contact. After establishing the detail the teacher then takes the children through these problem-solving steps:

How did each person perceive the behaviour of the others?

Why did he make the interpretations that he did?

How did he feel about what was happening?

What alternatives were possible?

What can be done now?

What consequences are likely to follow?

Teachers using the strategy find that other members of the class can often make valuable contributions and generate fresh perspectives both on situations and on individual behaviour. If a participant refuses to co-operate an onlooker will often be pleased to take part.

The activity is adapted from Spivak and Shure (1974).

FRIENDLY FEEDBACKS

'Friendly Feedbacks' is a simple strategy for use with younger children, which aims to have them focus on the friendly and co-operative behaviour of their classmates. When working in pairs or groups they can be asked to note helpful behaviours from others. Those to look out for can be mentioned at the beginning of the session, such as being prepared to lend things, listening to ideas, showing how to do something and so on. At the end of the activity children are asked to give feedback on the helpful and friendly behaviours of their classmates. The behaviours identified can be geared towards helping one particular child in order to give her opportunities to practise new social skills. It will also encourage others to focus on her changed behaviour.

RESOURCES

Changing behaviour

Cartledge, G. and Milburn, J. F. (eds) (1980) *Teaching Social Skills to Children*. Oxford: Pergamon Press.
This book contains an excellent chapter by S. Oden on socially isolated children which includes strategies for intervention.

Thacker, J. (1982) *Steps to Success*. Windsor: NFER – Nelson.
This is designed to enable individual children to use a problem-solving approach for interpersonal difficulties. It helps students to identify social and behavioural goals and what steps need to be undertaken towards achieving them. Although aimed at 11 – 12-year-olds it can be adapted for other age groups.

Weissberg, R. P., Gesten, E. L., Libenstein, N. L., Schmid, K. D. and Hutton, H. (1980) *The Rochester Social Problem Solving Program*. New York: Center for Community Study.
This is a programme for 8 – 12-year-old children designed to take place over 34 sessions.

Wragg, J. (1990) *Talk Sense to Yourself: Development of Self Management and Self Control in Educational and Clinical Settings*. Harlow: Longman.
This book is about the different messages we give ourselves and how some of them are helpful and some not. It encourages positive messages and the development of an internal locus of control.

Children and loss

Cox, K. and Desforges, M. (1987) *Divorce and the School*. London: Methuen.
> Intended to inform teachers about the effects divorce may have on children and to outline appropriate responses, this book also covers issues such as communication with the divorced parents.

Long, R. and Bates J. (n.d.) *Loss and Separation*. Devon Psychological Service.
> This is a booklet which outlines ways of supporting children through bereavement and loss. It is particularly directed at schools and teachers in giving them information about these issues, the responses that can be expected and ways to help.

REFERENCES

Berndt, T. J. (1979) Developmental changes in conformity to peers and parents. *Developmental Psychology* 15, 608–16.

Cowen, E. L., Pederson, A., Babigian, H., Izzo, L. D. and Trost, M. A. (1973) Long-term follow-up of early detected vulnerable children. *Journal of Consulting and Clinical Psychology* 41, 438–46.

Duck, S. (1986) *Human Relationships: An Introduction to Social Psychology*. Beverly Hills: Sage.

Frederickson, N. (1991) Children can be so cruel: helping the rejected child. In G. Lindsay and A. Miller (eds) *Psychological Services for Primary Schools*. Harlow: Longman.

Furman, W. (1984) Enhancing children's peer relations and friendships. In S. W. Duck (ed.) *Personal Relationships 5: Repairing Personal Relationships*. London and New York: Academic Press.

Manning, M. and Herrman, J. (1981) Relationships of problem children. In S. Duck and R. Gilmour, *Personal Relationships 3: Personal Relationships in Disorder*. London and New York: Academic Press.

Patterson, G. R., DeBaryshe, B. D. and Ramsey, E. (1989) A developmental perspective on anti-social behavior. *American Psychologist* 44, 329–35.

Piaget, J. (1965) *The Moral Judgement of the Child*. New York: Free Press.

Renshaw, P. D. and Asher, S. R. (1983) Children's goals and strategies for social interaction. *Merrill-Palmer Quarterly* 29, 253–74.

Rubin, Z. (1980) *Children's Friendships*. London: Open Books.

Spivak, G. and Shure, M. B. (1974) *Social Adjustment of Young Children*. San Francisco: Jossey-Bass.

Sullivan, H. S. (1953) *The Interpersonal Theory of Psychiatry*. New York: Norton.

Youniss, J. (1980) *Parents and Peers in Social Development: A Sullivan–Piaget Perspective*. Chicago: University of Chicago Press.

Chapter 8

A Friendly School – A Safe School

'Bullying is picking on someone all the time, especially when they can't fight back.'

'Bullying is pushing people around and making them do things they don't want to do.'

'Bullying is making fun of people and their families.'

'Bullying can be a group of people or just one person.'

'Bullying is hurting people and humiliating them.'

'Being bullied makes you feel ... worthless, miserable, frightened, lonely and left out, upset, angry and hopeless.'

'Bullying someone makes you feel ... tough and good when everyone is on your side, but afterwards you can feel uncomfortable, ashamed, confused, horrible and scared.'

REJECTION

Jennifer has now left the nice middle-class school in which the following events occurred. She was 9 years old when her parents moved into the area and within three weeks things had begun to go badly wrong at school. No one wanted to play with her and every time she tried to join a group she was ignored. It got worse as time went on. Other girls in her class would refuse to sit with her and turned their noses up whenever she went past. One girl in particular, called Stella, seemed to be central to what was happening. Stella had always been an influential person in the class and she appeared to be displaying the extent of her power by mounting the vendetta against Jennifer. Anyone who didn't join in risked being chastised as 'not one of us'. Within a few months Jennifer had changed from being a well-adjusted, happy little girl into a thin, anxious and withdrawn child. Her parents came up to school time after time and teachers promised to look out for incidents of bullying but were never able to pinpoint anything. After a while they lost some sympathy for Jennifer themselves as she always seemed to be a misery and not 'making an effort' herself.

Several years later some of the girls involved in this episode were asked about their feelings, both at the time and now. They all felt badly:

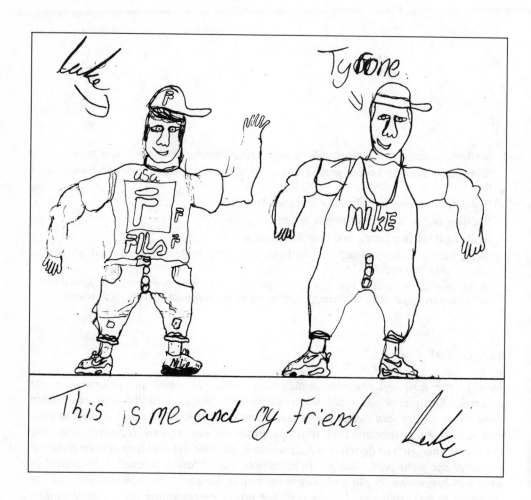

'I knew we were being horrible and I was really sorry for Jennifer sometimes, but what could I do on my own? I suppose in a way I was scared that it would be me they might start treating like that, instead of her.'

'I am really ashamed and embarrassed now but I just didn't want to think about her feelings at the time.'

None of the girls involved knew what she could do to stop this bullying without exposing herself to risks; the teachers did not know what to do and in the end more or less gave up trying; Jennifer became less and less able to deal with anything as her self-esteem was torn to shreds. In the end her parents did the only thing they could do and removed her from the school.

INTIMIDATION

Michael is 10, is small for his age, and has trouble with reading and writing. Life at school has been a miserable experience for him for nearly two years:

'It's always the same group of boys. They tell me I'm stupid all the time and call me names like "dumbo". I did tell my teacher but nothing happened except then they called me a sneak. Lately they have been throwing my things into a patch of waste ground on the way home and said they are going to beat me up. My dad thinks I ought to stick up for myself and my mum is just worried that I can't read very well. But I can't work at school, I just keep thinking of what will happen at playtime. I feel sick in the morning and don't want to go to school but I have to go.'

Michael's mother has had a word with the teacher, who always turns the conversation round to the difficulties Michael is having with the work. Last time she hinted that he was lazy and that was why he was not learning. When concerns are raised about bullying they are quickly dismissed: 'I expect he gives as good as he gets – it's just boys at this age, you know.'

NAME-CALLING

Warren is 12 and in Year 8 where he is one of very few children who are not white. His mother is Irish and his father is from Trinidad. Warren is doing well with his work in school and he does have some good friends. There is one boy, however, who taunts and abuses him virtually every day with racist comments and remarks. These often include insults about his family. Warren sometimes gets very upset by this and has on occasions lashed out in fury. He gets into trouble for misbehaving and his parents have been called to school to talk about Warren's 'uncontrolled outbursts'. The school don't think they need an equal opportunities policy because they 'have so few black children'. They also say they don't tolerate 'any bullying here' either.

ACKNOWLEDGING THE EXISTENCE OF BULLYING

The conspiracy of silence in schools about bullying is beginning, at last, to wear thin. Several headlines about incidences with particularly tragic outcomes have been followed by a growing recognition that bullying is a feature of most, if not all, schools. A current British research project in Sheffield, funded by the government, has found that one pupil in five reported being bullied 'now and then' and one in ten 'at least once a month'. Delwyn Tattum and David Lane (1989), reviewing the available research statistics to date, supported these figures by estimating that bullying may involve at least ten per cent of all children. The numbers of pupils affected by bullying are even greater if you take into account those who are fearful of it happening to them and those who feel helpless or guilty as bystanders. It is possible every child may be affected at some time or another in their school life either directly or indirectly – and yet at present few have the opportunity either to discuss or to develop strategies to deal with bullying and its consequences.

The example at the beginning of the chapter illustrates that bullying is certainly not confined to the inner city or to those that might be labelled 'problem schools'. British public schools have had a notorious history of bullying which, in the past, has been virtually institutionalized. Tom Brown's description of his schooldays may have been fictitious at one level but the story was based on well-documented facts of 'fagging', 'beating' and abuse of power in many private schools of the time. Although these extremes of torture are now rare and would not be tolerated knowingly in any school, less obvious but just as damaging bullying behaviours are frequently left to flourish (La Fontaine, 1991).

Any school which claims 'we don't have any bullying here' is either a long way on the road to developing whole-school policies where everyone knows what is being done to prevent bullying and how to deal with specific incidents or, more likely, it is burying its head in the sand and reassuring no one. In these days when schools are beginning to see themselves in competition with each other there may be a reluctance to admit to anything not being perfect.

Nevertheless, as children anticipate their move into high school they have hopes and fears and fantasies about what they might expect. Uppermost in many minds is an anxiety about the other pupils, especially the older ones, and what sort of treatment will be meted out by them:

'Do they put your head down the toilet?'

'My brother says that some of the big boys make you give them money. Is it true?'

These youngsters need to know that they will be taken seriously if they complain of intimidation or victimization. The school which is able to give pupils and parents clear, positive answers to their concerns ('What happens about bullying here?') must surely be at a competitive advantage in the long run over the one which denies its existence.

As with worrying behaviour of all kinds, bullying is frequently a subject for informal discussion in the staff-room. Although this may lead to the devising of useful and effective individual responses, it cannot deal with incidents in other than a piecemeal and potentially inconsistent way. Neither does it explore preventive strategies. Inevitably, some teachers find themselves at a loss to know what to do for the best and under pressure may resort to some responses which are dismissive or otherwise not helpful, such as 'don't tell tales' and 'sort it out for yourself'. Unfortunately those weaker pupils who do attempt to 'fight back' sometimes come off much worse and the situation is exacerbated.

The other conspiracy of silence comes from this very exhortation not to 'tell tales'. When used by perpetrators of bullying the threat 'or else' is implicit. Unless children feel that telling someone is going to be both safe and effective this threat will work. They need to know that when they confide in an adult they will be taken seriously.

SIGNS OF BULLYING

Half of those children who report to researchers that they have been bullied have not previously told an adult. There are often other indications to suggest that someone has been bullied and it is possible to identify a problem in other ways. Both parents and teachers need to be sensitive to these signs, which could include one or several of the following:

- a sudden change in demeanour – for example, from being outgoing to being withdrawn
- lack of appetite
- deterioration in concentration and unusually poor attainments in school
- disturbed sleep and/or nightmares
- unexplained loss of money or belongings
- unexplained scratches, bruises or signs of other physical assault
- increasing reluctance to go to school
- frequently feeling unwell or making more of slight ailments
- reluctance to talk about school
- wanting to be taken to and from school
- unexplained bouts of crying or unusually anxious behaviour
- unusually aggressive behaviour towards others, perhaps siblings

DENYING BULLYING BEHAVIOUR

The quotations at the beginning of the chapter are from a group of 11-year-old pupils who were trying to define bullying. Different people have different views and perspectives about what constitutes bullying but there is a growing consensus that it does not just occur when a couple of pupils have a fight in the playground. It occurs when there is a prolonged misuse of power and influence of one individual or a group over another. It's when someone is consistently left out, or harassed and picked on, when someone hears daily insults about themselves, their appearance, their family, their culture or their abilities. It's when they are pushed and shoved in the corridor, shunned and laughed at in the classroom and threatened and intimidated on the way home. There is no doubt that persistent bullying can make someone's life thoroughly miserable. It can lead, not only to a severely diminished sense of self-esteem, but sometimes to a desire to withdraw from any social contact where the bullying is taking place. This can result in poor attendance, real or imagined illness and increasing fear of facing others. Where a child's educational attainment as well as happiness is at stake, then the responsible adults around must take it very seriously indeed.

CHILDREN WHO MIGHT BULLY

One of the more difficult aspects of dealing with bullying behaviour is that there is sometimes, but not always, some role reversal of bully and victim. The actual behaviour may not be the same but it is possible that somone bigger and more powerful has at some time used his position to his advantage and to intimidate. This could involve outright abuse or making someone feel inadequate, putting him under pressure to succeed at all costs or to conform without question.

There is a well-known cartoon depicting a man being berated by his boss, coming home and screaming at his wife, who then takes it out on the children, who kick the cat. This may be a simplistic view but it contains an element of truth. Having a punitive response to the bully is therefore likely to be ineffective as it reinforces such behaviour as being acceptable.

Younger children who display bullying behaviour may well have not been given clear enough boundaries by adults and have got the impression that they can do what they like. Although it usually doesn't take too long in a school environment for them to understand that this is not the case, if this behaviour is allowed to continue the egocentric younger child will become the older bully.

Sometimes previously well-behaved children are accused of bullying, and a sensitive investigation may discover that there has been an event, such as loss of a parent through separation or bereavement, which has left them feeling angry and confused. Rather than risk taking out their anger on those close to them, such children find a 'safer' target in the guise of a fellow pupil who is unable to retaliate.

CHILDREN WHO MIGHT BE BULLIED

Children least able to retaliate and who have fewer resources than others at their disposal are often those with special needs. Pupils with learning difficulties may have some support in the classroom, but might very well be left to their own devices in the playground. They may be more used to a protected environment and may not have had the opportunity to learn either independence or assertion skills. Unless the school has recognized the need for social integration and has thought about what might be appropriate interventions, these children might become the butt of taunts or aggression and be unable to counter them.

This may also be true of those with fewer physical skills. Often children who are popular in school are those who have good motor skills and are good at sports. This is even more true in the United States. Conversely, those who might have a harder time in being accepted and valued are those who have difficulties with co-ordination. Strength of other qualities often overcomes these problems but unless the school is aware of their potential vulnerability, it is those children least able to 'stand up for themselves' who may be at the mercy of the aggressors.

Yet another group of children who may be especially at risk are those who have very low self-esteem. Incidents of bullying may simply confirm their expectations of themselves. These are the children who may give messages about their vulnerability by their body language. They may become very defensive when it is not appropriate, and misinterpret jokes and teasing as verbal aggression when none is intended. There is a very fine line between good-humoured joky behaviour between friends and taunting. Friendly bantering can easily turn into an exchange of insults, which in turn may result in physical retaliation. It is necessary for both parties to consider the underlying motivation of the interaction. 'I was only joking, miss' is so often an excuse for inexcusable verbal bullying.

REDUCING VULNERABILITY

Sometimes simply teaching children what they might do to appear more confident can reduce their vulnerability and consequently the extent to which they are the target of such bullying. If they also have a range of responsive behaviours to choose from then they will discover that some ways of dealing with situations make them worse and others are surprisingly successful. Early evidence from continuing research would appear to suggest that assertiveness training is among the most effective types of intervention in reducing bullying behaviour.

LONG-TERM OUTCOMES FOR BULLIES

Allowing bullying in school to continue is not only detrimental for the victims of such behaviour, but also ultimately for the perpetrators. Long-term studies show that children who have been persistently involved in bullying behaviour in school are four times more likely as adults to be involved in violent crime, be in prison, be involved in domestic violence, abuse their children and be unable to hold down a job (Eron *et al.*, 1987). Actively promoting social development and giving children strategies which enable them to interact more successfully at school may prevent this sort of behaviour continuing into adulthood with its inevitable consequences.

A PRO-BULLY ENVIRONMENT OR A SAFE SCHOOL?

There is a growing body of research that indicates which features of a school are likely to nourish and promote bullying behaviour and which will help to make a school a friendly and safe place. The following fictitious examples illustrate the best and the worst of these environments.

Shoutenthump School

Shoutenthump School has firm discipline. It stands no nonsense and there is no such thing as an excuse. The headmaster sits in his study, usually with the door closed, and comes out at regular intervals to shout at whoever happens to be passing at the time — this could be either a pupil or a member of staff. He has been known to humiliate members of staff at school assemblies and was outraged when caning of pupils was outlawed. He is a great sportsman and proud of his school's performance in games. In his view anyone who isn't athletic is a wimp. And if someone is not heading for university then that person must be thick. Half of the staff agree with him. There is a very long list of school rules which are written in a book somewhere. The words 'It's against the rules' are frequently shouted in the corridors and the classrooms, but no one quite knows what the rules are. Teachers appear to make them up on the spot for the sake of convenience.

The school is a large, rambling old building which is not too well heated or lit. The toilets are in the playground. No member of staff ever goes near them – nasty smelly places. There are very few staff meetings; they are not needed as the senior management have decided that notes will be sent round if there is something that people need to know – like fire drill. There are some policies somewhere – there's one about the science curriculum certainly and, oh yes, there's something about health and safety. Parents are very welcome to come to the school – but only once a term between 6 and 8 p.m. when it is their turn. Occasionally parents have complained about bullying and have been told in no uncertain terms, 'We expect children to stand up for themselves here.'

Allagreed School

Allagreed School tells its pupils right from the start that they are all important people. If a pupil has a difficulty of any sort he knows that he can talk to a member of staff and that he will be listened to. Parents also know that appointments will be made for them as soon as possible if they have a worry. The school has both an equal opportunities policy and a behaviour policy; they are reviewed every year with the entire staff. Parents, pupils, governors and school board officials are given the opportunity to contribute to the review process. There are very few school rules, and those that do exist are given to pupils in written form before they start. The rules are also written up in the hall and in classrooms. They say what is expected, not what is not allowed. The personal and social curriculum includes modules on appropriate assertiveness, group support, communication skills and 'valuing each other'.

The staff meet regularly and have their own professional code of conduct which includes expectations of behaviour towards each other and towards the pupils. There is a problem-solving group which addresses difficulties that individual staff may have and provides them with support. There are excellent links with outside agencies so that communications and support networks work at an optimum level. Whenever an incident of bullying is brought to the attention of staff, including midday supervisors, there are clear guidelines laid down as to the expected sequence of responses.

Pro-bullying factors

All schools, though not so extreme as the fictitious examples given above, tend to fall into one of these two broad categories of either encouraging or discouraging bullying behaviour. The following factors have frequently been identified by teachers and other educationists as promoting an environment which is '*pro-bullying*' and which enables such behaviour to flourish:

- no clear expectations of behaviour within the school as a whole
- a lack of consistency among staff in dealing with behavioural difficulties
- poor communication between staff
- poor communication between school and home
- bullying behaviour by at least some of the adults in the school
- lack of training, especially for midday supervisors
- unsupervised corners of the school and playground
- poorly maintained, shoddy-looking buildings
- a 'conspiracy of silence'
- a 'philistine' philosophy which tells children to 'stand up for themselves'
- a competitive atmosphere rather than a co-operative one
- an overemphasis on academic achievement at the expense of all other skills

Anti-bullying factors

Conversely, the following are features which have been identified as being typical of a *'safe school'* where bullying is less likely to occur:

- clear expectations of behaviour generally
- a code of conduct developed by the whole school and agreed to be fair and just
- a 'positive' behaviour management ethos where the emphasis is on acceptable behaviour and rewards rather than unacceptable behaviour and punishments
- consistency among all staff in their responses to behavioural difficulties
- acknowledgement that bullying occurs, that it is unacceptable and that it must be taken seriously
- a clear understanding by pupils that physical, verbal and psychological aggression will not be tolerated in any form
- an understanding that complaints of bullying are always investigated and dealt with
- a 'telling' ethos, where the issue of bullying in the school is out in the open and discussed, including a system which enables incidents to be communicated to staff
- adequate supervision of areas where bullying may occur together with the consideration of other ways of making them safe, such as improved lighting
- consideration given to the management of the playground so that it meets the needs of all children, not just those who want to play ball-games
- staff monitoring their own behaviour and the models they are providing for pupils
- support and collaboration between staff and a problem-solving framework for the discussion of behaviour difficulties
- the development of support and collaboration between pupils
- a focus on social behaviour which involves monitoring those children who are having difficulty fitting in or making friends, discussing issues around friendship and providing skills training for those who need it (e.g. assertiveness)

- strong home – school links and a 'partnership' approach towards parents
- a 'living' equal opportunities policy which is effective and promotes the value of all individuals and groups in the school

MAKING CHANGES

This section of the chapter shows ways in which a whole-school policy on bullying can be activated. It gives ideas and resources to raise awareness and some strategies for active intervention.

It must be stressed that selecting just one activity to deal with the whole issue of bullying is going to have little effect. Strategies need to be rooted within a whole framework which deals with prevention as well as response. There is, as yet, little evaluation of specific intervention although it would appear that those schools which take the issue seriously can reduce the incidence of bullying by as much as 50 per cent in a comparatively short time.

TAKING ACTION

A framework for developing a whole-school approach

Putting bullying on the agenda

It is likely that there at least a few individual adults in any school, either teachers or parents, who are concerned about children being bullied. To encourage the school to take responsibility for addressing the issue they may consider one or more of the following initiatives. These are written in the sequence in which it may be most beneficial to consider them:

- making an informal survey of the staff to find out who else shares their concerns
- keeping records of incidents and encouraging others to do the same
- asking for bullying to be discussed at staff meetings
- asking for bullying to be addressed as part of the formal school development programme
- if there is a behaviour policy or an equal opportunities policy, asking for a review and putting bullying on that agenda
- carrying out a survey of the children to find out the extent of bullying, where and when it occurs and the forms it takes
- showing staff a video such as *Sticks and Stones* (particulars at the end of this chapter)
- asking for training
- raising bullying at meetings of governors or the school board, via either the headteacher or the parent representative(s)

By the end of this stage there should be an acknowledgement that bullying happens and a willingness among the staff as a whole to do something about it.

Devising a policy

The process of coming to any firm decisions about dealing with behavioural issues in a school is not easy. There should, however, be the opportunity for every staff member in the school to contribute to the process and have her views heard. Ideally, this should extend also to the pupils themselves, the parents, governors or school board and all support staff. Whatever method of consultation is employed in the end there should be a sufficient degree of consensus to ensure that the policy will be effective.

Different schools will have different policies, but it is important that consideration is given to these points:

- Is there agreement about what constitutes bullying behaviour?
- How are pupils going to be encouraged to think about bullying and what it might mean for all those involved? What might be done to: (a) develop their empathy with those who are bullied? (b) increase their determination to stop it? How is the school going to communicate to pupils that bullying in all forms is unacceptable?
- Are staff willing to monitor their own behaviour so that they provide appropriate models?
- How is the school going to foster an ethos in which children feel comfortable talking about bullying incidents that have happened either to them or to someone else? To what extent can pupils be reassured about confidentiality? Is there going to be a system whereby teachers can be informed about bullying incidents?
- Are records going to be kept? By whom? What will be recorded?
- What are teachers or support staff expected to do when a child reports an act of aggression in the playground?
- Is there a graded system of sanctions which is clear to everyone?
- At what stage are the parents/carers of children who bully or who are bullied involved?
- Are children taught how to respond appropriately if they are being bullied or if they witness it happening to someone else?
- Are 'friendship-building', 'supporting others' and 'assertiveness' part of the curriculum in some way? Are links made between theory in the formal curriculum and practice in the informal?
- Is consideration given to the alternatives open to pupils who bully to develop their self-esteem in more acceptable ways?
- Is there a need to change the supervision arrangements for some areas in the school and grounds?
- Does the policy make efficient use of time? Are teachers doing things differently rather than additionally?

Putting a policy into operation

To ensure that a policy is active and living several things need to happen. First, it must be communicated to everyone in the school. A publicity campaign could include letters home to parents, plus perhaps a question-and-answer evening to 'launch' the initiative. Governors or school board officials also need to be involved. Training for support staff could be part of the 'package'. Most importantly, pupils require clear guidelines about what is expected of them and what they can expect of the school.

Things will not change dramatically overnight; it takes time for new attitudes, skills and strategies to become integrated into the existing structures. This means that monitoring the effectiveness of the policy will need to be built into a review process. Deciding who is responsible for this and how and when it will happen are questions that are more usefully answered at the outset rather than six months later when there might be a feeling that something is not working but no one quite knows what to do about it.

Empowerment

There are many teachers at the present time who feel that they have less say in what happens in school, less time to do what they consider important and more pressure to perform in ways that are dictated to them from outside. It is a small step from here to their feeling very disempowered themselves and feeling helpless to make significant changes of their own in the way their school functions. A few might even consider that they are being 'bullied' by a stream of dictates from 'above'. It might be worth exploring in the staff-room how people reinforce this helplessness for each other and in what ways teachers can support each other in seeing something through. Although it will inevitably take time to develop a whole-school approach to bullying, in the end it will save time and will also reduce stress. If teachers are prepared to say to each other, 'this is important and we *will* deal with it', they will also be communicating a message to their pupils that there are some things about which it is both right and possible to take control and effect change. By empowering themselves they will be empowering their pupils.

ACTIVITIES RESOURCES

The following activities are divided into sections which are intended to help schools to address bullying at different levels, beginning with strategies which may be useful in setting up a policy. Later ideas are for dealing with specific incidents and promoting behaviours which will inhibit bullying.

Raising awareness

There are a number of short films available which are excellent and generate a good deal of discussion. They are listed in the resources section at the end of this chapter.

ARRIVING AT A DEFINITION

People have very different ideas about what constitutes bullying. This is one way of exploring the definition which can be used with a school staff or with a class. It is useful to enact an awareness-raising activity beforehand.

1. Everyone is given a few moments to think of an incident of bullying that is known to them, possibly a personal experience or something they have witnessed. It could be recent or in the past.
2. Everyone then brainstorms what bullying is. There are no comments during this part of the activity.
3. All contributions are written down so that everyone can see them.
4. The class or group divides into smaller groups.
5. Each group is given ten minutes to come back with a definition of bullying.
6. There is a further discussion to come up with one agreed definition.

SCHOOL OR CLASS SURVEY

It is often useful to carry out a survey of bullying which not only provides information but also raises awareness of the issues and brings them into the open. You may wish to refer to or adapt the questionnaire in *Bullying: A Practical Guide to Coping for Schools* (Elliot, 1991). The things to remember are:

●   It *must* be anonymous and confidential or it will not give a true picture.
●   Be clear about and communicate the reasons for the survey. You need to find out what is actually happening in the school so that it can be dealt with. The purpose is *not* to discover individual instances or to find out who is bullying whom. If these are reported during the survey, however, they do need to be followed up.
●   You will need to ask questions to find the answers to these questions: How much bullying is going on? What form does it take? How bad is it? Where is it happening? When is it happening? What, if anything, is being done about it?
●   Pupils could be asked about their own experiences and information gathered about the nature of the bullying, the ages and gender of the perpetrators and whether they are individuals or groups.
●   You may also want to ask pupils who they think should be responsible for dealing with bullying and what sorts of things might be done to prevent it.

Whole-school/whole-class strategies

THE BULLY CIRCLE

This is an activity for a group of ideally from 12 to 20 people, although it is possible for a larger class to participate.

An empty chair is placed in the middle of the group who sit around it in a circle. The teacher or facilitator begins by asking the group to imagine that a bully is sitting in the chair.

The question is asked,

'What is the bully like?

Participants are encouraged to describe the bully.

'What gender are they?'
'What do they look like?'
'What expression is on their face?'

The following questions should be answered with a bully in mind.

'What has the bully done?'
'How did it make you feel?'
'What did you do?'
'What happened next?'
'What, if anything, happened later on?'
'What might have changed the situation?'

The facilitator then goes on to encourage the class to think more deeply about how this bullying behaviour is being supported.

'Why are we so afraid of this person?'
'How have they become so powerful?'
'Does the bully have friends in this class?'
'What are they like?'

These questions help the group to think up some solutions.

'Does there need to be a bully in this class? Why is that?'
'How can we solve this problem of having a bully here?'
'How can we solve the bully's problem?'
'Do we need help to solve this problem?'
'What else could we try?'

The facilitator or one of the group will need to write down all the strategies that are suggested at this point and before the end of the exercise there should be agreement to put at least one of them into practice immediately.

Finally, if this exercise is carried out with a class group, a date should be agreed to review the strategy and how well it is working.

THE VICTIM EXPERIENCE

This is an exercise similar to the bully circle except that the chair in the middle contains an imaginary victim. The questions asked of the group are identical except those about the bully's power to make people afraid. Instead the question asked is:

'Why do we feel sorry for this person?'
'Why have they become so powerless?'

Both of these activities encourage the whole group to consider their responsibility to each other. Had this exercise been carried out in the class where Jennifer was at school it is probable that the problem would have been dealt with by the pupils themselves with no further intervention necessary by staff.

THE BULLY BOX

This is very simply a version of a suggestion box that has been used in some schools. It provides a way for pupils to communicate incidents without going directly to a teacher. Schools that use this method of creating a 'telling' ethos need to ensure that they have devised the follow-up strategies clearly so that hopes are not raised and then dashed as nothing much happens. There also needs to be an awareness of the potential abuse of this system and thought given to whether pupils will be allowed to write anonymously. If it is the only way of communicating it may effectively bar those students who have difficulty with writing.

THE BULLY COURT

'Bully courts' are designed to empower pupils to deal with bullying themselves at a group level. There is some controversy over their use, and Michelle Elliot (1991) recommends that they are used only in schools where there is already a strong anti-bullying policy which is supported by all staff, parents and pupils.

Pupils elect representatives to sit on a bully court. This can be for a limited time or for each sitting. Classes, years or the whole school can have their own court, depending on what is most appropriate. There must be at least one member of staff to ensure that procedures are carried out properly and that any decision made is in accordance with the school's policies. The disadvantage of bully courts is that they are better designed to deal with the acute problem than with the chronic: that is, extreme individual instances rather than the individual who persistently 'picks on' another.

Each person involved in an incident, including any witnesses, is required to give her version of events to the court. At the end of the court's sitting a verdict is pronounced and a 'sentence' imposed. This could include menial tasks, a private or public apology, being banned from certain areas or activities for a period of time or a 'suspended' sentence.

COUNCILS

School, year or class councils can be effective in giving pupils a voice in expressing their concerns and asking for strategies to be discussed. They deal with issues on an organizational and impersonal level so that it may be easier for individuals or groups to feel comfortable in bringing the subject up. Councils also give young people a greater sense of responsibility and ownership of strategies.

CONTRACTS

Contracts are simply agreements that are signed by all new entrants to the school. They are explained and discussed with new pupils and their parents or carers at the initial interview. Schools will want to ensure that any contract they draw up is compatible with their own policies. A typical contract, however, might look like this:

Allagreed School wants all its pupils to be happy in school and to enjoy learning. Bullying is therefore not acceptable.
Bullying includes picking on someone, ganging up on someone, making unkind remarks about them, or in any way making them miserable and unable to enjoy school. You are asked to read and sign the following contract.

I (name)........... will try to be friendly to my fellow pupils.
I will not use physical force in any way at any time.

I will not make comments which are hurtful about anyone's appearance, race, gender, family, ability, beliefs or circumstances.

I will not threaten or frighten anyone.

I will not try to force anyone to do anything.

I will not join in with anyone who is bullying.

I will let my class teacher know about any incident of bullying that I see.

I will report to my class teacher any bullying that happens to me.

I understand that if I am accused of bullying on three or more occasions my parents will be asked to come to school to discuss this.

Signed: Pupil. . . . .

Countersigned by Parent. . . . .

Witnessed by. . . . .

A copy of the signed contract should be given to the pupil and a copy kept in the pupil's school file.

Dealing with bully gangs

Often groups of people, incited by individuals seeking power over them, will behave in ways that they would not if they were on their own. Where a group of pupils are throwing their weight around in school in a way that intimidates others, it is necessary to deal with each of them individually at some stage. Written accounts of incidents from all involved will help to identify the roles that each is carrying out and may give guidance as to how the bully gang could be dealt with most effectively.

THE PIKAS APPROACH

The Pikas approach, also known as the common concern method, refers to group bullying as 'mobbing', a Scandinavian term. The aim of this method, as above, is to 're-individualize' the group members. Each individual is seen for interview both to discuss the incident itself and to explore his anxieties and reservations. It helps if this happens as soon after an incident as possible. The 'victim' is not seen until after everyone else to reduce accusations of informing. At the end of the interview there is a discussion about how each person will behave with the others involved and what he will be saying to them. Everyone is then brought together to agree on their 'common concern' and the action they will take. The situation is reviewed a week later. The aim is to increase tolerance, promote communication and generate strategies by the students themselves.

THE NO-BLAME APPROACH

This is illustrated in a video and pack produced by Lame Duck Publishing. It offers an approach to dealing with specific incidents in school. The feelings of those concerned are the focus of the discussion and of the intervention, not the details of what actually happened.

The teacher has a discussion with the child who has been bullied. The emphasis is on how the child feels although the names of those involved are also ascertained. The teacher asks the child to produce something, such as a picture or a poem, to illustrate her distress.

The teacher then meets with all the group of children who were involved, whether by bullying, colluding or observing. She tells them about the unhappiness of the person they bullied and uses the drawing or writing for emphasis. Although no blame is attributed and the details of the incident are not discussed the group are left in no doubt that they have a responsibility to make this person feel happier. They are asked about their ideas but no promises are extracted.

It is then left up to the group to take initiatives further.

The teacher arranges to meet everyone, including the child who has been bullied, individually a week or so later to see whether things have improved. The schools that have used this approach feel that it has a lot to offer, especially as no one is in trouble and there are positive consequences all round.

Excuses, excuses

'I was just only joking.'
'It was a bit of a laugh.'
'It was an accident.'
'We didn't mean to upset her, it was only a tease.'

It is difficult for busy teachers not to accept these well-worn excuses for bullying, but there needs to be a clear sequence of responses. Ideally, the first response should come from the student. Laughing it off or ignoring is always a possibility and shows that it has not had the desired effect. Otherwise, looking at someone in the eye and saying very firmly 'This isn't funny' and walking away may work. Sometimes it really has been a joke that has gone wrong or an accident, and all that needs to happen is an explanation and an apology. If it happens for a second or a third time, however, it must be take much more seriously and dealt with as an incident of bullying. Fostering a 'telling' ethos and keeping records are therefore essential.

Bystanders

A school which is determined to stamp out bullying will ensure that the message comes across that there are no 'innocent' bystanders. Anyone who sees bullying happen or knows that someone is being picked on becomes responsible. If that person chooses to do nothing then he is effectively condoning or collaborating with the bullying behaviour. One way of getting pupils to think through the role of the bystander is to work on some 'What if?' scenarios. Hypothetical situations are presented to small groups who discuss the alternative responses.

WHAT IF

Here are some examples of scenarios that could be used. Of course, many other situations could be discussed, including incidents where the perspectives both of the bully and of the victim are given.

1. You walk into your classroom with a friend and you both see an incident in which three or four pupils are throwing someone's schoolbag around. The person is clearly upset by this. Do you:
    (a) catch the bag, give it back and leave it at that
    (b) do nothing but later agree that if you see it happen again you will tell
    (c) tell the bullies that they are being horrible and not to be so unkind
    (d) try to be friendly to the victim afterwards
    (e) think that it's none of your business
    (f) anything else.

2. Someone has recently arrived at the school. She is very shy and has a stutter when she speaks. She is also quite plump. One other girl mimicks her all the time and has started calling her names: Do you:
    (a) not join in but otherwise do nothing
    (b) tell the teachers what is happening
    (c) try to get the bully to see how unkind she is being
    (d) talk to other pupils in an attempt to get them to be friendly to the new girl and give her some protection
    (e) anything else.

It is important to stress that there isn't one correct answer to these alternatives. They are there as a basis for discussion. More ideas for 'What ifs' can be found in the Kidscape booklet on bullying.

Individual interventions

It is a fine balance that adults have to take between doing something about a child being bullied and helping them to do something themselves. Generally, especially with verbal bullying, it is better to offer empowering strategies to the child concerned first. This requires some clear guidance, monitoring and reassurance that there will be back-up if the abuse continues. See also Chapter 2.

Looking confident

It may seem a cliché but it is true that looking confident can actually increase confidence. It can also give others the message 'don't mess with me'. Pupils who walk around with their heads down and with a slumped posture, who are reluctant to look straight at anyone and who mumble when they speak are more likely to be seen as potential targets than those who 'stand tall', can look others in the eye and speak directly. Showing children how to look more confident and encouraging them to try out different ways of standing, looking and speaking can be a start in increasing their self-esteem and ability to cope with difficult situations.

GO WITH THE FLOW

Although there may be some people who will think that the 'go with the flow' strategy is tantamount to collusion it can in reality be very effective. Encouraging children to react differently and to 'go with the flow' is a way of empowering children who are bullied verbally to help themselves. It tends to pull the rug from under the feet of the bully, who usually does not know how to respond. It also raises the esteem of the child concerned both in her own eyes and in those of others. It should not, however, be used with a bully who is volatile and may resort to physical abuse.

Many young people become highly defensive when 'teased'. They strongly deny the accusations or taunts and become very upset. This is understandable, but sadly this reaction is often rewarding and may simply encourage the verbal bully. A 'go with the flow' response is a statement which is not a denial but which nevertheless gives the 'victim' something to say which will surprise and undermine the bully. It might be useful to discuss the exact form of words which might be used and encourage practice in role play or in front of a mirror at home. Body language is also important if this strategy is to be successful.

It is difficult to give exact forms of words that will deflect verbal bullying because it will depend on the children involved and exactly what the problem is. Phrases which show a sense of pride and/or humour will make the 'victim' feel good about herself as well as surprise the bully. General comments might be:

'I love you too.'
'You could win prizes with all the stories you make up.'
'Do you know any words with more than four letters?'

It is necessary to discuss with the child what she will feel comfortable with and encourage her to come up with her own ideas.

After the response has been made it is best to move away in the direction of a supervising adult, without seeming to hurry. The aggressor might want to retaliate verbally but it will probably take him some time to think something up, so moving away from the situation confidently is effective.

This strategy is unlikely to be successful with very withdrawn pupils whose self-confidence is rock bottom, and should not be suggested if the person is unlikely to be able to carry it through.

GETTING IT DOWN

One way of empowering an older child who is subject to verbal abuse is to give him a notebook in which he makes a note of the time, place and actual words used in any incident. This will also provide evidence for taking further action if necessary. This worked brilliantly in one high school, where a 13-year-old boy had been the butt of incidents for some time. The first day he used this strategy he took his notebook out of his back pocket and, pencil poised, asked 'What was that you said?' It didn't happen again.

These are only a few of the strategies that can be used to intervene in schools. Many more can be found in the books and resources listed below. If a school is developing a 'friendly' ethos where relationship building and co-operative ventures are a significant part of the agenda then dealing with bullying is likely to be easier and more at a pro-active than at a reactive level.

RESOURCES

The short films listed below are very useful at the initial stages of raising awareness of bullying behaviour.

Sticks and Stones is possibly the most immediate in its impact. It is important that teachers using this watch it through themselves first as some of the scenes are quite powerful. It will need careful introduction. It is the most professionally produced of the videos available and has a scene which portrays a 'bully court' in operation. Available from: Video Resource Unit, Central Independent Tele-vision, Broad Street, Birmingham B1 2JP, UK.

Only Playing Miss is produced by the Neti-Neti theatre company and is a video of the play that they have performed in many schools. It is bilingual in Ben-gali and English, supported by British Sign Language. The company publishes scripts and provides follow-up work to the video. This package can be used as a starting-point for developing school initiatives. Available from: Trentham Books Ltd, Unit 13/14, Trent Trading Park, Botteslow Street, Stoke-on-Trent ST1 3OY, UK. A script and full description of the workshops are also available.

The Neti-Neti company can be contacted at 44 Gladsmuir Road, London N19 3JU, UK.

Stamp Out Bullying is also a video accompanied by a handbook. It is primarily a video of activities taken in a school to address bullying; they include role play, discussion and creative work. It may give teachers ideas about a cross-curricular approach. Available from: Lame Duck Publishing, 71 South Road, Portishead, Bristol BS20 7DY, UK.

Information and support

In the last few years, several organizations have been set up in Great Britain specifi-cally to deal with a range of issues concerning child safety. These are some of the best known:

KIDSCAPE: provides materials and information as well as running courses and conferences. World Trade Centre, Europe House, London E1 9AA.

ABC 'Anti-Bullying Campaign': provides information and resources for parents who want to work with schools. 10 Borough High Street, London SE1 9QQ.

CHILDLINE is a telephone number for children in distress. 0800 1111.

A useful resource for teachers is TIPS: the Teaching Information Package (1985), published by Macmillan Education. It includes sections on bullying, extortion and blackmail in schools.

REFERENCES

Arora, T., Foster, P. and Thompson, D. (1990) A whole school approach to bullying. *Pastoral Care*, September.

Besag, V. (1989) *Bullies and Victims in Schools*. Milton Keynes: Open University Press.

Elliot, M. (ed.) (1991) *Bullying: A Practical Guide to Coping for Schools*. Harlow: Longman.

Eron, L. D., Huesmann, R., Dubow, E., Romanoff, R. and Yarmel, P. W. (1987) Aggression and its correlates over 22 years. In D. H. Crowell, I. M. Evans and C. P. O'Connell (eds) *Childhood Aggression and Violence*. New York: Plenum Press.

Department of Education and Science (1989) *Discipline in Schools*, Report of the Elton Committee. London: HMSO.

Haringey Education Authority (1992) *Bullying: A Haringey Response*. Available from The Lodge, Church Lane, London N17.

La Fontaine, J. (1991) *Bullying: The Child's View*. An analysis of telephone calls to Childline about bullying. London: Calouste Gulbenkian Foundation.

Mooney, A., Creeser, R. and Blatchford, P. (1991) Children's views on teasing and fighting in junior schools. *Educational Research* 33, 2.

Olweus, D. (1984) Aggressors and their victims: bullying at school. In N. Frude and H. Gault (eds) *Disruptive Behaviour in Schools*. London: Wiley.

Pikas, A. (1989) The common concern method for the treatment of mobbing. In R. Roland and E. Munthe (eds) *Bullying: An International Perspective*. London: David Fulton.

Rutter, M., Maughan, B., Mortimore, P. and Ouston, J. (1979) *Fifteen Thousand Hours: Secondary Schools and Their Effects on Children*. London: Open Books.

Smith, P. K. and Thompson, D. *Practical Approaches to Bullying*. London: David Fulton.

Smith, P. K. and Whitney, I. Survey service on bully/victim problems in schools. Part of the Department for Education *Sheffield Bullying Project* (1990−3). PO Box 603, University of Sheffield, Sheffield S10 2UR.

Tattum, D. P. and Lane, D. A. (eds) (1989) *Bullying in Schools*. Stoke-on-Trent: Trentham Books.

SAIRA

Denia

Karen

Nicola
homewood

Jaclyn

Nicola

My Picture is about when me are and my friends play outside

Chapter 9

The School Playground

'What did you do in school today, then?'

  'We had this really brilliant game of football and I scored two goals.'
  'I had a fight with Rosemary at dinner time − she pulled my hair.'
  'Not much, it was wet and we had to stay inside all day.'
  'We went to the aerobics class Miss Brady is doing on Monday lunchtimes.'
  'The dinner lady made me and Terry pick up all the rubbish.'
  'Costas brought his Game-Boy into school and it got broken.'

THE IMPORTANCE OF PLAYGROUND EXPERIENCES

Children spend at least a fifth of their school day out of the class and away from a structured teaching environment. From the comments that they often make about what goes on in school you may be forgiven for thinking that it is the time spent out in the playground that is most meaningful, memorable and relevant to them. It is where friendships are made and broken, where, out of the watchful eye of teachers, the worst bullying takes place, where behaviour difficulties may spill over into violence and aggression and where children find themselves accepted or rejected. For some children the playground is a place to use up excess stores of physical energy or to talk about last night's television soap. For others it can be a place of daily misery with protective adults in short supply and no lesson to hide in. Although little teaching takes place it is nevertheless a learning environment, and the lessons that children learn about themselves and others during their 'free' time are brought back into the classroom.

If there has been a strong focus on developing friendships and social skills in the classroom it is the playground where we might hope to see this applied. In a way the school yard is a testing ground for school or classroom policies and ethos.

The benefits of play are widely acknowledged in the Western world today for promoting the development of language, creative thinking and problem solving: 'Play is indeed the child's work, and the means whereby he grows and develops' (Isaacs, 1933).

The complexity of a child's play is often assessed as an indication of the level of ability. The value of play for children in promoting development is reflected in the provision of a wide range of toys, books, games and activities for the very young. The continuing value of play for older children, with the possible exception of physical play, is often underestimated, especially in relation to the development of social competence.

In some schools there is now the recognition that in contrast with lively and stimulating classrooms, the playground is often a bleak place, both in terms of the physical environment and the lack of things to do. Break-times rarely have clear aims and objectives other than to provide a space of time in the day between sedentary, directed activities in which children can use up energy and interact freely with each other. Many would say that this is sufficient purpose and that any 'interference' by adults would be an infringement of pupils' rights to determine their own space and time. There is also an anxiety that the 'culture' of childhood, its games, rhymes and rituals, might be lost if teachers somehow took them over. Nevertheless, up to two-thirds of children have a negative view of their experiences in the playground (Tizard *et al.*, 1988), and there is a pervasive view among teachers that the quality of interactions in the school yard is often not high and that too much of what goes on is anti-social.

This chapter tries to take account of these different perspectives and looks at ways of improving aspects of the playground without imposing too much adult control. It explores opportunities to promote positive social interactions which meet the needs of different groups and individuals, and initiatives to make break-times more rewarding and enjoyable for everyone.

GRAVEL AND GRASS: THE PHYSICAL ENVIRONMENT

A generation or so ago it was much more common for children to 'play out' in the neighbourhood, in the streets, the parks and wherever opportunities for 'adventure' might be found. The greater availability of cross-age friendships meant that games were passed from older to younger children. Rules and expectations were learnt from other children and the variety of play environments lent itself to the development of imaginative games. Today, many parents are too fearful of potential molesters, of traffic and other accidents to let their children play outside without close supervision. Instead many children either have their time highly structured by adults who ferry them from one after-school activity to another, or become passive participants in the activities and adventures presented to them on television. Consequently the school yard may be one of the few places where children have the freedom to let their imagination run riot — but without the provision of an environment to stimulate ideas what often happens is the riot without the imagination.

Some schools, often those which are already situated in a 'richer' environment, are fortunate enough to have school grounds which include grassed areas, large equipment, 'natural' areas with ponds and trees and even a garden as well as a hard-surface area. Other schools, especially those in cramped inner-city areas where the need is even greater, are not so lucky. A school yard in a primary or elementary school which is surrounded by high walls or fences offers very little to children, who are often left to their own devices to relieve the boredom. The provision of one or two pieces of equipment to be shared by a large number of pupils may cause conflict rather than develop co-operation and also presents difficulties in ensuring safety. High schools usually fare better because they are built on larger sites with more opportunities for variety in the grounds.

Teachers often acknowledge the problem, but changing a flat piece of gravel into a source of interest and amusement is a daunting and potentially expensive task. Some schools have decided that improving the school grounds is a priority and have spent money accordingly, sometimes applying for special grants to help with finance. Others have taken the opportunity of rebuilding programmes to develop school grounds. Some improvements are always possible, however, and need not be costly or time-consuming. Even the minimum of changes can be worthwhile. Ideas that may be worth considering are given in the activities section of this chapter.

The experiences of several schools indicate that playground development is often piecemeal and takes more account of adult than of pupil perspectives. There is not much point in creating an aesthetically pleasing environment if it does not meet the needs of the children. According to Brown and Burger (1984), overall planning within a framework of clear objectives is essential if the amount of energy and resources is to be justified by the end result – that is, an improvement in the playground experiences for all children.

BALANCING NEEDS

If one looks over the fence into an inner-city school yard the immediate impression is likely to be of quite large groups of boys running about kicking or throwing a large ball and smaller groups of girls walking around arm in arm talking – or perhaps playing with a skipping rope or small ball. There would also be several children who are either alone or walking around with a supervisor. Meeting the needs of all those who use the playground is not easy: there are different age groups, different interests and the different gender interactions to consider.

In the absence of intervention, the school yard is often dominated by bigger boys who want to play ball games and who consequently take up much of the available space. Girls' (and teachers') acceptance of this male monopolization is not uncommon (Dunn and Morgan, 1987). Some schools, however, aware of equal opportunities issues, have attempted to tackle the problem. Some have encouraged boys to include girls in their games. Others have given footballs to girls and encouraged them to play together, sometimes giving them separate instruction and practice first. Yet others have restricted the playing of football to certain times to enable girls to 'reclaim' the space. The success of these ventures has been mixed and has depended on many factors, including the initial acceptance of gender inequalities by both children and staff. In several inner London schools where there has been a long-term commitment to equal opportunities policies there are now a significant number of girls who consider football to be a legitimate female play activity, although teams remain segregated by gender (Lewis and Roffey, in press).

In the United States the great emphasis on sport generally is a difficulty for those children, especially boys, who are not so athletic. 'Unsporty' individuals risk being ostracized by their peers. Children with special needs also often have poor physical co-ordination and this is in an area which must be addressed if social integration is to have meaning. Placing high value on and promoting other social activities would go at least some way to giving both the less academic and the less sporty some status among their peers.

ZONING

'Zoning', that is, providing separate areas, is one way of meeting the needs of different groups of children. One school in England has an area which has been devoted entirely to skipping, with appropriate rhymes painted on the adjoining wall. Another has ball games on the 'lower' playground only. It takes few resources and not a great deal of space to devote an area to the practising of basketball, which can be encouraged as a mixed-gender activity. It may be worth spending some time drawing the school grounds to scale and looking at how different activities might fit in. Carol Ross and Amanda Ryan (1990) have some thoughtful and imaginative ideas on zoning in their book on improving the school playground, *Can I Stay In Today, Miss?*.

There may not be enough space, however, to divide into zones, and other ways of balancing needs will have to be considered. Offering different activities at different times is a possibility, though it must be ensured that everyone knows what to expect when; looking forward to something and finding that it does not happen is not likely to improve behaviour. Other schools have tried 'staggering' break-times themselves so that there are simply fewer children in the area at one time. The policy of allowing the youngest children time outside separate from everyone else is now quite common and allows for a gradual integration into the main school. This does not, however, encourage cross-age friendship, and a more adventurous initiative is to divide and mix age groups at break-times so that the older children have some responsibility for the younger ones. A school in Devon took this one step further and 'matched' pairs of grade three (7–8-year-old) and grade six (10–11-year-old) children who took part in a collaborative activity on Friday afternoons. Playtime experiences for the younger children improved as they were no longer intimidated by the 'big boys', and the older children's self-esteem was enhanced (Blatchford, 1989).

STRUCTURES AND SKIPPING ROPES: EQUIPMENT

When improvements to the playground are being considered, the provision of stimulating pieces of large equipment is often uppermost in people's minds. The decision-making process centres around whether or not to have a climbing frame. A great deal of thought will also be given to the health and safety factors involved. Less thought may be given to exactly what will be provided in terms of children's experiences. This is not to say that installing a large, interesting and safe structure is a bad idea but it is often expensive and it may be wiser to spend limited funds on things that will meet the needs of more children or be open to a greater variety of uses. Large play items that have been used in school, some more permanently than others, include old fire-engines, tractors and other vehicles (with any potentially dangerous parts removed), old rowing boats, a Noah's ark, a lifeboat, a lizard made out of old car tyres, forts and castles, theatre structures and space rockets. If there are many children wanting to play with a piece of equipment that will only hold a limited number then there must be a way of organizing its use so that everyone gets a turn.

Children over the age of about 7 are likely to be more interested in smaller pieces of equipment, such as balls, ropes and rings. Supplies of these can be circulated among classes so that all children have a regular turn if they wish. A selection of games which might be played with various items of equipment could be introduced in PE lessons. A successful ploy in some schools has been to give responsibility for taking out equipment to those children who are finding it more difficult to integrate into social groups because of shyness or lack of ability. Other children are informed that the pupil with responsibility for the ball, rope, etc. can choose who can join in with the game. The choosing process needs to be supervised in the first instance to ensure that it works well.

There will be times when children bring things to school themselves, either toys or games of their own or things that are the current craze, from marbles to transformers to yoyos. Whatever it is there needs to be explicit understanding about the management of these items. Are they only allowed in children's possession at breaktimes? Where will they be kept and are there expectations about 'sharing', 'lending' and 'borrowing'? What will happen if they are the focus of disputes? The worst scenario is the one where an expensive new toy such as a computer game gets broken or lost when it has been 'borrowed' without permission. Not only is the owner very upset, but so also are the parents, who come to school with complaints. To prevent such difficulties from arising these decisions need to be made before anyone even thinks of putting their treasured new toy in their schoolbag.

GAMES, RHYMES AND RITUALS

Games, rhymes and rituals are playground activities which need little more than the children themselves. Few props, equipment or supervision are necessary. Most adults will remember something of the 'culture' of their own childhood when there were set sayings for being 'safe', choosing who goes first or who is 'out' and so on. In 1969 Iona and Peter Opie published their research into children's street games, which revealed a richness and diversity of children's games throughout Great Britain. These included games involving chasing, hiding, catching, acting, pretending, racing, guessing, daring and duelling (combat with conkers, lolly-sticks, knuckles and so on). The Opies discovered that similar games were played from the north of Scotland to the Scilly Isles but that there were clear regional variations on themes. There are both American and European versions of some of the rhymes, which is an indication of how long they have been around and how well they travel.

Ways of starting games are sometimes known as 'dipping'. There are over fifty rhymes in the Opie book alone connected with this activity. Some versions are so complex that they are virtually a game in themselves. Counting fists is standard practice in many countries, and throughout the twentieth century this has been accompanied in school yards throughout Britain and America with a 'potato rhyme' such as this (The player whose fist is tapped on the last word puts that fist behind his or her back. Players are 'out' when both fists have been hit.):

One potato, two potato,

Three potato, four,
Five potato, six potato,
Seven potato, more.

The advantage of 'dipping' is that it is seen by children to be fair. It can prevent one aspect of domination in the playground by more powerful individuals.

Since publication of the Opie research there have been major social changes throughout the Western world, such as the impact of television and the influence of the wider multicultural communities in which we now live. Some authors have lamented the decline in the use of traditional games and there does seem to be some evidence for a decline (Blatchford, 1989). There is also, however, a view that younger children below the age of 11, and in particular girls, have a private world in which they do participate in such activities (Grudgeon, 1991). It would be interesting to see how much of this 'culture' still exists, and how it may have changed and developed.

Some schools which serve a number of different communities have decided to enlist the help of parents in bringing into the school yard the rhymes and rituals which represent the cultural backgrounds of all the children in the school. This not only preserves an element of individual cultures but also shows that each is valued by the school. Children's 'ownership' of games can be protected if they are simply asked to teach others about them. Structured opportunities to do so may need to be set up, perhaps in the classroom first. Children may then appreciate being left to themselves. There is an element of childish humour and 'rudeness' to many of these rhymes which pupils may feel uncomfortable about sharing in front of adults!

SUPERVISION

For teachers, break-times are often a welcome relief from the incessant demands of the classroom and offer the chance to have a cup of coffee, to chat with colleagues for a few moments, to prepare lessons, or to help an individual child. In some schools, notably in the United States, teachers go out with their own classes at recess. They have a break when their classes are with subject specialists. In Great Britain primary school teachers usually cover the entire curriculum and there is no space in the day for each teacher to have an individual break on a regular basis. There is instead a duty rota for members of staff to keep an eye on things in the playground.

At lunchtimes there is no such obligation on teachers to involve themselves with the children and for the most part supervision is carried out by ancillary staff who are employed for that purpose. No qualifications are required, the pay is very low and training is rarely given. Supervisors are expected to oversee the dining areas as well as the school grounds and to manage wet lunchtimes indoors when necessary. It is a difficult and arduous job which is not helped by the fact that supervisors are often not regarded with the same respect as the teachers. Yet it is the attitude of supervisors in the playground that, more than anything else, affects playground use (Brown and Burger, 1984).

Many supervisors feel that their job is to make sure that lunchtimes run smoothly and interact with pupils to sort out problems rather than try to involve children in activities or encourage them to play together.

TRAINING

Training for lunchtime supervisors is seen as a high priority in many schools but finding the time and funding presents difficulties. In some schools senior staff agree to cover in order to enable the training to take place. Others have tried to include ancillary staff on their own training days, especially when devising school policies about behaviour.

Betty is a senior midday supervisor in an inner-city school. She is a grandmother herself and clearly likes children. She has a way of talking and listening which makes each student feel important. Sometimes she starts up one of her large repertoire of games, including children who are otherwise left out. After a while, when the game has a momentum of its own, she withdraws. She seems to be able to anticipate trouble and sort things out before they blow up. When there is a crisis she is seen to be listening to all involved and takes children to one side to hear what they have to say. She smiles a lot and shouts little. New pupils are occasionally rude to her and new lunchtime staff don't always have the same attitude towards children that she does or have the same skills. But Betty is both a good manager and a strong influence. It isn't long before both staff and children learn what is acceptable in the playground and what isn't. Betty is greatly treasured by the teaching staff, who rely on her for calm lunchbreaks.

It is hard to teach this quality of supervision but it is possible to give alternative strategies for handling situations and to look at what would make the job more rewarding. There are several training packs available to help with supervisor training. Some of these are listed in the resources section of this chapter.

STATUS

In addition to providing training, schools can increase the status of lunchtime supervisors. It helps to have clear liaison between teachers and midday assistants, for teachers to be seen to back decisions made by them and for consistent sanctions to be applied to children who are rude or disrespectful. Discussions with supervisors about how they might go about winning that respect in their own right may also be useful. Wherever possible inclusion in, or at the very least communication about, the development of whole-school policies on relevant topics such as behaviour, play and parents should be made available to all support staff.

MANAGING UNFRIENDLY BEHAVIOUR

There will be fewer problems at break-times if there are a variety of activities on offer which appeal to many pupils. It helps to have good supervision which reinforces the school policy on behaviour. Even in an ideal world, however, there are going to be conflicts and disputes.

A few straightforward playground rules help both to limit difficulties and to provide back-up when things go wrong. These would have to relate to the school concerned and the age of the students but might include where students are allowed to go during break-times and what their responsibilities are in the dining area.

A more specific playground code for younger pupils might include:

'Everyone must have their feet on the ground at all times.'

'You must come straight away when a supervisor asks you to come and explain something.'

Once the expectations are made clear it is easy for supervisors and teachers to remind children if they seem to be breaking the 'playground code'.

TELLING TALES

'Telling' is a behaviour that causes particular difficulties. On the one hand pupils are advised to inform a teacher or supervisor if someone is bullying or behaving unfairly. On the other hand both children and adults do not warm to those who are constantly complaining about the behaviour of others, seeing them as 'whingers'. A first response could be for the supervising adult to agree to come and watch how games are proceeding. This in itself will help to prevent unfriendly behaviour. It also provides opportunities to comment on and otherwise reinforce more positive social interactions. Not taking immediate action will also protect the complaining child from later repercussions and also give her a chance to find ways of influencing the situation herself − perhaps with some advice on how to do this. If unacceptable behaviour in the playground is either extreme or continuous, it needs to be addressed at a class level with the teacher.

BEGINNING AND ENDING BREAK-TIMES

The way in which break-times begin influences what happens in the playground, and how they end can affect what happens in the classroom.

In primary and elementary schools it is probably better to do away with bells and whistles altogether and have children go out in small groups rather than in a great rush all together. Accidents are less likely to happen and it promotes a calm rather than a frenetic atmosphere. The teacher 'on duty' can make sure that her class goes out a few minutes earlier so that there is supervision for everyone. Coming in can also happen gently. This may be organized in several ways:

1. A teacher walks around telling groups of children that break-time has ended. They are expected to stand still. Others who see that this is happening also stand still. Once everyone is quiet and still classes or groups of children are directed back into school.

2. There is an expectation that children will tell each other to stand still and listen when a signal is given by a teacher or supervisor. This promotes both individual responsibility and co-operation. Pupils can then be directed back into class quietly where they are more likely to settle down quickly to work.

3. Where older pupils are given responsibility to look after younger children they can be asked to make sure that they return to their classes at the correct time.

They may need to be taught how to do this well. Practice and supervision will be required at first.

BREAK-TIMES FOR HIGH SCHOOL STUDENTS

Much of the available research on school playgrounds and what happens during breaks has been carried out in primary and elementary schools and is therefore most relevant to younger children. Although some of what we have summarized here is applicable to senior schools this is clearly an important area for further study.

Schools which have realized that the overall well-being of students is affected by social interactions during break, especially lunchtimes, have made efforts to provide a variety of clubs and activities. These often depend on the goodwill of the teachers to either run or supervise. Cross-age links could, however, be promoted by having older students run some activities. Some ideas are given in the activities section of this chapter. People from outside the school may also be interested in coming in at lunchtimes to offer their particular expertise to students, possibly conversation in another language or a creative skill.

Giving access to curricular areas at lunchtime may also be helpful for pupils to complete work. Some of these would, of course, need to be supervised by staff but in some cases more senior students could again be given responsibility. Library facilities need to be made available together with other areas where students can do homework if they wish.

There are schools which have turned their special needs department into an 'exceptional needs' facility. They have made extension work available for students who are particularly able as well as those who are having difficulty. Paired reading schemes as well as other activities to meet a variety of needs are on offer at lunchtimes and meet academic as well as social needs.

Being 'let out' is an important element for many older students at break-times. The issue for schools is, let out where? And what happens on wet days? Having somewhere informal to sit and chat, perhaps listen to music or play cards, is crucial. Problems for schools include the management of these areas, especially when there are large numbers. Warm, comfortable common rooms are ideal but out of the reach of many schools with tight budgets. The first step in any planning to improve break-time experiences for students is to discover what is happening now, and what both students and teachers would like to happen. It is then up to the school to look at what the possibilities are within the constraints of space and resources. It is probable that more is open to change than is at first apparent.

TAKING ACTION

There are a number of ways in which break-times can be made more actively enjoyable and encourage friendly interactions between children. The physical environment of the playground and how break-times are supervised influence what happens socially. It is important that a wide variety of activities is on offer and that participation is made possible for everyone.

Ideas for improving the school grounds

1. Ensure that everywhere is regularly supervised, including outside toilets. There should be no dark, unsupervised corners where bullying could flourish.

2. Paint game markings on the ground and on the walls. If there are some in existence already such as for hopscotch, brighten them up. Show children the different games they could play on them.

    Pupils could be involved in a playground project from beginning to end, collecting ideas, discussing options, making decisions and carrying out the work. They could also be involved in discussing how games should be played and what rules might be established. Having a system where older children introduce newcomers to the playground would maintain knowledge of and interest in the games that could be played, including any new versions that children had thought up.

3. Painting murals on walls brightens up grey areas but active involvement of children is restricted to those who do the painting unless the murals themselves stimulate play. If they depict scenes which lend themselves to stories and the children's awareness of these is raised by supervisors then this can lead to adventure games that need only the minimum of props. Ideas could include magic, space, travel, animals or mysterious caves. If some simple props could be made available, such as items of clothing, old 'magic' carpets, shells for hearing messages and so on then the playground can be turned with ease into a potential fantasy world.

4. Many schools have dug up part of the asphalt and created green spaces which can be used for educational purposes as well as providing somewhere more pleasant to sit. The provision of a quiet area with seating meets the needs of older students and those children who appreciate the opportunity just to talk freely with each other. This could be doubled up as an outside 'waiting area' for parents who are collecting their younger children. Tables on which quieter games could be played, especially in summer, are even better but not always practical if there is very limited space and resources.

5. An extension of the above might include a garden area, perhaps with a pond, where children can take responsibility for maintenance. Parents' groups are often happy to be involved in digging and planting as it gives them a more active and focused involvement in the school community. Some schools have successfully kept animals on the school grounds and for those children who are experiencing social difficulties this is very useful. They can learn caring skills in a non-threatening situation and can then be helped to apply these, where appropriate, in situations with classmates. Looking after an animal also lends itself well to paired or small-group activities where everyone is given a role in a collaborative task. If social learning is to take place with this or with any similar activity, there needs to be a raised awareness and focus on the interactions of the participants, not only on the task itself.

6. Although curriculum extension games and activities are an adult imposition on the playground they do provide a clear purpose to break-times which encourages both learning and positive social interaction. Recess in one American elementary school, described by Peter Blatchford (Blatchford, 1989), has been turned into

'Play and Learn Time' (Wholf, 1984). Thirty 'graphics', designed by teachers but painted professionally, support areas of the curriculum such as the development of reading and vocabulary, number concepts and the understanding of fractions. The aim is for classroom concepts to be reinforced in the playground but in a way which makes it fun. For example, the names of all the American states have been written around the walls. The simplest of games is for someone to call out 'Go to Ohio', 'Now, go to South Carolina'. This can be extended by calling 'Go to where you'd find the White House' or 'Travel to the West Coast'.

GAMES AND ACTIVITIES

We have already discussed the need for balancing activities in the playground so that one game does not continually dominate, nor one group of pupils.

There are literally thousands of children's games, many of which require little or no equipment. All that is needed is the idea and showing children what to do. These can include hand-clapping games, pretend games, 'circle' and 'line' games, word games and so on. There are many excellent books which contain details of different types of activities suitable for children of different ages. We have listed some of these in the resources section. Here are two examples of very simple activities.

ONE WORD AT A TIME

'One Word at a Time' is most suitable for children over 8. A small group of children sit in a circle. One of them starts a story with one word. The person on her right continues with the next word – anything that fits and makes sense. This goes on round and round the circle until the sentence or story comes to an end. Another child takes a turn at being the one to start. Supervisors could suggest some words to start with which might make funnier or more unusual stories, for example 'crocodiles' or 'grandma'.

RESISTANCE

Push your arm (but not your body) hard against a wall for about thirty seconds. When you move away from the wall your arm will lift up all by itself. Children of all ages are intrigued by this and will enjoy finding out for themselves and then showing others their discovery.

Activities which require a small amount of equipment can include:

Skipping. With individual ropes or a long one for group games. Children may already know some skipping rhymes and games. Supervisors could get the children to teach them as well as perhaps showing them some more games.

Ball games. Small balls could be used for individual or paired games, larger ones for group games. Using basketball nets to practise 'shooting' is quite an energetic activity but usefully confined to a small area. Children enjoy circle ball games as well as team games. There are schools which allow only 'soft' balls out in the playground for safety. One school, having had the experience of rapidly depleting stockpiles of such balls, decided to sell them to the children for a few pennies each. They now appear to be taking better care of them.

Games with rings, hoops and beanbags.

Paper planes, and other origami activities.

Simple magic tricks. Teaching these to children who need a boost to their self-esteem will give them skills which are unique. They can show other children 'how it works'.

Card games. Only for indoors or very calm days. They can be very simple paired games such as 'Pairs' or 'Snap' or more complex games.

Activities for older children and high school students

Some of the above are suitable for older pupils but there is a need to consider a much wider range of activities, especially for lunchtimes, in senior schools. The following are just a few of the possibilities. Some will require instruction and/or supervision and some will need less or none at all.

- Producing a school or class newspaper. This includes writing, illustrating, layout, printing, collating and so on. There are roles, therefore, for a range of abilities.
- Musical activities, both listening to music and playing. 'Band' practice may need less adult support than orchestra practice. Music is a vital interest for many young people and to some extent the group that someone belongs to will be partly determined by the music he likes. It may be helpful for pupils who are finding it difficult to 'fit in' to share their enthusiasm for a particular kind of music with others who feel the same.
- Drama. Putting on performances is a very unifying social activity. A group of people share hard work, anxiety and exhilaration together. It is important that no one is cast into a 'scapegoat' role in times of difficulty. Drama is excellent, both within the curriculum and as an extra-mural activity, for those individuals who need to channel their extrovert energies in a positive and fulfilling way.
- Physical activities. These need not only mean ball games. Some teachers, students or outside volunteers may be prepared to run classes for aerobics, dancing or weight training. What use can be made of the gymnasium so that students can have a work-out at lunchtimes if they wish? Tennis, badminton and table-tennis are popular, as are pool and snooker, but providing a table is expensive.
- Board games. Chess immediately comes to mind but there are also Scrabble, Trivial Pursuit, Pictionary, Cluedo and a host of others. Some individuals like fantasy games such as Dungeons and Dragons.
- Card games are also enjoyed by all ages. They range from the ones based on pure luck (and concentration) to those which require a high level of skill.
- Clubs can be set up for almost any interest. The most common ones in schools are for computers, art and photography. Others could be for collectors (stamps, coins, postcards), foreign countries and languages, specific religions, craft interests or special activity interests such as horse-riding or bikes. Also fan clubs.

- Films and videos. These could either be restricted to wet days or be available on a regular, perhaps weekly, basis. The titles of films should be communicated well in advance and the system set up so that it runs as smoothly as possible, with all the necessary equipment in the right place and working properly.

DEALING WITH DIFFICULT BEHAVIOUR

It is hoped that the suggestions made in this chapter and others will help to limit the extent of difficult behaviour in the playground. See especially Chapter 8, which deals with bullying. The following strategy has been adopted by several schools, which find that it works well.

THE CARD SYSTEM

This is a straightforward method of dealing with behaviour difficulties in the primary or elementary school playground which was developed by a behaviour support teacher and an educational psychologist (Imich and Jeffries, 1987). It is structured around a system used in football matches with which many pupils will be familiar. It gives supervisors clear strategies for intervention and helps to avoid arguments.

Teachers and other adults supervising the playground have a yellow and a red card with them – in the same way as a soccer referee does. When an incident comes to their attention (i.e. they observe one child verbally or physically abusing another) they hold up a yellow card to the aggressor telling him exactly why (e.g. 'I saw you punching Martin – this is a warning'). As on the playing field, arguments are not allowed. If this pupil receives a second yellow card in the same playtime he is 'sent off' with a red card.

The school needs to ensure that everyone knows what happens to pupils who are sent off the playground. There is a danger that it could be seen as a soft option. Some pupils may enjoy being sent indoors on cold days or receiving the attention. Children who are always being 'sent off' will need a different, more specific intervention.

Adaptations to this system could include:

1. Giving silver and gold cards to pupils who are behaving in a particularly supportive way to others. This would ensure that staff give attention to acceptable behaviour and are not scouring the playground looking out for the miscreants. It will need to be tied in with the whole-school system of rewards and attention for good behaviour.
2. Telling pupils who inform about unseen incidents that they will make a note of it and keep an eye on the person for a while. If several children complain about the same person then action must be taken.

TRAINING FOR SUPERVISION

The quality of the supervision on the playground is a crucial factor in the smooth running of break-times. Few non-teaching staff have the benefit of training, although such training is clearly identified by many schools as a priority. We have listed in the resources section some of the training packs for supervisors that are presently available.

RESOURCES

The following is a selection of books which contain activities that are suitable for break-times. Most of them will need some introduction and some require supervision. It may be wise to teach a small group informally first and let that group teach others so that 'ownership' remains with the children as much as possible. Sometimes children only require a basic outline and will make changes and adaptations to suit themselves. Supervisors may need to remember the original rules in case they need to arbitrate!

Games for playing outside

Play Outside Book. David Wickens and Sharon Finmark. Studio Vista.
   How to turn outside spaces into places of imagination and fantasy with the minimum of materials. Some adult supervision needed.

Games for All Seasons. Emanuela Bompiano. Methuen.
   These are games from all over the world for groups, pairs and individuals.

Crackerjack Book of Games. BBC Publications.
   These are fun ideas but need careful planning if the participants are not to get over-excited. Supervision needed.

Body Tricks to Teach Yourself. Puffin.
   They probably need teachers to have a go first. Many children like to master such skills as juggling and enjoy the opportunity to do so. Even those who are not sport fanatics may want to try some of these ideas.

Games and How to Play Them. Hamish Hamilton.
   Games for different occasions with the advantage that they require little or no equipment and once taught they need no adult supervision.

Wet-weather games

Indoor Games for Rainy Days. Sid Hedges. Ward Lock, 1975.
   Games for individuals and groups including card games, pencil and paper games and potentially noisier games.

Why Don't You? BBC Knight Books, 1982.
   All sorts of things to do instead of watching TV – including magic tricks.

Pencil and Paper Games and Puzzles. Gyles Brandreth. Carousel, 1976.
   Some more difficult than others – best played in small groups or pairs.

Co-operative games

Let's Co-operate. Mildred Masheder. Peace Pledge Union, 1986.
   Some of these games are more likely to work than others and will need discussion first.

The Great Playtime Games Kit. National Playing Fields Association.

The Cooperative Sports and Games Book. T. Orlick. Pantheon, 1978.

Challenge without Competition. T. Orlick.

Playing for Life. New Games.

How Do People Play? Games from Many Lands. MacDonald.

Training for supervisors

Guidelines for Primary Midday Supervisory Assistants. Written by Jenny Mosley and published by Wiltshire County Council.

Not so much a training pack as a booklet full of ideas. It is divided into three sections. The first deals with approaches to children which are more likely to be successful, the second gives some suggestions for games both indoors and out and the final section outlines what the school needs to do to support their lunchtime supervisors in doing a good job. It is a simple guide but very clear. The games are generally suitable for the younger age range only.

Primary Lunchtime Resource Pack. Published by Newcastle Education Committee, 1990.

This pack is divided into two. The first section covers in detail the content of four hourly sessions of a training course for lunchtime supervisors. Activities are timed and deal concisely with the major issues of clarifying roles, encouraging good behaviour and dealing with difficulties. Session 4 is about beginning to develop a school lunchtime policy. Handouts are included in each for each session. The second half of the pack contains activities and games. Some of these are useful; many could be gleaned from any puzzle book in a magazine rack.

Working Together: Lunchtime Supervision. Published by OPTIS (Oxfordshire Programme for Training, Instruction and Supervision), 1986.

This booklet is one of several in the pack 'Working Together' which is specifically aimed at non-teaching staff supporting pupils with special needs. It is not necessarily a training pack but could be used to support a training course. It appeals to a slightly wider age range than most but has a section specifically for activities with younger children. Although it is not geared specifically to mainstream schools the vast majority of the information and ideas are applicable to any lunchtime anywhere. It is full of examples of situations that supervisors might meet and explores possible options for dealing with them. For those who have more time to give to training it covers more ground than the other packs, including such issues as smoking and irate parents.

REFERENCES

Blatchford, P. (1989) *Playtime in the Primary School.* Windsor: NFER – Nelson.

Brown, J. G. and Burger, C. (1984) Playground designs and pre-school children's behavior. *Environment and Behavior* **16** (5), 599–626.

Dunn, S. and Morgan, V. (1987) Nursery and infant school play patterns: some related differences. *British Educational Research Journal* **13** (3), 271–82.

Grudgeon, E. (1991) Girls play. *Language and Learning* **5,** February.

Imich, A. and Jeffries, K. (1987) Showing the yellow card. *Times Educational Supplement,* 6 November.

Isaacs, S. (1933) *Social Development in Young Children.* London: Routledge & Kegan Paul.

Language and Learning (1991), 5 February. Resource section, 'The School Playground'.

Lewis, C.L. and Roffey, S. (In press) Developing the friendly school. Paper presented at the Division of Education and Child Psychology Conference. British Psychological Society, 1993.

Opie, I. and Opie, P. (1969) *Children's Games in Street and Playground.* Oxford: Oxford University Press.

Ross, C. and Ryan, A. (1990) *Can I Stay in Today Miss?* Staffordshire: Trentham Books.

Sluckin, A. (1981) *Growing Up in the Playground.* New York: Plenum Press.

Tizard, B., Blatchford, P., Burke, J., Farquehar, C. and Plewis, I. (1988) *Young Children at School in the Inner City.* Hove: Lawrence Erlbaum Associates.

Wholf, F. (1984) Playground PALS. *Instructor,* May, 46–8.

Me   My best friend
      Ruksharia   Julie

these are My best friend and I like them alot
chey allway help me at my work.

Chapter 10

The Social Climate of the Classroom

'Tricia, our newly qualified teacher, has worked wonders with Year 5. They really work and play together as a class now.' (Headteacher)

'They all think the world of Mr Denton; he has a certain way with them.' (Parent)

'It's surprising to see how they've grown up since they've been in Gillian's class.' (Teacher colleague)

'Last year we mucked about quite a bit. It's much better now, we really get a lot of work done.' (Pupil aged 10)

'I didn't used to like coming to school but this year I've made more friends and people are nice to me. I had a broken arm and people in my class wrote and said they missed me and what they were doing. I wanted to come back quickly so I didn't miss anything.' (Pupil aged 12)

PROGRESS FOR A CLASS

Last year was a bad one for the Year 4 class. They had several different teachers because of the long-term sickness of their class teacher. No one stayed long enough to know them well and to use that knowledge to build class pride and confidence. The behaviour of some pupils deteriorated, especially those who were having difficulty with learning. The classroom usually looked a mess and the attendance of the class was unsatisfactory. When the new class teacher took over at the beginning of the year she had a tough job. By the end of the first term, however, the class was almost unrecognizable as the same group of children. They were co-operative, on-task most of the time, interested and enthusiastic. The attendance figures were much higher and the behaviour in the playground no different from that of pupils in the rest of the school: better than most, if anything. The differences had been brought about by the teacher and what she was able to do to influence both the quality of the learning experiences for the pupils and the relationships in the class.

PROGRESS FOR AN INDIVIDUAL

When Hannah arrived in her new class she had a long record of problems with school attendance. She had been 'ill' on a number of occasions in the past and her parents had often had difficult decisions to make when she complained of illness. They were worried that she simply did not want to go to school — but found it hard to force her because she disliked it so much. She did not seem to have friends and would not say anything about school. Hannah seemed to be becoming more withdrawn at home and rather depressed, although she played happily with the younger children next door, and seemed to boss them about!

When the family moved house, Hannah moved to a new school. Her parents had been worried about this. Although friends and neighbours said it was a good school, some of the pupils did seem to look rather tough. Indeed Hannah's parents had been worried that she might never attend at all, but quite the opposite happened. From the first few days she cheered up and no longer complained of stomach-ache or headaches. Hannah began to talk to her parents about homework and about some of the lessons. Other children began to call for her on the way to school and she walked home with a group.

When Hannah's parents met the class teacher, he had little to say about it except that she was an asset to the class, reliable and responsible. She tried hard and would always help anyone if she could. What might have gone wrong in the previous school was not understood by the adults but happily was not a mystery they needed to unravel. One of the visible things that had been happening was that two children were assigned to make sure that every new pupil was all right for the first week. This involved not only basic things like being in the right place at the right time but also introductions to the rest of the class, making sure they met everyone. There was an expectation that any new pupil would be helped socially and be included and encouraged to join in. There was a discussion between the three pupils (Hannah and her two buddies) and the teacher at the end of that week and also at the end of the second. This covered all sorts of things but included social progress and problems. One aspect of the positive climate was discussion and being upfront about any problems. The teacher wanted to know of any bad news as well as good; you were expected to sort out most issues but would not have to do it all by yourself.

But what had made it easy for Hannah was not just, or even especially, the two 'buddies' so much as the welcoming and cheerful nature of the class as a whole. They all told her that she was welcome and that she'd be fine, they'd make sure, although she would have to settle down and mix in. It was nice to have somebody new join the class. They talked to each other and with her and the teacher and it was no great problem joining in a conversation or opting out to do something else.

PROGRESS FOR THE TEACHER

When Joanne first had the class, each day was stressful and little was achieved. The children were attention seeking and exhibited difficult behaviour. They also seemed to have daily conflicts which made the teaching and learning process an uphill struggle. Children would argue or even fight over equipment, taunt and bully quiet children and deliberately interrupt the work of others. Joanne seemed to spend half of the time as an arbitrator for parties who did not want arbitration. She had two parents visit to support their children in disputes and these were ready to argue with her. Gradually the overall discipline of the class improved and the worst of the conflicts disappeared. Joanne thought it was more a case of her suppressing problems through strong behaviour management than any fundamental change.

She had insisted on some basic rules of class conduct including seating arrangements. She also insisted on groupwork with very clearly defined tasks. This made things better and by the end of school year Joanne felt that she had made a lot of progress. She also felt that it had been hard work. As she said to her colleagues, it had been like running through sand. If only the pupils had been more willing and used to mixing better together and with others, it would have all been a lot more pleasant and much more would have been achieved. Perhaps Joanne had laid the basis to build on, but continuous and specific work would be needed in the following year to take the class forward.

WHO WILL BE THE TEACHER?

For parents who know a first school well, one of their earlier questions and worries before a child starts school or moves to a new class is 'Who will be the teacher?' For young people who attend high school where a choice of option group is pending, the key question is the same: 'Which teacher will we have?' This question is more important than others we might expect about which other children or young people will be in the class. Parents, teachers and children feel strongly that being in the 'right class' is very important. Being in the right class means having the right teacher.

For teachers the challenge is to establish social progress whatever the initial level of social competence in the class. The question is, 'How can I move this class forward to create a positive climate?' It is also interesting to remember the answers that parents, children and young people give when asked what the teacher is like: 'She's nice', or 'He's great.' Positive answers usually express aspects of a positive social nature, as well as competence in establishing good behaviour and promoting learning, establishing a good climate for the business in hand. To have a good teacher is to have a teacher who can keep order, develop academic skills and teach children how to relate to others, and who provides a model of adult social skills.

THE SOCIAL CLIMATE

Adults too need a positive social climate at work. Management in business and administration has increasingly looked at ways of establishing and maintaining a positive organizational culture (e.g. Deal and Kennedy, 1982). To some extent and in many contexts this has replaced the 'macho management' of former years. Attention to total quality management (e.g. Bank, 1992) includes the development not only of specific techniques to create and maintain positive working relationships but also the beliefs which accompany and support them. Some of the basic values listed by Tom Peters and Robert Waterman (1982) as the essentials found in the best companies can be applied to and translated for the school as an organization. What is more, they focus to a considerable extent on aspects of the organization which are socially relevant. Some can be applied almost exactly as they are. Taking these values, one might suggest equivalents for the class:

- 'a belief in being the best' might become 'a belief in being a great class'
- 'a belief in the importance of the details of doing a job well' could stay the same
- 'a belief in the importance of people as individuals' could stay the same
- 'a belief in superior quality and service' might become 'a belief in high-quality work and presentation'
- 'a belief that most members of the organization should be innovators ... and a willingness to support failure' might become 'a belief that all can change and progress and that failure is part of trying'
- 'a belief in the importance of informality to enhance communication' might become 'a belief that all can and should communicate with all'
- 'a belief in the importance of growth and profits' becomes 'a belief in the importance of progress and learning'

While exploring these concepts might be helpful for a school, schools can go well beyond borrowing from industry. Schools are places where large numbers of people work together and learn to do so; building in the value of people and the skills needed to make the most of them is central to their purpose.

Business writers have struggled to define organizational culture. One useful if general definition is 'the way we do things round here'. John Bank identifies six key aspects which organizations attempting to create a strong and positive culture need to address:

- regular ways of doing things
- norms and expectations for work performance, which are set both formally and informally
- the main values held
- the philosophy towards customers and employees
- the rules of the game for getting along well
- feeling or atmosphere created by the physical layout and decoration.

(Bank, 1992, p. 114)

These give basic and valuable guidelines for any organization to promote a positive and helpful culture and can be applied to the school as a whole and to individual classes.

Business analysts are also exploring the importance of leadership skills. These are important not only in achieving specific goals but also in building beliefs and commitments throughout the organization. Just as a positive organizational culture is seen as vital, so too are the leadership skills to achieve it. One key feature of business leadership which is singled out by workers is the ability to promote change. Similarly, there is a growing interest in leadership in education. This applies not only to headteachers and other managers; each teacher is a leader and needs to develop leadership skills accordingly. These include assertion skills, consultation skills and the definition of specific goals. The enthusing about visionary goals is also critical. This is the belief that what is being done is important and the ability to make others feel it is important too.

A POSITIVE CLIMATE

Barry Schneider (1993) makes some excellent points about who can help to create a positive school climate and how, together with some cautions about how much more there is to find out about this. Yet for many years teachers have planned and designed activities for classes and groups which address class climate as well as specific academic or other goals. Teachers spend great amounts of time and energy helping, organizing and encouraging children in some of the following:

- class assembly presentations
- dance, music, drama and other productions for school and community audiences
- study trips
- practical activities in groups
- social events, parties, discos
- trips for mainly social reasons
- sports and exercise events
- school journeys, field trips and adventure pursuits activities
- hobby activities and clubs
- discussion and debating activities
- class conferences, involving parents
- class newspapers and other publications
- classroom layout and décor
- rituals, gifts, celebrations, birthdays, leavers' events and reunions
- class events reported in the local media
- twinning with other organizations, and support of community initiatives, for example with older people
- cross-age responsibilities and tutoring
- class organizations, for example council/consultation group
- visitors, greetings and displays
- links with other classes and schools
- fund-raising events

All these and many more are part of a successful and happy school. (The happiness is necessary as well as desirable.) They also give opportunities to build positive relationships between staff and with parents and others in the community. One favourite for starting off with good relationships with teachers, pupils and parents is an ice-rink trip. Helping each other to stay upright regardless of age and rank does wonders to create a good class atmosphere in a single event. Perhaps the simplest events can be identified and sustained even at the busiest times. These may involve community support, or consist of activities which also address academic goals.

THE INDIVIDUAL, THE GROUP, THE CLASS

Children and young people need to learn the social skills to relate to others in one-to-one situations, and in small and larger groups such as the class. These are not always easy for children or for adults. Adults are often anxious about having to speak in public if they are not used to it. Children are often worried about reading or asking questions in front of the whole class. Learning to relate appropriately in one-to-one, small-group and more public situations is part of developing social competence. The audience in the public situations can support those who speak out or make it hard for them; the ritual of whole-class communication contributes to the background against which friendliness may thrive or struggle.

How a child fares in whole-class situations can make a considerable difference to her social confidence. Children who seek attention by disrupting the whole class are likely to be rejected as possible friends and excluded from play and other group activities. Yet such disruption can be actively supported by others at the time. Social development and social problems do not take place in a vacuum. Children spend many hours each day in school, and the school environment is very important. Barry Schneider, however, describes the literature on the possible contribution of the school as 'limited and highly fragmented' (1993, p. 116), especially when compared with research on the effect of the family. As schools in general and classes in particular give so many opportunities for social contact and learning it is surprising that the school contribution to social development has not been more thoroughly researched. There can be few doubts that schools and classes within them do have considerable effects on children's social development. Future research is likely to find most positive effects when the school is working closely with the community on social and other issues. Parents, teachers and children and young people feel strongly that being in the 'right class' is important. For teachers, having a class that is friendly and positive is a substantial improvement to their quality of working life. It is much more productive to feel part of the community and working with it than separate and working against it.

At work we usually have to follow rules for our work and also social relationships in the workplace. There are both formal rules and goals and informal rules for effective and productive social relations at work. Schools have rules, both formal and informal, some of which relate to social behaviour. The link between social skills and social rules is one which schools are well placed to teach, along with social skills themselves.

Specifically, these rules, expectations and skills help children and young people to build relationships of various kinds both with other individuals and with groups. The interactions of all class members will also have a substantial effect on how successful any strategy with an individual is. While we need to identify and work with those children, relatively few, who have a great need to learn and practise basic social skills, strategies at a range of levels are all helpful. A focus on giving a few the skills to integrate socially with others has more chance of working if those 'others' are in a class where the social climate is positive. They will be more successful in applying these skills if the social climate and expectations are for inclusion, acceptance and mutual value, support and enjoyment. For all children a positive social climate in a classroom and in a school has effects which reach wider than individual social success: there are many implications for the wider society and perceptions of humanity. For the teacher, addressing social skills at a whole-class level is an effective use of time rather than having too many small-group and individual interventions to run and monitor.

For children who have effective social skills, improving the social climate of the classroom has many benefits. It will help them to be effective in helping others in the class as there will be an overall framework of expectations, and active adult support for their positive social initiatives. There will be an expectation made of all children and adults, so that positive and socially successful children will not be wholly responsible: the responsibility will be shared. This shared responsibility will also include the children who are not finding friendship and skills in friendliness and progress easy. In a positive climate everybody makes the effort. Other benefits for children who have adequate social skills and experiences can be predicted. If children feel part of a class it will make the emergence of negative groups less likely. Limitation of friendship opportunities because of inequality of opportunity will be less likely the more positive the climate is.

Creating such a climate involves attention not just to objectives but also to the process. This not only involves where we want to go to but also how we want to go there and what we will learn from our progress. Social development means learning the benefits of collaboration, assertion and listening. The process can be hard, but should also be enjoyable — for the teacher too — and go close to the fulfilment that keeps teachers motivated. Some occasions will require quiet and concentration, others cheerfulness and laughter. The children need to have the rules and expectations clear but to use these to ensure they can feel safe in growing more independent socially, in preparation for situations away from direct adult control and situations in the future. Attention to the social climate brings about shared responsibilities and a climate of collaborative problem-solving. These are general and fundamental lessons for life which benefit all children. They are also lessons which make life more pleasant for the teacher; nothing wrong in that!

One intervention in a large high school was carried out to help a withdrawn and isolated child. Clive was especially unhappy at break-times, so was given the task of organizing the watering and care of the plants in the school. It was a very large school and there were possibly hundreds of them to list and care for. He was given clear guidance on plant care and spent some time with a technician from the science faculty learning and observing exactly what to do. Then Clive was provided with pupil helpers to whom he assigned tasks. These were often children who were in trouble, yet the combination of Clive's sense of the importance of the job and their extroversion led to several successes. Most of the helpers proved to be happy to do something useful and responsible over break-time which also kept them out of trouble. Once the system was set up, little staff time was needed. The outcomes were:

- Clive had a task to fill up the difficult recess times
- he had clear instructions to give his 'team'
- his team saw the job as helpful and a good way of staying out of trouble
- within two weeks Clive was known to and liked by many of the most talkative children in the school
- the plants were well looked after and the appearance of the school improved

Replicating this kind of responsible activity using whole classes or part of a class is easy and can save staff time. What is essential is that it is well planned and that children have precise guidelines for what they do, both for the task and for the social requirements of the task.

CLASSROOM QUALITY, VISIBLE AND INVISIBLE

Anyone who regularly visits classrooms knows the care and attention that many teachers pay to the physical environment of their classroom, especially in the early years. The walls and even the ceilings are often covered with examples of children's work, and stimulus materials for curiosity and more formal learning. Displays of materials, clearly labelled, are evidence of the topics and projects which are in progress at the time.

The quality of the classroom environment is not only defined by physical attributes; the social environment is also an important indicator of quality. By this we mean such factors as the level of noise and the way people talk to each other, the degree to which students are actively engaged in tasks, levels of support and co-operation. Some of these are clearly evident, some more subtle; all are important. Strategies which may be less obvious are the teacher's creating opportunities for building the self-esteem of each pupil and positive behaviour management once initial good order has been established. Because some aspects of a positive social environment are not obvious, the observation and study of classroom interaction is required. This has proved to be helpful in giving feedback to teachers: we are not always behaving in the way we think we are. Jane French (1992), for example, describes some of the issues in studying classroom interaction but also notes some priorities for attention, for example the dominance by boys of much classroom discussion. Teachers who believe they give equal attention in discussion are not always able to do this; some kind of feedback system is necessary for teachers to understand their own behaviour and to develop what they do accordingly. Using a self-record system to share out teacher attention is feasible; it can be effective and easy if managed and planned, has an excellent outcome for the class and is seen as fair. It needs to be done largely on a group basis to avoid breaking up the whole-class atmosphere that is so important and to avoid undue pressures on the teacher. Asserting that all children are equally valued can be matched by recording their engagement in activities and access to adult guidance.

A positive social climate is supported by and in turn supports a high level of engagement in academic tasks. This is partly because meeting core objectives is necessary for any organization to create and maintain positive attitudes. Failure to pursue the main task and failure to pursue it effectively produce stress; when people are under stress they are likely to project this on to those around them by blame, fault-finding and irritability. In a classroom, failure to promote and achieve academic goals will undermine the social climate. In the business literature noted earlier, the style of leadership, the social climate and the effectiveness of the organization were closely linked. In the current educational context with a focus on the formal academic curriculum, the importance of these links needs to be asserted, especially where there are pressures on time and funding. In today's high schools, time with the class teacher may be eroded for lesson time. Perhaps the social development of the class is becoming less central to schools. Even where time is at a premium, the quality of relationships which teachers promote and in which they participate is still an essential part of a successful working environment for adults and pupils.

In a competitive educational world, there is a great deal of interest in school effectiveness. School effectiveness and improvement studies are becoming complex and many influences are being identified. It is not an easy area in which to conduct research, especially when data about schools can affect their funding, reputation or pupil intake. However, Peter Mortimore and colleagues, for example, do conclude that where schools have a similar intake there can be significant differences in effectiveness as indicated by a range of measures (Mortimore *et al.*, 1988). Peter Mortimore's findings from a primary school sample are broadly consistent with the findings of Michael Rutter and colleagues with a smaller sample of secondary schools (Rutter *et al.*, 1979).

One difference in effectiveness between schools appears to be 'school ethos' – the human side of the school. The ethos of the school permeates what happens because it links with the expectations of those who are part of the school. School improvement teams are interested in building positive attitudes and relationships not only within a school but between a school and the community. The Yale Child Development Study, for example, looks at the process of school improvement, at how the people relate to each other. James Comer, the Director of what is now called the 'Comer Process' of school improvement at Yale, emphasizes that the process of bringing the people together for common progress is essential.

The social climate of a school is inseparable from other aspects of the ethos. Recent research discussions concern the possibility that effectiveness is significantly influenced by what happens at the class level, that an effective school has a large number of effective classrooms. This is something of a circular agreement but does suggest that what happens in the individual class may have the key effect on what happens across the school, rather than the other way round. Differences in effectiveness between classrooms in the same school may be as important and worthy of study as differences between schools. As noted before, this is consistent with the key question of parents and children: 'Who will be the teacher?'

Creating a social climate in the classroom offers many comparisons with the real climate. There can be bleak or fruitful seasons, mild days and stormy ones, unexpected events and problems in forecasting. Yet within a particular climatic zone things even out over time and one can make fairly good judgements about what to expect and how to deal with events. In the classroom there are also preferences, from a quiet atmosphere reminiscent of a library to one where there is a higher level of excitement and busy, perhaps noisy, activity.

EXPECTATIONS AND STRATEGIES

Building an effective class and classroom climate requires clarity about responsibilities. The key person is the class teacher. This is not to say that the class teacher has to involve herself personally in every aspect of the class's schooling. Social difficulties are most likely to occur, however, in situations in which adult involvement is absent or limited, where the school permits the adults to be seen as of low status, or where boundaries of responsibility are unclear.

Expectations can be developed, and need not be identical between schools. These relate not only to staff and pupils, but also to parents and others. Effective involvement in children's learning by parents and others is well established in many schools, especially in the early years, usually through shared reading schemes. In these, the responsibilities of school and family are explicit and actions recorded.

The usual responsibilities of the school are to hear the child read regularly, identify reading material at an appropriate level, and to devise guidelines and a record format for reading at home. In turn, parents are asked to read with their child regularly and according to the guidelines and to fill in the reading record. Paired reading involving parents is effective academically but is also likely to have substantial social and other benefits. Such schemes do need clear guidelines, planning and management. Similarly, peer tutoring in schools can work for mutual benefit, promoting cross-age mixing and friendly relations. Within a class, peer tutoring can help to ensure that learning problems bring a child or young person closer into class networks rather than being pushed to the margins.

Collaborative learning can benefit not only the pupil who is being tutored, but also the pupil in the tutor role. The interest in the work of Vygotsky has promoted research on the relationship between learning and language, and the social process of developing thinking skills. Jonathan Tudge, for example, concludes that 'children who collaborated with an adult (generally a mother) were most likely to complete the task successfully. This research strongly suggests that children come to learn adult meanings, behaviors, and technologies in the process of collaboration (Tudge, 1990, p. 156).

Robert Slavin summarizes a large number of studies on co-operative learning among pupils and presents the benefits as:

- improved academic performance
- development of interracial friendships
- helping to overcome barriers to include children with learning difficulties and physical handicaps
- enhanced self-esteem
- group norms promoting positive school learning
- pupils spending more time 'on task'
- increased within-class friendships

(Kutnick, 1988, pp. 182–3)

Slavin discusses methods for promoting co-operative learning, especially four which have been extensively developed and researched. Two relate to general co-operative learning methods which can be applied to most subjects and levels, while the other two are curricula designed for use in particular subjects at particular grade levels: 'These four methods all incorporate team rewards, individual accountability, and equal opportunities for success, but in different ways' (Slavin, 1990, p. 230).

A magic circle can be a vital part of every week for every class (Fearn and McCabe, 1975) in building a positive climate. This is a time when all sit together in a circle for discussion. Emphasis is given to listening to others and turn taking in speaking. The Human Development Program 'is designed to help students develop useful insights in regard to themselves and others, while they practice communication skills. Circle topics are experiential approximations of these topics' (Fearn and McCabe, 1975, p. 31). The activities give a clear progression for individuals and a class, and many suggested topics are given, for example 'something that I did that I felt good about, but somebody else felt bad about'. Because of the clear progression and structure, the magic circle offers security and support in exploring personal issues in the classroom.

TAKING ACTION

Starting out

For a positive class ethos there are particular reasons for starting well, at the beginning of the year, the week, each day and lesson. Starting well sets expectations about behaviour, work completion, punctuality and attitude. It is always best to prevent problems by starting well; socially this reduces the likelihood of dominance, rejection, isolation, conflict and other social problems, which are more prevalent in a social vacuum. It also reduces the vulnerability of many children. It is useful to give some time at the outset, not only to starting these activities, peer tutoring, group-work, etc., but also to discussing why it is important to do so. Some children may not understand why a positive social climate needs to be established – and some parents may not see the link between a healthy social environment and learning. All these things need to be communicated; most social skills groups start with an outline of the reasons why such groups are helpful. Asking students to think about hypothetical class situations can be useful and can promote discussion of issues of bullying, relationships, reluctance and enthusiasm to attend, co-operation, self-esteem and confidence. Behind these lie a range of powerful concepts and forces which are to do with access to rights and resources, responsibilities, belonging, quality of care, challenge, achievement and ethics.

GROUP PROBLEM SOLVING

The problems can relate to specific curriculum goals, especially in technology and in science; building in expectations and instructions for group co-operation makes these subjects enjoyable and productive. An example of a task is to ask the children to make a structure out of newspapers as a bridge, capable of supporting a person's weight, between two points, or to build a structure which a person can sit inside. Feedback is needed on the brainstorm process and to encourage analysis of tasks, looking at the task creatively and listening to the ideas of all. Discussion of the assigning of tasks is needed and each person can ask for help or can be offered help.

SHARED STORY WRITING

Shared story writing can help to develop language, literacy and social skills. Children form groups to discuss and write a story together, and a large colourful book is then produced by them for the school or class library. Different groups may be given a similar theme, for example 'the day everything went wrong'. They need to brainstorm ideas for the story, allocate tasks and work together. Adult support for this process is valuable, particularly where groups include children with learning difficulties. Children take great pride in these books, and many of them choose to read them in quiet sessions, and want to take them home at the end of the year.

PROJECT/COLLAGE WORK

The groups decide on organization, following guidelines so that the rules and expectations are explicit, for example taking turns to speak, deciding and allocating tasks and resources, finding out the specific skills of individuals (e.g. artistic ability, research).

THE CRITICAL FRIEND

Discussing and applying the concept of needing and benefiting from feedback so long as it is well-meant and honest. This can apply to class work, music, performances, etc., and is structured in at an early or rehearsal stage. The person who is giving the feedback has to be honest, supportive, specific and helpful; the outcome will be better quality for the final product.

CLASS DIARY

The children write in or say things to be written in for a display or record of events and feelings. Children can write in positive things, trips, events, incidents, or comment on playtime. This can be done by having one person each week fill in the diary on behalf of the class, by asking everyone for possible entries. The diary can be designed to comment on positive contributions by individuals, groups, parents, etc. A class book of jokes, stories, games, etc. is also valuable.

POSTCARDS

Everyone in the class asks a relative to send them a postcard. Where pupils have relatives abroad or in another part of the country, these are the relations they ask. The postcards become part of a class display and can relate to aspects of the curriculum depending on the age of the class.

CLASS PHOTO ALBUM

Children write a brief description of themselves: likes, dislikes, personality, languages spoken and signature. These are displayed with individual and whole-class photographs. Discussion of the photographs on a regular basis can encourage informal mixing across the class. Photographs and videos of the whole class working or of other activities can be used to discuss whole-class functioning and ways of improving it. Bringing in somebody else to discuss this can also be helpful and interesting.

SETTING UP A BUSINESS

The class set up and run a 'business'. This can involve many kinds of activities depending on the age of the class. A primary school class decided that they would like to cook and sell biscuits. Children were given roles which were rotated, worked in teams, and there was discussion of how best to plan the business. They spent part of the profits on a whole-class outing.

CELEBRATIONS

Decide what to celebrate and how. This is a big issue; most schools we know do excellent work for Christmas and other celebrations. This takes time but can be used as part of developing class ethos as well as contributing to the whole school. Taking part is important for each child so some of the successful activities that achieve this can be repeated for different classes. All of this takes time, and major productions and celebrations can interrupt the work and ethic of a school; small-scale celebrations work well and lighten the atmosphere. Birthdays are fine, with cards and singing a song, but it is possible to use other events and to involve the class in planning what an individual would appreciate most. Class cards for those who are ill or having problems are valued. Celebration of achievements of different kinds can emphasize the social development of the class. Recognition rather than reward systems can also highlight and sustain social achievement. This could involve wall stickers or having a jar in which the teacher puts a marble when there is a personal or group achievement, but the jar contains the achievements of the whole class.

BIRTHDAY LINES

In this activity, derived from Watkins (1989), p. 93, the class line up in order of their birthdays. The challenging part is – they have to do this without talking! The purpose is to develop ways of co-operating. Discussion afterwards can cover:

- which strategies were helpful?
- what does co-operation mean?

RESOURCES

Leif Fearn, Robert McCabe with Geraldine Ball (1975) *Magic Circle: Supplementary Idea Guide*. Uvaldo Hill Palomares: Human Development Program.
  This gives an outline of the principles and examples of practice in the planning and running of magic circle activities.

Robert E. Slavin (1983) *Cooperative Learning*. New York: Longman.
  Provides guidance about principles and practices of a range of co-operative learning techniques.

REFERENCES

Allen, G. (1989) *Friendship: Developing a Sociological Perspective*. Hemel Hempstead: Harvester Wheatsheaf.
Argyle, M. and Henderson, M. (1985) *The Anatomy of Relationships*. London: Heinemann.
Bank, J. (1992) *The Essence of Total Quality Management*. New York: Prentice-Hall.
Deal, T. and Kennedy, A. (1982) *Corporate Cultures: The Rites and Rituals of Corporate Life*. Reading, Mass.: Addison-Wesley.
Epstein, J. L. and Karweit, N. (1983) *Friends in School: Patterns of Selection and Influence in Secondary School*. New York: Academic Press.
Fearn, L., McCabe, R. with Ball, G. (1975) *Magic Circle: Supplementary Idea Guide*. Uvaldo Hill Palomares: Human Development Program.
French, J. (1992) Social interaction in the classroom. In C. Rogers and P. Kutnick (eds) *The Social Psychology of the Primary School*. London: Routledge.
Kutnick, P. J. (1988) *Relationships in the Primary Classroom*. London: Paul Chapman.
Mortimore, P., Sammons, P., Stoll, L., Lewis, D. and Ecob, R. (1988) *School Matters: The Junior Years*. Wells: Open Books.
Newton, C. and Tarrant, T. (1992) *Managing Change in Schools: A Practical Handbook*. London: Routledge.
Peters, T. and Waterman, R. (1982) *In Search of Excellence*. London: Harper & Row.
Rizzo, T. A. (1989) *Friendship Development among Children in School*. Norwood, NJ: Ablex.
Rutter, M., Maughan, B., Mortimore, P. and Ouston, J. (1979) *Fifteen Thousand Hours: Secondary Schools and Their Effects on Children*. London: Open Books.
Schneider, B. H. (1993) *Children's Social Competence in Context: The Contributions of Family, School and Culture*. Oxford: Pergamon.
Slavin, R. E. (1983) *Cooperative Learning*. New York: Longman.
Slavin, R. E. (1990) Co-operative learning. In C. Rogers and P. Kutnick (eds) *The Social Psychology of the Primary School*. London: Routledge.

Smilansky, M. (1991) *Friendship in Adolescence and Young People*. Gaithersburg, Md: Psychosocial and Education Publications.

Tudge, J. (1990) Peer collaboration in the ZPD. In L. C. Moll (ed.) *Vygotsky and Education*. Cambridge: Cambridge University Press.

Watkins, C. (1989) *Your New School*. Harlow: Longman Tutorial Resources.

Wilmott, P. (1987) *Friendship Networks and Social Support*. London: Policy Studies Institute.

Name Index

Subject Index